HIGHER EDUCATION ADMINISTRATION WITH SOCIAL MEDIA: INCLUDING APPLICATIONS IN STUDENT AFFAIRS, ENROLLMENT MANAGEMENT, ALUMNI RELATIONS, AND CAREER CENTERS

CUTTING-EDGE TECHNOLOGIES IN HIGHER EDUCATION

Series Editor: Charles Wankel

Recent Volume:

Volume 1: Educating Educators with Social Media –
Edited by Charles Wankel

Forthcoming Volume:

Volume 3: Teaching Arts and Science with the New Social Media – Edited by Charles Wankel

CUTTING-EDGE TECHNOLOGIES IN HIGHER EDUCATION
VOLUME 2

HIGHER EDUCATION ADMINISTRATION WITH SOCIAL MEDIA: INCLUDING APPLICATIONS IN STUDENT AFFAIRS, ENROLLMENT MANAGEMENT, ALUMNI RELATIONS, AND CAREER CENTERS

EDITED BY

LAURA A. WANKEL
Seton Hall University, New Jersey, USA

CHARLES WANKEL
St. John's University, New York, USA

IN COLLABORATION WITH

**MATTHEW MAROVICH
KYLE MILLER
JURATE STANAITYTE**

United Kingdom – North America – Japan
India – Malaysia – China

Emerald Group Publishing Limited
Howard House, Wagon Lane, Bingley BD16 1WA, UK

First edition 2011

Copyright © 2011 Emerald Group Publishing Limited

Reprints and permission service
Contact: booksandseries@emeraldinsight.com

No part of this book may be reproduced, stored in a retrieval system, transmitted in any form or by any means electronic, mechanical, photocopying, recording or otherwise without either the prior written permission of the publisher or a licence permitting restricted copying issued in the UK by The Copyright Licensing Agency and in the USA by The Copyright Clearance Center. No responsibility is accepted for the accuracy of information contained in the text, illustrations or advertisements. The opinions expressed in these chapters are not necessarily those of the Editor or the publisher.

British Library Cataloguing in Publication Data
A catalogue record for this book is available from the British Library

ISBN: 978-0-85724-651-6
ISSN: 2044-9968 (Series)

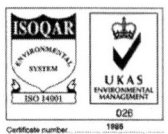

Emerald Group Publishing Limited, Howard House, Environmental Management System has been certified by ISOQAR to ISO 14001:2004 standards

Awarded in recognition of Emerald's production department's adherence to quality systems and processes when preparing scholarly journals for print

INVESTOR IN PEOPLE

CONTENTS

LIST OF CONTRIBUTORS ix

CONNECTING ON CAMPUS WITH NEW MEDIA: xi
INTRODUCTION TO HIGHER EDUCATION
ADMINISTRATION WITH SOCIAL MEDIA

PART I: SOCIAL MEDIA AND ENROLLMENT MANAGEMENT

HYBRID ENGAGEMENT: HOW FACEBOOK HELPS
AND HINDERS STUDENTS' SOCIAL INTEGRATION
Bree McEwan 3

SOCIAL MEDIA FOR SOCIAL RESEARCH:
APPLICATIONS FOR HIGHER EDUCATION
COMMUNICATIONS
Nicolle Merrill 25

SOCIAL MEDIA USE BY ENROLLMENT
MANAGEMENT
Philip Griffiths and Anthony Wall 49

PART II: SOCIAL MEDIA IN ADVISING AND MENTORING

SECOND LIFE: THE FUTURE OF EDUCATION IS
HERE TODAY
P. Charles Livermore 71

MENTORING 2.0 – HIGH TECH/HIGH TOUCH
APPROACHES TO FOSTER STUDENT SUPPORT
AND DEVELOPMENT IN HIGHER EDUCATION
    Melanie Booth and Arthur Esposito   *85*

LEARNING TOGETHER: USING SOCIAL MEDIA TO
FOSTER COLLABORATION IN HIGHER EDUCATION
    Neil Ford, Melissa Bowden and Jill Beard   *105*

USING SOCIAL MEDIA IN STUDY ABROAD
    Penny Schouten   *127*

USING SOCIAL NETWORKING SITES DURING
THE CAREER MANAGEMENT PROCESS
    Nancy Richmond, Beth Rochefort and Leslie Hitch   *147*

PART III: SOCIAL MEDIA AND PUBLIC RELATIONS

AMPLIFICATION AND ANALYSIS OF ACADEMIC
EVENTS THROUGH SOCIAL MEDIA: A CASE STUDY
OF THE 2009 BEYOND THE REPOSITORY FRINGE
EVENT
    Nicola Osborne   *167*

CONNECTING FANS AND SPORTS MORE
INTENSIVELY THROUGH SOCIAL MEDIA
    Karen Weaver   *191*

PART IV: SOCIAL MEDIA AND ALUMNI RELATIONS

ENGAGING ALUMNI AND PROSPECTIVE
STUDENTS THROUGH SOCIAL MEDIA
    Eric Kowalik   *211*

AM I INVITED? SOCIAL MEDIA AND ALUMNI
RELATIONS
   Heather M. Makrez   *229*

TWITTER IN HIGHER EDUCATION: FROM
APPLICATION TO ALUMNI RELATIONS
   Jon Hussey   *249*

ABOUT THE AUTHORS   *273*

SUBJECT INDEX   *281*

LIST OF CONTRIBUTORS

Jill Beard	Bournemouth University, Bournemouth, UK
Melanie Booth	Marylhurst University, Marylhurst, OR, USA
Melissa Bowden	Bournemouth University, Bournemouth, UK
Arthur Esposito	Virginia Commonwealth University, Richmond, VA, USA
Neil Ford	Bournemouth University, Bournemouth, UK
Philip Griffiths	University of Ulster, Jordanstown, Northern Ireland
Leslie Hitch	Northeastern University, Boston, MA, USA
Jon Hussey	American University, Washington, DC, USA
Eric Kowalik	Marquette University, Milwaukee, WI, USA
P. Charles Livermore	St. John's University, Queens, NY, USA
Heather M. Makrez	University of Massachusetts, Lowell, MA, USA
Bree McEwan	Western Illinois University, Macomb, IL, USA
Nicolle Merrill	Aalborg University, Aalborg, Denmark
Nicola Osborne	EDINA, University of Edinburgh, Scotland, UK

Nancy Richmond	Massachusetts Institute of Technology, Cambridge, MA, USA
Beth Rochefort	Northeastern University, Boston, MA, USA
Penny Schouten	NAFSA 2010 Technology Task Force, Washington, DC, USA
Anthony Wall	University of Ulster, Jordanstown, Northern Ireland
Charles Wankel	St. John's University, New York, NY, USA
Laura A. Wankel	Seton Hall University, South Orange, NJ, USA
Karen Weaver	The Pennsylvania State University – The Abington College, Abington, PA, USA

CONNECTING ON CAMPUS WITH NEW MEDIA: INTRODUCTION TO HIGHER EDUCATION ADMINISTRATION WITH SOCIAL MEDIA

Since the advent of the digital campus, numerous changes have occurred. In early developments, we were able to improve efficiencies and eliminate the need for human intervention to conduct routine activities. The power of processing massive amounts of data moved from mainframes to desktops and mobile computers. The transition to a ubiquitous computing environment was a relatively quick transition and one that has had a profound impact on the work we do and the way we do it. The presence of information technology has actually transformed the teaching, learning, and administrative environment in post-secondary education world-wide.

These technologies have not only revolutionized data processing and administrative tasks but also created new forms of interpersonal communication. The opportunity to connect and be connected has forged new frontiers in the development and transference of knowledge. Additionally, the emergence of social media technologies has brought an exciting new wave of innovation and opportunity to educators and administrators across the university campus. Leveraging these new forms of technology to communicate, market, inform and further the achievement of institutional goals is opening new venues within which universities can explore and innovate.

In addition to providing essential services, developing community has long been a fundamental element of university life programs. The potential opportunity to enhance university life and community development through the creative and effective implementation of social media technologies is an important and emerging phenomenon. Social media initiatives and activity are transforming the very nature of collegiate life.

As with all emerging technologies, an initial phase that seems chaotic will eventually give way to more integrated and mainstream applications. Consideration for the educational applications, efficiencies, and community development opportunities that attach to the leveraging and integration of social media technology is an important area for innovation and study. In the chapters that follow an overview of the diversity of applications of social media across multiple university-based functions will provide a mosaic of creativity and innovation in action.

In Chapter 2, "Hybrid Engagement: How Facebook Helps and Hinders Students' Social Integration," Bree McEwan examines the role of Facebook and other social networking sites (SNSs) in providing students with new ways to become socially integrated within a campus community. Considering the implications for social engagement that websites like Facebook provide is important for student affairs professionals because research has shown that the social adjustment of students within college communities is correlated with student retention rates. Understanding the potential of SNSs is an important consideration for student affairs professionals charged with the responsibility of fostering campus climates that support engagement and success. Monitoring the potential pitfalls and limitations that these SNSs may present in hindering social integration, the development of effective interpersonal communication skills and the development of meaningful friendships is also considered. McEwan also presents information pertaining to the current utilization patterns of SNSs of traditional and non-traditional students. Understanding the ways that students utilize social networking to form connections with resources and others will help guide practitioners in adapting programs and understanding the role of SNSs in the social integration of students on campus.

In Chapter 3, "Social Media for Social Research: Applications for Higher Education Communications," Nicolle Merrill presents and tests new methods for conducting research on the use of social media tools such as Twitter and Facebook in outreach activities across universities in the United States. The author argues that despite the increase in utilization of these tools, the availability of information that identifies and validates best practices in higher education remain sparse. Merrill presents the case that digital ethnographic methods should be incorporated into the higher education researcher's toolkit. Merrill conducted an exploratory online survey utilizing Twitter and LinkedIn to gather data on the use of social media in international higher education recruiting and outreach. The survey sought information on which social media tools were being used by university staff, the perceived benefits and drawbacks of social media use in international recruiting and outreach, and how universities measured social media for international recruiting purposes. Using a digital ethnographic approach, Merrill gathered relevant, timely data from international higher education professionals and gained insight into the norms, rules and workings of social networking communities. Results point to new methods for understanding the evolution of higher education communications for researchers and university staff alike. Data from the exploratory study of international higher education communications are presented as an example of the rich amount of data obtained through this approach.

In Chapter 4, "Social Media Use by Enrollment Management," Phillip Griffiths and Anthony Wall investigate two different uses of SNSs within the same higher education institution (the University of Ulster). While both were primarily focussed on retention, one SNS attempted to communicate with students whilst they were still making their choices about where and what to study, whereas the second aimed to create a medium for students to interact with one another before arriving at university. The chapter first outlines the theory behind SNSs before highlighting both the rationale behind the decision to use them and the experience of both users. It then describes how lessons learnt led to changes being made in the following year, both in the way the sites were managed and changes to the SNSs used. The authors found that the creation of a dedicated SNS needs to be carefully planned, designed, disseminated, and monitored. Project managers need to closely monitor progress on all activities throughout the life-cycle of a project to ensure its success. Additionally, since the potential for inappropriate postings and cyberbullying exists, policies and guidelines for dealing with inappropriateness need to be considered. The authors recognize the potential and widening accessibility of SNS applications and see value in encouraging their use as a learning/reflecting tool; they are less certain that students will adopt university-sponsored SNSs as a means to find and prepare themselves for a course at the university.

In Chapter 5, "Second Life: The Future of Education is Here Today," P. Charles Livermore discusses the value of Second Life (SL) as an educational tool that he argues will be increasingly utilized for the education of students at all levels. He believes that the use of virtual environments are destined for expanded use as a result of the growth in online and distance education in both high school and post secondary education, the relationship between SL and games or gaming along with the interest of college students in gaming; the similarity between education and the problem-solving nature of games, the transition and sophistication of computers from simply being a "tool" to that of "team member," and the increase in online databases and decline of physical use of libraries. The author describes how one might participate in SL, how he conducts library sessions with students, identifies multiple sites that are available to educators in SL and argues for the expansion of adoption of SL by educators. The author provides a vivid description of islands, avatars, SL sites and experiences using SL in instruction. The author concludes that SL offers an excellent opportunity for today's educator to experiment with the future.

In Chapter 6, "Mentoring 2.0: High-Tech/High-Touch Approaches to Foster Student Support and Development in Higher Education," Melanie Booth and Arthur Esposito argue that Web 2.0 technologies are resulting in great shifts to networks from institutions, out of vertical structuring into horizontal structures, from bureaucracy to individual judgment, from centralization to decentralization, and from constrained territories to working with the world. Considering how these shifts apply to their experiences advising and mentoring students in higher education, they do not think it is a stretch to say that when these technologies are employed thoughtfully and strategically these shifts likely do occur in particular ways and can, in fact, facilitate student support, development, and learning in new ways. Though they use a variety of social media applications to facilitate their practice as mentors and advisors, they acknowledge concerns about technology and information overload yet value the solutions that technology provides for community in the time of globalization.

In Chapter 7 "Learning Together: Using Social Media to Foster Collaboration in Higher Education," Neil Ford, Melissa Bowden, and Jill Beard focus on how social media tools can be used to enhance collaboration in higher education and the benefits and challenges that this can bring. They investigated how two social media tools, social bookmarking and microblogging, can be utilized to foster collaboration and determine why this is important in contemporary higher education. Case studies of social media use at Bournemouth University show how social bookmarking and microblogging have already yielded benefits.

The case studies are grounded in the challenges facing higher education in 2010. They explore how social media has been used in the context of a need to enhance academic excellence and drive efficiencies in the face of funding constraints and changing demographics. The case studies illustrate: first, how social bookmarking has been used to foster group cohesion, reflective practice and evaluative skills in students, as well as being used at an institutional level to drive professional and administrative efficiencies; and second, how microblogging has made a difference in promoting reflective learning, group cohesion, and professional awareness in students and how this style of social networking has contributed to enhancing academic and professional networks. While the tools, uses, and stakeholders vary, the case studies show how social media has enabled collaboration between, students, academics, librarians, learning technologists, and even professional groups beyond the institution. They conclude that, when used appropriately, social media can facilitate the collaboration that will be essential to overcoming the challenges facing higher education.

In Chapter 8, "Using Social Media in Study Abroad," Penny Schouten discusses how NAFSA: Association of International Educators recognizes that their membership needs training in technology and social media. The author asserts that social media helps international educators and study abroad service providers do their job more effectively and efficiently. She provides evidence that social media helps to keep advisors up-to-date with world events with immediate news reporting, and lowers advertising costs. Schouten describes how using social media can reduce time spent on general inquiries, increase an advisor's access to industry experts and resources, strengthen relationships among partnered institutions abroad, reduce travel costs, and facilitate fundraising efforts by cultivating donor groups.

The author argues that social media and study abroad programs share the commonalities of connecting the world, and being able to share and unite across cultures and continents. Schouten concludes that as technology continues to evolve, study abroad professionals will need to adapt to effectively deploy these technologies and, in so doing, are much like their students studying in foreign countries who must adapt and evolve in their newly adopted cultures and environments.

In Chapter 9, "Using Social Networking Sites during the Career Management Process," Nancy Richmond, Beth Rochefort, and Leslie Hitch describe how higher education professionals and college students can use SNSs and technology to manage their careers. Recognizing that individuals can expect to change careers several times in a lifetime, they point out the importance and role of social networks as a central component to the career management process. They discuss how individuals' communication and interactions on SNSs plays an important role in one's career development. The authors examine SNSs as an important resource in exploring career options, learning, networking, searching for jobs, professional development, and making career decisions. They also discuss the importance of maintaining a professional image online. A model is presented on using SNSs to gather information and feedback during the career management process. Scenarios and examples are provided from higher educational professionals, hiring managers, college students, job seekers, and career changers. The chapter envisions the future of career management specific to higher education and addresses how higher education career advisors can respond to SNSs and technology.

In Chapter 10, "Amplification and Analysis of Academic Events through Social Media: A Case Study of the 2009 Beyond the Repository Fringe Event," Nicola Osborne provides an overview of the use of social media tools across higher education describing how Twitter hashtags, live blogs, Facebook events, and Flickr groups are becoming a regular feature of academic conferences and events. Osborne reflects on the experience of planning, moderating and analyzing social media amplification of the 2009 "Beyond the Repository Fringe" event organized by EDINA, the Digital Curation Centre (DCC) and the University of Edinburgh School of Informatics. The author describes how this "unconference format" with a physical audience of approximately 90 individuals was broadened through online participation with colleagues, peers, and interested onlookers accessing live coverage of the event through Twitter, CoverItLive, a live blog, an event Wiki, video feeds, and a Flickr pool. Osborne, based on this experience, raises several important issues regarding social media usage and provides a series of practical guidelines for planning amplification of higher education events.

In Chapter 11, "Connecting Fans and Sports More Intensively through Social Media," Karen Weaver discusses strategies used by contemporary intercollegiate athletics programs to promote their teams. Weaver provides an understanding of the use of social media to engage fans, stakeholders, prospective student athletes, and donors in the high stakes game of revenue generation. She guides the reader to understand the evolution of social media as it applies to athletics external relations. Weaver's analysis includes the leveraging of video technology across multiple "platforms" – television, broadband, and mobile applications – and demonstrates how these allow departments to deepen the ties between fans and teams.

In Chapter 12, "Engaging Alumni and Prospective Students through Social Media," Eric Kowalik argues that the Web is changing the focus of modern advertising, which for many years was focused on drawing associations from the physical qualities of products to the unfulfilled yearnings of potential customers. The author asserts that although emotion continues to play an important role in marketing, the web has created a new type of customer who is becoming immune to the hard sell of traditional marketing. In fact Kowalik states that if you need to sell it, it may not be worth buying. He goes on to say that Web, blogs and social media have enabled a customer revolt. The Web is a more rational space and it thrives in open, questioning cultures.

The author discusses that according to McGovern, a new type of customer is emerging. This customer is less emotional and more rational. This customer does not believe in blind faith. They are on the Web to research, compare, to find out for themselves what they need to know to make a rational, rather than an emotional choice. Kowalik urges that the modern customer should be treated as an inquisitive stranger to achieve marketing success. Consequently, marketing one's institution should focus on engaging with the customer and showing them the desirable products, services and/or experiences that connect to the university. Through the use of "The Conversation Prism," created by Brian Solis, the author represents the evolution of social media's multiple channels as they emerge, fuse and dissipate conversation. Kowalik describes how social networks can be used to build trust and relationships. He discusses how recognizing that one's message exists within a larger ecosystem that is often beyond control.

In Chapter 13, "Am I Invited? Social Media and Alumni Relations," Heather M. Makrez focuses on the initial implementation of social media as it pertains to alumni relations, along with the relevance it plays within the advancement world. Makrez discusses social media strategies that are a creative and powerful way to connect, educate, and energize those interested in the university. The author describes how this technology and related change in interpersonal behavior allow us the capabilities to create a complex, tightly-woven, and diverse university community – a hotbed for innovative ideas, energetic conversation and practical networking. This chapter outlines the implementation of social media initiatives for someone at any comfort level. It explores the societal norms and beliefs that need to be institutionalized before one can be truly successful in implementing a strategic investment of time, money and brainpower. The chapter discusses the experimental uses of social media within the context of a diverse alumni community – which connects seamlessly to emerging campus-wide initiatives. It will challenge the reader to think out-of-the-box when it comes to finding an answer that suits their specific institutional goals. The author hopes to inspire a creative, fun, innovative and interactive flow of ideas, along with the courage to try new things. Be bold. Be brave. Be here. Yes, you are definitely invited!

In Chapter 14, "Twitter in Higher Education: From Application to Alumni Relations," Jon Hussey provides an understanding of the rapid growth of Twitter use as a marketing tool or means to communicate directly with prospective and current students as well as alumni. This chapter provides a broad outline on what Twitter is, how it can be used in higher education, and how some professionals are already using it. Hussey walks you through the unique opportunities for engagement that Twitter offers and how to build a university-wide Twitter strategy to successfully develop relationships in all aspects of university life.

Twitter use in higher education is not going away, and the 30.7 percent of higher education professionals using Twitter are the trendsetters leading a new era of real-time, interactive communication. They may have started a university Twitter account a couple of years ago to test the waters and explore its uses. When they started, Twitter – or social media in general – was probably not part of their job description. Today, universities are following the success of businesses like Comcast – which has 10 employees dedicated to social media – by adding social media skills to job requirements and recreating Web sites to include social media plugins and Twitter landing pages. As more higher education professionals begin to see the value of Twitter, so do the 300,000 people joining the service daily. Hussey discusses the continued growth and evolution of Twitter as it continues to meet the demand and needs of new users with expanded features and better usability. He asserts that ongoing development make Twitter easier to use, easier to understand, and more effective as a business and communications tool. More importantly, he describes that Twitter's success is linked to its accessibility and that it enables everyone in a higher education community – students, faculty, alumni, and staff from every office across campus – to *act*, *interact*, and develop a community.

Implementing the use of a new networking technology, whether it be through Google Apps, Skype, or other Web 2.0 platforms can be a learning experience whether or not a full-blown initial success. It is incumbent upon members of our university communities to arrive in the future by taking the path to it. That path includes the use of social media with their sustainability, cost, agility, and range. Indeed it will become increasingly impossible to be competitive while using the communications media of the past.

Laura A. Wankel
Charles Wankel
Editors

PART I
SOCIAL MEDIA AND ENROLLMENT MANAGEMENT

HYBRID ENGAGEMENT: HOW FACEBOOK HELPS AND HINDERS STUDENTS' SOCIAL INTEGRATION

Bree McEwan

ABSTRACT

The social integration of students within a campus community is vital in enhancing their college experiences. Researchers have sought to determine how best to promote successful social integration for university students. Traditionally, on-campus orientations and residence hall activities have been used to foster student social integration. However, Facebook and other social networking sites (SNSs) can be used for social integration among students in ways that were never before possible. It is important that student-affairs professionals explore the supportive roles for this that SNSs like Facebook might play, since successful student adjustment within a campus is positively correlated with student retention rates.

College students are already using Facebook to bolster their social networks within the university, but it is worth considering the advantages and disadvantages of promoting the use of SNSs for social integration. Facebook is favored because it offers low levels of self-disclosure in social interactions, it increases the social capital of the university, and it offers students with a unique means of acquiring academic support from both their professors and their peers. Unfortunately, extensive Facebook use can also create a social skills deficit in students, lead students to experience information overload, and cause them to shirk their academic responsibilities.

Facebook is neither a panacea for student engagement nor a signal of the end of meaningful interpersonal connections on campus. Student-affairs professionals should become aware of the ways that students engage with SNSs to leverage opportunities for furthering student integration while remaining aware of the limitations for community building that SNSs present.

INTRODUCTION

Higher education researchers and practitioners have spent considerable effort researching and implementing strategies to facilitate students' social integration (Astin, 1993; Bean, 1990; Christie & Dinham, 1991; Skahill, 2003; Stoecker, Pascarella, & Wolfe, 1988; Thomas, 2000; Titus, 2004; Tinto, 1993, 2000). Successful social integration requires students to create and maintain university-affiliated social relationships. Traditional means used by students to build their social networks include activities such as befriending residence hall mates or joining campus organizations. However, the internet- and computer-mediated communication technology provides modern students new ways to build social networks. Students can create and maintain university-affiliated connections by communicating via online social media websites such as MySpace, Twitter, and of course, Facebook. These types of social media allow students to post information about themselves and interact with "friends" who have also created profiles. Social media has allowed the university social community to become what Aleman and Wartman (2009) term a "hybrid environment" meaning that students are able to interact with their social networks both on- and offline (p. 50). Social media websites provide a unique opportunity for students to connect with multiple, intersecting social networks. Students could potentially "friend" new university classmates, roommates, fellow campus organization members, as well as family members and high school friends.

Social networking sites also create new challenges and potential pitfalls for student engagement professionals. Websites such as Facebook may help students engage in relationship-building communication, increase social capital, and provide increased access to academic resources. However, such sites may also contribute to a diminished communication skill, information overload, problems associated with disconnecting from the pre-university network, and decreased academic performance.

SOCIAL INTEGRATION, ADJUSTMENT, AND UNIVERSITY RETENTION

An important concern for educators is how students adjust academically to the university. Academic adjustment is certainly a critical part of adapting to the university environment. Furthermore, academic advancement should be the primary goal of any higher educational experience. However, for students to be able to achieve academically they must also socially adjust to the university community (Giannini, Hamilton, & Spitzberg, 2007). Researchers have found that student social integration into the university community plays a large role in student retention. Higher education researchers have defined retention as whether students persist at a particular university until graduation (Astin, 1993; Berger & Milem, 1999; Hays & Oxley, 1986; Napoli & Wortman, 1998; Skahill, 2003; Tinto, 2000; Titus, 2004). Lack of student retention is a widespread problem for higher education. Nationally, more students leave their first higher education institution before degree completion than those who persist (Carey, 2005; Tinto, 1993). Statistics collected by American College Testing Programs (2009) indicate that 55% of college students leave their institution before receiving a degree. Although some students are forced to leave the university due to academic failure, Tinto (1993) found that over 75% of students who leave do so voluntarily and for nonacademic reasons. It seems, as Bean (1990) argued, "the social environment is crucial to forming the attitudes associated with fitting into and staying enrolled in school" (p. 160).

Social adjustment is a particular concern for students who are new to the university and for the student affairs professionals who care about such students' ability to succeed. Research has found that social adjustment may help students cope even better with their new university life than academic adjustment (Giannini et al., 2007). First year students face the challenge of breaking away from their pre-university social network and establishing a new university-affiliated network (Paul & Brier, 2001). The friendships that make up a student's university-affiliated social network are critically important for their adjustment to the university (Chapman & Pascarella, 1983). These friendships can provide the resources students depend on to remain engaged in university life and persist until graduation (Grant-Vallone, Reid, Umali, & Pohlert, 2003–2004; Samter, Whaley, Mortenson, & Burleson, 1997; Skahill, 2003; Thomas, 2000).

One concept that helps illuminate how students utilize social network connections to adjust to the university is the idea of social capital. Social capital refers to resources individuals perceive are available through their network of acquaintances (Coleman, 1988; Putnam, 2000). Putnam further delineated social capital as two distinct types; bridging and bonding social capital. Bridging social capital refers to accruing resources from individuals with whom one shares a loose social connection. These loose connections are also termed weak ties (Granovetter, 1973). Bonding social capital refers to resources that are available from close relationships such as family or close friends. Student affairs professionals interested in freshmen adaptation and integration into the university environment should be particularly interested in bridging social capital. As freshmen come into the university, their initial connections are likely to be weak ties. The resources available from these weak ties may drive how connected freshmen feel to the university community. These feelings of connectivity may in turn drive freshmen persistence and success.

Previous research on university retention has examined a variety of ways that students build social capital offline. Student engagement studies have found a wide range of social capital building behaviors to be correlated with institutional commitment and retention. These behaviors include joining student organizations (Tinto, 1993; Titus, 2004), interacting with peers (Astin, 1993; Berger & Milem, 1999; Grant-Vallone et al., 2003–2004), work-study (Tinto, 1993), participating in extra- and co-curricular activities (Tinto, 1975; Stoecker et al., 1988), creating study groups (Titus, 2004), attending religious services (Astin, 1993), and engagement with other types of student affairs programming (Stoecker et al., 1988).

Similarly, retention scholars have found that the availability of social support or social capital from one's social network is also related to university retention. Social network variables found to be related to retention include the size of a student's social network (Hays & Oxley, 1986; Skahill, 2003), social network structures (Thomas, 2000), types of friendships (Bean, 1990), and availability of social support (Napoli & Wortman, 1998). Other research has examined students' perceptions of their own sense of belonging (Hausmann, Schofield, & Woods, 2007), feelings of social integration (Napoli & Wortman, 1998), feelings of a sense of congruence with campus values and norms (Berger & Milem, 1999), and sensing an available student community (Astin, 1993).

The earlier variables are useful for examining how today's college students engage with the university community. However, modern students have a new world of technology at their fingertips. Communication technologies can further students' ability to engage in specific behaviors related to retention, maintain their social network, and also increase their sense of belonging and community. Students can find student organizations, peers, and extracurricular activities using message boards and social networking sites. They can utilize email, instant messaging, chat services and social networking sites in order to form, build, and maintain both their university-affiliated and external social network. These activities may in turn lead to greater feelings of university integration. Social networking sites provide students with a variety of the communication tools listed earlier. Students can use these websites, to form groups, send private messages that are similar to email, engage in one-on-one chat, as well as post public messages to other students' profiles. Currently, one of the most popular websites students use to manage their social networks is Facebook. The remainder of this chapter focuses specifically on college students' use of Facebook and how the popular social networking site may contribute and detract from social engagement.

COLLEGE STUDENTS AND FACEBOOK

More and more college students are turning to social network sites to help them build and maintain friendship networks (Lenhart, Purcell, Smith, & Zickuhr, 2010). Boyd and Ellison (2007) defined social network sites as:

> Web-based services that allow individuals to (1) construct a public or semi-public profile within a bounded system, (2) articulate a list of other users with whom they share a connection, and (3) view and traverse their list of connections and those made by others within the system. (p. 1)

As stated earlier, one of the most popular social network sites for today's college student is Facebook.com. Facebook meets all of Boyd and Ellison's criteria for social networking sites. Individuals on Facebook construct a profile using Facebook's standardized template. Although users can set privacy settings (and some research suggests that students are becoming more savvy in regard to privacy settings; Lenhart et al., 2010), their profiles are generally open to their selected list of friends. These "friends" are the list of others with whom the user has chosen to share a connection. Users may seek out "friends" by searching for a specific person or by browsing categories. Facebook will also suggest possible new friends based on the networks of users' current friends. Finally, students can share information about their extended peer network (Lampe, Ellison, & Steinfield, 2008). Through Facebook, individuals can view friends of friends and depending on privacy settings click through to those individuals' profiles and pictures.

Mark Zuckerberg founded the Facebook.com in 2004 as a way for students at Harvard University to connect with each other online. By May 2005, Facebook.com supported 800 different college networks. In 2006, Facebook began to allow nonuniversity-based users. Today, Facebook has 500 million international users from both university and noneducational networks. The average user has approximately 130 friends and spends about 55 min a day on Facebook (www.facebook.com/facebook).

Students could use Facebook and other social networking sites to connect with individuals anywhere in the world. In reality, they tend to use social networking sites to keep track of their current social network. Rather than supporting purely online relationships, Facebook may be another way that students attempt to build and maintain their offline social networks to fulfill their need for companionship (McMillan & Morrison, 2008; Subrahmanyam, Reich, Waechter, & Espinoza, 2008). Thompson (2008) argued that individuals use Facebook to connect with people with whom they already share proximity. Several other researchers have also found that people use Facebook primarily to communicate with individuals whom they already know offline (Boyd & Ellison, 2007; Ellison, Steinfield, & Lampe, 2007; Joinson, 2008; Lampe et al., 2008; McMillan & Morrison, 2008). However, there seems to be two specific types of relationships young adults have with those they add to their Facebook friend list. One, they add people who they already know well. Second, young adults add contacts that they have recently met and think that they may wish to interact with more in the future (Bryant & Marmo, in press; Lampe et al., 2008). Lampe, Ellison, and Steinfield (2006) termed this activity social searching. Social searching refers to using Facebook to keep track of people one already knows offline. Social searching is in contrast to Lampe et al.'s (2006) term social browsing. Social browsing involves attempting to form online connections to people whom one does not already know. Lampe et al. (2006) found that first year students were more likely to use Facebook for social searching than social browsing. Students rarely report using Facebook to find new friends whom they have never met offline (Lampe et al., 2008; Subrahmanyam et al., 2008).

Facebook use appears to be nearly ubiquitous on college campuses (Subrahmanyam et al., 2008; Lampe et al., 2008). Although in the not-too-distant past freshmen might not have become aware of Facebook until they reached the college campus (Lampe et al., 2006), today's freshmen typically enter the university already aware of and comfortable with use of social networking sites. A report by the Pew Research Center found that 73% of American teenagers with internet access already use social networking websites (Lenhart et al., 2010). Young adults simply continue this use in the college environment. Seventy-two percent of young adults aged 18–29 use social networking sites and 45% of young adults aged 18–29 visit a social networking site at least once on a typical day (Lenhart et al., 2010). Data collected by the Higher Education Research Institute in 2007 showed that 94% of first year students had spent some time on a social networking site and that most students spent between 1 and 5 h a day on such sites. Other recent studies show a similar rate of use. For example, Lampe et al. (2008) found 96% of Michigan State University students reported they were Facebook users. Lampe et al. also found that Michigan State students spent an average of 82 min a day on Facebook. Barkhaus and Tashiro's (2010) participants reported accessing Facebook anywhere from once to 20 times per day (5.3 times per day on average). A majority of Joinson's (2008) participants reported visiting the site at least once a day and also spent between 1 and 5 h on Facebook. The amount of time that students spend on Facebook may increase even more as the availability of online access increases. These days students are able to access Facebook continually throughout the day not only through stationary desktop computers, but also via laptops, and increasingly their mobile phones (Thompson, 2008).

Facebook seems to be particularly important for students just joining the university. Researchers have found that freshmen and sophomores tend to use Facebook more than upperclassmen (Aleman and Wartman, 2009; Ellison et al., 2007; Lampe et al., 2008). Other studies have also found that younger students have heavier Facebook use than older students (Joinson, 2008). One explanation for this effect is that younger students may be more comfortable with adopting social network technology. However, given that Facebook's spike in popularity is approximately 2007 (when today's seniors, Class of 2011, were freshmen) an alternative explanation for this effect might be that Facebook is particularly important for students who are in the process of growing their university-affiliated social network. Once these networks stabilize students may become less dependent on social network sites.

In fact, Facebook may be just one strategy that freshmen use in order to build their social networks. The Higher Education Research Institute (2007) found that the more time students spent on Facebook the more likely they were to report partying and alcohol consumption. It is likely that this correlation is spurious with neither Facebook use driving alcohol consumption nor partying driving Facebook use. Rather these activities may all be strategies that students use to try to engage with their university peers. Although parents and educators might frown on students engaging in any of these activities, Astin (1993) found that both attending parties and alcohol consumption were positively related to university retention. It may be that students who possess the time to invest in developing a rewarding and diverse social network are more likely to spend a considerable amount of time engaging in a variety of social strategies.

The research reviewed above investigating Facebook usage suggests that college students are indeed using Facebook as a strategy to build and maintain social networks. However, the question remains, Is such a strategy a productive one? Throughout the history of the expansion of communication technologies, scholars have expressed fears that improvements in technology would weaken interpersonal contact and community (see Hampton & Wellman, 2003 for a review). Such fears include that online interaction will prevent people from engaging in the "real" community and that Internet driven or supported communities are not as meaningful as offline connections. Bugeja (2005) also argued strongly that electronic communication might complicate relationships and prevent us from truly connecting with others. However, others (including Hampton & Wellman) have argued that communication technologies may help bring people closer together. It is likely that student use of social networking sites might both facilitate campus engagement as well as detract from the student experience, and ultimately retention and persistence rates.

FACEBOOK FACILITATION OF SOCIAL INTEGRATION

Student affairs professionals know that students' social integration is crucial for their success at any institution of higher learning. Facebook and other social networking sites provide a rich opportunity for students to form and maintain the network connections that may lead to greater social integration. In order to fully capitalize on the opportunity provided by Facebook, student affairs professionals should familiarize themselves with the multitude of ways Facebook can facilitate integration into a university-affiliated social network.

Facebook and Disclosure

According to social penetration theory (Altman & Taylor, 1973), individuals attempting to create new social relationships must engage in low levels of self-disclosure. Social media provides students with novel ways to engage in this type of self-disclosure (McElvain & Smyth, 2006). The perception of social distance provided by computer-mediated communication may allow students to feel more comfortable reaching out to others in their new social environment (Ellison et al., 2007). Social networking sites such as Facebook constitute an extremely casual form of communication. Messages can be sent, received, replied to, and even ignored quite easily (Barkhaus & Tashiro, 2010). In face-to-face communication, students may be tentative to engage in self-disclosure because such disclosures may be face threatening. Individuals experience face threats when others in their social circle disagree with the identity the individual has chosen to present (Brown & Levinson, 1987). Expressing self-disclosures to new acquaintances is both necessary to form new social connections but also fraught with potential complications. Individuals are sometimes hesitant to disclose for fear that those whom they are disclosing to will not be understanding. However, the casualness of the medium of social networking sites allows students to transmit and control their social communication and disclosures in ways that may feel less face threatening because they are less immediate.

Another communication behavior that is considered face threatening is requests for individuals to engage in a desired behavior (Brown & Levinson, 1987). These types of requests are called negative face threats. Negative face threats are considered face threatening because the requested individual might not wish to engage in the behavior. These types of requests could be asking for favors or compliance. However, a request to be someone's friend or acquaintance could also be considered a negative face threat. Again, the ability to present a social request via a social networking site might be considered less face threatening than attempting to make such a request in person or even over the phone. Indeed, Barkhaus and Tashiro (2010) found that students often used Facebook to reach out to recently formed acquaintances in situations where before they would not have communicated with this person at all. Before Facebook the potential cost of face-threatening behaviors, such as running the risk of being turned down when inviting someone to a social event, may have prevented the formation of these social connections. The mediation of Facebook as a message channel may seem to remove the direct threat to face. In fact, research has shown that Facebook may be particularly useful for students who feel uncomfortable initiating direct contact due to shyness and low self-esteem (Barkhaus & Tashiro, 2010; Ellison et al., 2007). However, computer-mediated communication is quickly becoming a default method of communicating for all students. As one of McMillan and Morrison's (2008) participants commented, "[the internet] is the only real way to contact someone at college" (p. 83).

In addition, following similar things on Facebook may provide students with an updated version of "watercooler" talk. Freshmen using Facebook have a wealth of information to fall back on when starting conversations with fellow students. It is not uncommon in the halls of academia to hear two students conversing about "so-and-so's" Facebook update, relational status, or tagged photos. This phenomenon is similar to what Hampton and Wellman (2003) discovered in their ethnography of a wired Toronto suburb. Neighbors in "Netville" had ready-made conversation starters available from their common email listserv.

Increased Social Capital

When students stay connected to university-affiliated social ties they have an increased sense of involvement at the institution (Kavanaugh, Carroll, Rosson, Zin, & Reese, 2005). Students use the status, messaging, and wall post functions of Facebook to spread information and news about both the social network and the university (Aleman & Wartman, 2009). This type of communication may help students feel a greater sense of belonging to the university community. There is also evidence to suggest that increased Facebook use is associated with increased involvement with campus groups. Heiberger and Harper (2008) found that 78.1% of students who spent more than an hour a day on Facebook participated in at least 1 student organization whereas only 63.3% of students who spent less than an hour a day on Facebook participated in at least one student organization.

Students can connect to campus organizations as well as learn about a variety of other university-affiliated social activities by using Facebook. Indeed, student affairs professionals are beginning to utilize Facebook to promote university clubs and activities. In general, research has found that the internet can provide an easy way to communicate about community events (Hampton & Wellman, 2003). Facebook is designed to further facilitate this use of the internet by providing mechanisms for community building. Many students report using Facebook as a way to plan gatherings and keep track of social events (Aleman & Wartman, 2009; Barkhaus &

Tashiro, 2010; Heiberger & Harper, 2008; Lampe et al., 2006; McElvain & Smyth, 2006). Students may also use Facebook to identify common interests with other students through use of "Group" or "Fan" pages (Heiberger & Harper, 2008; McElvain & Smyth, 2006). In some cases event planning and interest identification may become intertwined as student groups use Facebook to plan organization events, campus protests, and political rallies around their common interests. Although, initially students primarily used Facebook purely for their own social events and parties, research suggests that students are becoming more likely to use Facebook to find out about various campus activities (Heiberger & Harper, 2008; Joinson, 2008; Lampe et al., 2008). Campus organizers and student affairs professionals might consider using Facebook to increase awareness of organizations and activities (Heiberger & Harper, 2008).

As discussed earlier, students rarely create brand new relationships purely through Facebook (Boyd & Ellison, 2007; Ellison et al., 2007; Lampe et al., 2008; McMillan & Morrison, 2008). However, they do report using Facebook to solidify fledgling face-to-face connections. Facebook and other social networking sites seem to be particularly useful for the light maintenance of weak ties (Ellison et al., 2007). People use relational maintenance strategies to help sustain relationships (Dindia, 2003). Maintenance strategies identified pre-Facebook included communication behaviors such as attempts to make interactions pleasant, self-disclosure, or sharing tasks (Canary, Stafford, Hause, & Wallace, 1993). Bryant and Marmo (in press) have identified maintenance strategies that college students use on Facebook including a Facebook-specific strategy called surveillance. Surveillance includes behaviors such as looking at Facebook friends' news updates and reading their profiles without commenting on them. Generally, people use similar relational maintenance strategies to maintain weak and strong tie relationships (McEwan & Guerrero, 2010a). However, Bryant and Marmo's participants reported that surveillance is a particularly useful strategy for maintaining connections to casual friends and acquaintances. Maintaining relationships via Facebook can help college students perceive the availability of resources from their social network (McEwan & Guerrero, 2010a).

Ellison et al. (2007) found that students report Facebook to be particularly useful for accruing perceived resources from weak tie relationships, i.e. bridging social capital. Earlier research on Internet facilitated community building also found that the effects of online connection are generally stronger for weak tie than strong tie relationships (Hampton & Wellman, 2003). Although close relationships are important for student satisfaction, the maintenance of a weak tie network may also help students feel connected to the university. Perceptions of the availability of network resources from both weak and close ties have been linked to how committed students are to graduating from their current university (McEwan, 2009). In addition, Ellison et al. (2007) found that bridging social capital was highly correlated with student satisfaction with university life. The Higher Education Research Institute (2007) also reported that the more time students spent on social network sites the more likely they were to be generally satisfied with their social life. Similarly, Heiberger and Harper (2008) found that the 92.2% of students who spent more than an hour per day on Facebook rated their connection to the university community as high or very high (compared to only 73.4% of students who spent less than an hour per day on Facebook and rated their connection to the university community as high or very high).

Although maintenance of the weak tie network on Facebook may contribute to a student's general satisfaction with university life, Facebook can also help maintain strong tie relationships (Ellison et al., 2007). Maintaining strong tie relationships may help students perceive the availability of social support (McEwan & Guerrero, 2010a) as well as actually obtain social support (Thompson, 2008). Social network sites and other types of mediated communication might allow students easy access to their support networks. For example, Gemmill and Peterson (2006) found that students use computer mediated communication to connect with close friends after a stressful day.

Academic Support

Finally, students may use Facebook in ways that directly relate to their academic performance. Today's students are accustomed to use the internet to complete school assignments and group work (McMillan & Morrison, 2008). Thompson (2008) found that it was common for students to list their classes on their Facebook page in an attempt to connect with others in those classes. However, after Facebook opened up to nonuniversity affiliated networks, this feature has been removed (Lampe et al., 2008). Despite the removal of this feature, students still report other ways they use Facebook for academic purposes. These purposes include sharing notes and class information (Heiberger & Harper, 2008; McElvain & Smyth, 2006), arranging group meetings, and asking each other questions about assignments (Thompson, 2008).

CHALLENGES FACEBOOK PRESENTS FOR SOCIAL INTEGRATION

Although Facebook can provide benefits for social integration as described earlier, many are concerned that Facebook and other forms of Internet communication may also hinder students from fully integrating into campus life (Engelberg & Sjoberg, 2004; Lloyd, Dean, & Cooper, 2007; Nalwa & Anand, 2003). As with any new communication technology, there are fears that the new technology may displace "real" offline relationships and contribute to isolation from the greater community (Bugeja, 2005; Hampton & Wellman, 2003). Facebook is no exception and may in fact detract from students' ability to integrate and engage in some very specific ways.

Communication Skill Deficit

One way that Facebook may hinder social integration is that the communication tools provided by Facebook might contribute to a communication skills deficit. The freshman experience provides a wide range of opportunities for freshmen to practice a variety of communication skills that will be useful throughout their academic career and beyond. McEwan and Guerrero (2010b) found that being skilled at self-disclosure and issuing invitations were particularly important for freshmen to be able to form rewarding social networks. However, social media such as Facebook may allow freshmen to avoid developing these important communication skills. Freshmen in Barkhaus and Tashiro's (2010) study reported using Facebook to avoid the "weirdness" of calling someone on the phone. Lloyd et al. (2007) argued that students might substitute Facebook for direct contact. Similarly, Rainie, Lenhart, Fox, Spooner, and Horrigan (2000) found that people might use mediated forms of communication such as email to avoid conflict or as a screen to say things they were unwilling to address face to face. Thompson (2008) stated, "Freshmen viewed Facebook as generally the easiest way to contact other students because students had become so accustomed to communicating via [computer-mediated communication] CMC" (p. 132). Given the previous discussion of face threats it makes sense that students may find that communicating through Facebook is helpful for mitigating potentially threatening communication. However, it is also important that students learn how to manage these types of communication without hiding behind Facebook. Using mediated forms of communication for friendship initiation may prevent students from forming communication skills that are essential for developing rewarding social networks. Student use of Facebook and other forms of mediated communication as a conflict management tool may simply backfire if students use the medium to engage in conflict communication that is more face threatening than they would be willing to use in person (Zornoza, Ripoll, & Peiro, 2002).

Information Overload

One of the benefits of social networking sites is the amount of information they can provide students about current and potential social network members. However, there is some concern that Facebook and similar social networking sites could also contribute to information overload. Heiberger and Harper (2008) argued that some students might feel intimidated by the sheer amount of information available on Facebook. McMillan and Morrison's (2008) participants also reported that they fear information overload from social network sites.

Furthermore, the type of information that is available on Facebook and other social networking sites might actually increase students' feelings of loneliness. Increased internet use has been linked to higher loneliness scores in adolescents (Engelberg & Sjoberg, 2004; Nalwa & Anand, 2003). Loneliness is defined not just as feeling alone, but also as feelings that there is a deficiency in one's social opportunities (Perlman & Peplau, 1982). College students, although surrounded by peers, rank themselves as far lonelier than other age cohorts (Cutrona, 1982; Brennan, 1982; Ponzetti, 1990). Freshmen are particularly susceptible to loneliness (Giannini et al., 2007). This effect is thought to be caused by college students overestimating how much fun their university peers are actually having. Facebook may exacerbate this effect by skewing students' perceptions of others social activities. On Facebook, people may try to present themselves in what they feel is the best possible light. For college students this may involve showcasing themselves attending social events and generally enjoying life. Students might then view their friends' profiles and pictures and feel that their own social life does not measure up to the social life their Facebook friends are presenting.

Academic Concerns

Research is mixed on the academic implications of Facebook. Some faculty have negative perceptions of Facebook and student Facebook use (Heiberger

& Harper, 2008). Students have also stated that Facebook can distract them from academic pursuits (Yazedjian, Toews, Sevin, & Purswell, 2008). Gemmill and Peterson (2006) argued that synchronous forms of computer-mediated communication such as the chat functions on social network sites might disrupt schoolwork. Some research has found Facebook usage is negatively correlated with lower levels of education involvement (Lloyd et al., 2007), time management skills, and the development of effective study skills (HERI, 2007). However, Ellison et al. (2007) found that Facebook did not have an effect on participant's grades.

The Existing Network

Facebook also helps students stay connected to others who could provide social support including family, distant friends, and other social network connections they had before entering the university. Ellison et al. (2007) found that 96% of student Facebook users in their sample reported that they used Facebook to keep up with people they knew from high school. Subrahmanyam et al. (2008) found that students reported their primary reasons for using social media was to keep in touch with friends they do not see often and to keep in touch with family. McMillan and Morrison's (2008) participants also reported using the social media to stay connected to distant family members and international students found computer-mediated communication particularly important for staying connected with communities in their home countries.

At first glance, the maintenance of external ties may not seem like a negative consequence of Facebook use. However, using Facebook to maintain one's pre-university network may cause students' difficulty integrating into the new university environment. Previous research has shown that when students maintain connections to their pre-university friend and family networks they have a harder time becoming involved with the university community and shifting their values and expectations to match those of the university community (Christie & Dinham, 1991).

In addition, reliance on the external network may come at the expense of forming new social connections at the university. When students use Facebook to keep track of old friends rather than making new friends, their ability to perceive resources from the university-affiliated social network may be reduced (Subrahmanyam et al., 2008). According to Heiberger and Harper (2008), faculty and administrators reported that they felt Facebook and other social media websites might isolate students from forming new relationships. Students who concentrate on maintaining their precollege social network are more likely to experience loneliness and "friendsickness" (Paul & Brier, 2001). Paul and Brier defined friendsickness as grieving over the loss of precollege friends. Although all new students may experience friendsickness to some degree, the constant reminder of the activities of old friends on Facebook may intensify feelings of friendsickness. Research by Lloyd et al. did find that Facebook use had a negative effect on peer relationships. (Although it should be noted that while the relationship was statistically significant, the effect size was negligible ($r^2 = -.015$)).

More evidence for the effect of students' experiencing isolation when they concentrate on the external network is illustrated by one of McMillan and Morrison's (2008) participants. "Stacey," an international student, reported that she enjoyed using the internet in the morning in order to chat with friends back in her home country, Greece. However, her engagement in this morning network maintenance lead her to begin to resent her morning classes and other university related activities that kept her from working on her previous friendships. Maintenance of the external network can lead to dissatisfaction with the university (Astin, 1993; Hausmann et al., 2007).

FACEBOOK AND STUDENT AFFAIRS

Student affairs professionals may consider embracing Facebook for the good things that it contributes to student integration while at the same time preparing for some of Facebook's more negative consequences. Facebook can be useful for students forming new weak tie relationships and can help students identify groups and individuals with whom they might wish to associate. Student affairs professionals might be able to use some features of Facebook to help students identify relevant groups, activities, and shared interests. These connections may in turn allow students to create a rewarding network at the university, which may lead to greater commitment to that university. However, student affairs professionals should also make certain that freshmen have opportunities to engage socially offline as well, as offline engagement seems to be vital for the development of communication skills. Providing offline engagement may also help students to build a new university-affiliated social network, rather than over-relying on their family and high school friends for their social needs.

Another area of concern is how useful Facebook truly is for student affairs professionals. Student affairs professionals are learning to utilize Facebook for student engagement in a variety of ways, including setting up group and fan pages for their universities, colleges, departments, athletic teams, and campus organizations. However, studies by Lampe et al. in 2006 and 2008 found that most students do not expect to interact with university faculty or staff on Facebook. In fact, some students report that they prefer not to be contacted via Facebook and view such contact as intrusive (Berg, Bergaum, & Christoph, 2007). Student affairs professionals must exercise caution when considering when and how to connect with students via Facebook.

Researchers in higher education, human communication, and technology should begin to give more directed attention to the effects outlined in this chapter. From previous research, we understand that sometimes Facebook use facilitates networking building and sometimes it leads to information overload and a lack of growth in communication skill. Sometimes Facebook use provides assistance with academic achievement and sometimes it leads to a decreased focus on academics. Sometimes students' connections to their precollege network can provide valuable social support while for others these connections can lead to feelings of loneliness, a sense of disconnection from the university, and failure to persist. Investigations that look beyond the effects of Facebook use and begin to explore the nuances and theoretical explanations of these effects are needed. Are there mediating variables that determine the utility of Facebook for student integration and retention? Are certain students more likely to experience either the enhancing or the debilitating effects of Facebook? Or are these aspects of Facebook experienced as dialectical tensions? That is, opposing tensions which successful students learn to manage (for a review of dialectical tensions see Baxter & Montgomery, 1996). Finally, and perhaps most importantly, can higher education institutions and student affairs professionals learn how to help students navigate Facebook usage in a way that helps increase student success?

In addition, higher education and communication technology researchers might consider the various ways that Facebook may help or hinder nontraditional students. Much of the research drawn upon for this chapter has been conducted with a traditional college student sample. Nontraditional students may show different patterns of Facebook use and find different components of Facebook useful or harmful for staying connected to the campus community.

CONCLUSION

In the end, it is likely that Facebook is neither a panacea for student engagement nor a signal of the end of meaningful interpersonal connection on campus. Rather, Facebook likely has a similar effect on student community as the effect of the Internet on the wired neighborhoods studied by Hampton and Wellman (2003). They argued that:

> The Internet is neither weakening nor radically transforming community, but is instead adding onto existing forms of communication. We have argued that online socialites are not a distinct social system, separate and cut off from existing foci of activity and existing social network members. Rather, the Internet affects community as one form of communication among many, whose use and implications are intertwined. (p. 303)

Facebook and other social networking sites operate as an extension of the type of internet communication studied by Hampton and Wellman. As such, they do provide new ways for students to connect and new challenges for student social engagement, but such innovations and challenges are not drastically different from those previously encountered in endeavors to find interpersonal connection and community on university campuses. Student affairs professionals should become aware of the ways that students engage with social networking sites in order to leverage opportunities for furthering student integration while remaining aware of the limitations for community building that social networking sites present.

REFERENCES

Aleman, A. M. M., & Wartman, K. L. (2009). *Online social networking on campus: Understanding what matters in student culture.* New York: Taylor & Francis.

Altman, I., & Taylor, D. A. (1973). *Social penetration: The development of interpersonal relationships.* New York: Holt, Rinehart, and Winston.

American College Testing Programs. (2009). National collegiate retention and persistence to degree rates. Available at http://www.act.org/research/policymakers/pdf/retain_2009.pdf

Astin, A. W. (1993). *What matters in college?* San Francisco, CA: Jossey-Bass, Inc.

Barkhaus, L., & Tashiro, J. (2010). Student socialization in the age of Facebook. In: *Proceedings of the 28th annual SIGCHI conference on human factors in computing systems*, Atlanta. ACM, New York (pp. 133–142).

Baxter, L. A., & Montgomery, B. M. (1996). *Relating: Dialogues & dialectics.* New York: Guilford Press.

Bean, J. P. (1990). Why students leave: Insights from research. In: D. Hossler & J. P. Bean (Eds), *The strategic management of college enrollments* (pp. 147–169). San Francisco, CA: Jossey-Bass, Inc.

Berg, J., Bergaum, L., & Christoph, K. (2007). Social networking technologies: A 'poke' for campus services. *EDUCAUSE Review, 42*, 32–44.

Berger, J. B., & Milem, J. F. (1999). The role of student involvement and perceptions of integration in a causal model of student persistence. *Research in Higher Education, 40*, 641–664.

Boyd, D. M., & Ellison, N. B. (2007). Social network sites: Definition, history, and scholarship. *Journal of Computer-Mediated Communication, 13*, 210–230.

Brennan, T. (1982). Perspectives on loneliness. In: L. A. Peplau & D. Perlman (Eds), *Loneliness: A sourcebook of current theory, research and therapy* (pp. 269–290). New York: Wiley.

Brown, P., & Levinson, S. (1987). *Politeness: Some universals in language use*. Cambridge: Cambridge University Press.

Bryant, E. M., & Marmo, J. (in press). Relational maintenance strategies on Facebook. *Kentucky Journal of Communication*.

Bugeja, M. (2005). *Interpersonal divide: The search for community in a technological age*. New York: Oxford.

Canary, D. J., Stafford, L., Hause, K. S., & Wallace, L. A. (1993). An inductive analysis of relational maintenance strategies: Comparison among lovers, relatives, friends, and others. *Communication Research Reports, 10*, 5–14.

Carey, K. (2005). One step from the finish line: Higher college graduate rates are within our reach. Retrieved from the Education Trust website: http://www.edtrust.org/dc/publication/one-step-from-the-finish-line-higher-college-graduation-rates-are-within-our-reach

Chapman, D. W., & Pascarella, E. T. (1983). Predictors of academic and social integration of college students. *Research in Higher Education, 19*, 295–322.

Christie, N. G., & Dinham, S. M. (1991). Institutional and external influence on social integration in the freshmen year. *Journal of Higher Education, 62*, 412–436.

Coleman, J. S. (1988). Social capital in the creation of human capital. *American Journal of Sociology, 94*, S95–S120.

Cutrona, C. E. (1982). Transition to college: Loneliness and the process of social adjustment. In: L. A. Peplau & D. Perlman (Eds), *Loneliness: A sourcebook of current theory, research and therapy* (pp. 291–309). New York: Wiley.

Dindia, K. (2003). Definitions and perspectives on relational maintenance communication. In: D. J. Canary & M. Dainton (Eds), *Maintaining relationships through communication: Relational, contextual, and cultural variations* (pp. 1–28). Mahwah, NJ: Lawrence Erlbaum Associates.

Ellison, N. B., Steinfield, C., & Lampe, C. (2007). The benefits of Facebook "friends": Social capital and college students' use of online social network sites. *Journal of Computer Mediated Communication, 12*, 1143–1168.

Engelberg, E., & Sjoberg, L. (2004). Internet use, social skills, and adjustment. *CyberPsychology & Behavior, 7*, 41–47.

Gemmill, E., & Peterson, M. (2006). Technology use among college students: Implications for student affairs professionals. *NASPA Journal, 43*, 280–300.

Giannini, G. A., Hamilton, K. A., & Spitzberg, B. H. (2007). Coping with college: Exploring loneliness through coping strategies enacted by incoming college freshmen. Paper presented at a meeting of the National Communication Association, Chicago, IL, USA.

Granovetter, M. S. (1973). The strength of weak ties. *American Journal of Sociology, 78*, 1360–1380.

Grant-Vallone, E., Reid, K., Umali, C., & Pohlert, E. (2003–2004). An analysis of the effects of self-esteem, social support, and participation in student support services on students' adjustment and commitment to college. *Journal of College Student Retention, 5*, 255–274.

Hampton, K., & Wellman, B. (2003). Neighboring in Netville: How the Internet supports community and social capital in a wired suburb. *City and Community, 2*, 277–311.

Hausmann, L. R. M., Schofield, J. W., & Woods, R. L. (2007). Sense of belonging as a predictor of intention to persist among African-American and White first year college students. *Research in Higher Education, 48*, 803–838.

Hays, R. B., & Oxley, D. (1986). Social network development and functioning during a life transition. *Journal of Personality and Social Psychology, 50*, 305–313.

Heiberger, G., & Harper, R. (2008). Have you Facebooked Astin lately? Using technology to increase student involvement. *New Directions of Student Services, 124*, 19–38.

Higher Education Research Institute. (2007). College freshmen and online social networking sites. Available at http://www.gseis.ucla.edu/heri/PDFs/pubs/briefs/brief-091107-socialnetworking.pdf

Joinson, A. N. (2008). 'Looking at', 'Looking up', or 'Keeping up with' People? Motives and uses of Facebook. *Proceeding of the twenty-sixth annual SIGCHI conference on Human factors in computing systems*, Florence, Italy, pp. 1027–1036. New York: ACM.

Kavanaugh, A., Carroll, J. M., Rosson, M. B., Zin, T. T., & Reese, D. D. (2005). Community networks: Where offline communities meet online. *Journal of Computer Mediated Communication, 10*. Available at http://jcmc.indiana.edu/vol10/issue4/kavanaugh.html

Lampe, C., Ellison, N. B., & Steinfield, C. (2006). A Face(book) in the Crowd: Social searching vs. social browsing. In *CSCW 06 Conference Proceedings*, Banff, Alberta, pp. 167–170. New York: ACM.

Lampe, C., Ellison, N. B., & Steinfield, C. (2008). Change in use and perception of Facebook. In *CSCW 08 Conference Proceedings*, San Diego, pp. 721–730. New York: ACM.

Lenhart, A., Purcell, K., Smith, A., & Zickuhr, K. (2010). *Social media and mobile internet use among teens and young adults*. Retrieved from the Pew Internet and American Life Project website: http://pewinternet.org/Reports/2010/Social-Media-and-Young-Adults.aspx

Lloyd, J., Dean, L. A., & Cooper, D. L. (2007). Students technology use and its effects on peer relationships, academic involvement and healthy lifestyles. *NASPA Journal, 44*, 481–495.

McElvain, K., & Smyth, C. (2006). Facebook: Implications for student affairs professionals. *Bulletin (ACUI), 18*–22.

McEwan, B. (2009). *Social integration and university retention*. Dissertation, Arizona State University, Tempe, AZ. Dissertation Abstracts International, publication number 02410939. Ann Arbor, MI: ProQuest.

McEwan, B., & Guerrero, L. K. (2010a). The social integration through maintenance model: A study of newly-formed friendship networks. Paper presented at a November meeting of the National Communication Association, San Francisco, CA, USA.

McEwan, B., & Guerrero, L. K. (2010b). Freshmen engagement through communication: Predicting friendship formation strategies and perceived availability of network resources from communication skills. *Communication Studies, 61*(4), 445–463.

McMillan, S. J., & Morrison, M. (2008). Coming of age with the Internet: A qualitative exploration of how the Internet has become an integral part of young people's lives. *New Media Society, 8*, 73–95.

Nalwa, K., & Anand, A. P. (2003). Internet addiction in students: A cause of concern. *CyberPsychology and Behavior, 6*, 653–656.

Napoli, A. R., & Wortman, P. M. (1998). Psychosocial factors related to retention and early departure of two-year community college students. *Research in Higher Education, 39*, 419–455.

Paul, E., & Brier, S. (2001). Friendsickness in the transition to college: Precollege predictors and college adjustment correlates. *Journal of Counseling and Development, 79*, 77–89.

Perlman, D., & Peplau, L. A. (1982). Perspectives on loneliness. In: L. A. Peplau & D. Perlman (Eds), *Loneliness: A sourcebook of current theory, research and therapy* (pp. 1–18). New York: Wiley.

Rainie, L., Lenhart, A., Fox, S., Spooner, T., & Horrigan, J. (2000). *Tracking online life: How women use the Internet to cultivate relationships with family and friends.* Retrieved from the Pew Internet and American Life Project website: http://www.pewinternet.org/∼/media//Files/Reports/2000/Report1.pdf

Ponzetti, J. J. (1990). Loneliness among college students. *Family Relations, 39*, 336–340.

Putnam, R. D. (2000). *Bowling alone.* New York: Simon & Schuster.

Samter, W., Whaley, B. B., Mortenson, S. T., & Burleson, B. R. (1997). Ethnicity and emotional support in same-sex friendship: A comparison of Asian-Americans, African-Americans, and Euro-Americans. *Personal Relationships, 4*, 413–430.

Skahill, M. P. (2003). The role of social support network in college persistence among freshman students. *College Student Retention, 4*, 39–52.

Stoecker, J., Pascarella, E. T., & Wolfe, L. M. (1988). Persistence in higher education: A 9-year test of a theoretical model. *Journal of College Student Development, 29*, 196–209.

Subrahmanyam, K., Reich, S. M., Waechter, N., & Espinoza, G. (2008). Online and offline social networks. Use of social networking sites by emerging adults. *Journal of Applied Developmental Psychology, 29*, 420–433.

Thomas, S. L. (2000). Ties that bind: A social network approach for understating student integration and persistence. *Journal of Higher Education, 71*, 591–615.

Thompson, B. (2008). How college freshmen communicate student academic support: A grounded theory study. *Communication Education, 57*, 123–144.

Tinto, V. (1975). Dropout from higher education: A theoretical synthesis of recent research. *Review of Educational Research, 45*, 89–125.

Tinto, V. (1993). *Leaving college: Rethinking the causes and cures of student attrition* (2nd ed.). Chicago: University of Chicago Press.

Tinto, V. (2000). Linking learning and leaving: Exploring the role of the college classroom in student departure. In: J. M. Braxton (Ed.), *Reworking the student departure puzzle* (pp. 81–94). Nashville, TN: Vanderbilt University Press.

Titus, M. A. (2004). An examination of the influence of institutional context on student persistence at 4-year colleges and universities: A multilevel approach. *Research in Higher Education, 45*, 673–699.

Yazedjian, A., Toews, M. L., Sevin, T., & Purswell, K. E. (2008). "It's a whole new world": A qualitative exploration of college students' definitions of and strategies for college success. *Journal of College Student Development, 49*, 141–154.

Zornoza, A., Ripoll, P., & Peiro, J. M. (2002). Conflict management in groups that work in two different communication contexts: Face-to-face and computer mediated communication. *Small Group Research, 33*, 481–508.

SOCIAL MEDIA FOR SOCIAL RESEARCH: APPLICATIONS FOR HIGHER EDUCATION COMMUNICATIONS

Nicolle Merrill

ABSTRACT

Social media tools such as Facebook and Twitter are increasingly being integrated into recruiting and outreach activities across the US universities. Despite their popularity among staff, resources on best practices in higher education remain sparse. As new communication tools evolve and transform higher education, researchers must adapt their approaches to understand these tools and collect relevant data. This study presents and tests new methods for conducting research in higher education communications. The author presents digital ethnography as a relevant methodological approach for researching and understanding online communities in higher education. Using an exploratory online survey distributed through online social networks as an example, the author gathers data on the use of social media in international higher education recruiting and outreach. The exploratory survey sought information on which social media tools were being used by university staff, the perceived benefits and drawbacks of social media use in international recruiting and outreach, and how universities measured social media for international recruiting purposes. Using a digital ethnographic approach, the author gathered relevant, timely data from international higher education professionals and gained insight into the norms, rules, and workings of social networking communities. Results point to new methods for understanding the evolution of higher education communications for researchers and university staff alike. Data from the exploratory study of international higher education communications are presented as an example of the rich amount of data obtained through the approach.

As the new decade unfolds, universities and colleges are increasingly using social media such as Facebook and Twitter to communicate with potential students. The trend toward increased usage of social media in higher education has produced social media boot camps for quick "how-to" workshops at higher education conferences, lists of the top 100 colleges on Twitter, and a scramble to articulate rules on "friending" for college admissions counselors. New media tools such as Facebook and Twitter are increasingly being integrated into recruiting and outreach activities across the US universities (Ganim Barnes & Mattson, 2009). Facebook, Twitter, blogs, and other social media have been identified as a "key to communicating with this generation of students," according to the CEO of National Association for College Admissions Counseling (NACAC), Joyce Smith (NACAC, 2009). University admissions and marketing offices use social networking sites to promote their schools, enhance their brand, and engage future students. Beyond information distribution, higher education is also using social media tools to gain insight into target audience needs and competitor practices, through information shared on social networking communities.

Though institutions are increasingly incorporating social media into communication strategies, there is a lack of academic research on its use in higher education communications. The University of Massachusetts Dartmouth published the first statistically rigorous longitudinal study on social media use in college admissions in 2008 (Ganim Barnes & Mattson, 2009). Extensive data, compiled in 2007 and 2008 from interviews with 453 four-year universities, revealed that universities engage extensively in blogging activities and participate on social networks like MySpace and Facebook. Two years later, Twitter and YouTube have increased in popularity in higher education communications, with MySpace declining in use. Thus, the information presented in a two-year old, large-scale study is already outdated. Yet questions still remain about the motivations, benefits, and success of social media communications in higher education.

The pace at which new communication technologies are introduced and incorporated into the higher education communications landscape presents challenges for administrators and researchers alike. How do institutions gather timely, relevant information on the use of new media tools? Moreover, as social media transforms communication and information distribution across industries, researchers have an opportunity to investigate how such tools can contribute to existing research methodologies. How can social media complement existing social research methods? As higher education embraces new communication tools, researchers must adapt to new research methodologies to understand the very tools they study.

This chapter presents digital ethnography as a relevant, useful methodology for social research in higher education communications. Using an exploratory study launched by GlobalCampus in February 2010 as a case study, the chapter examines the use of social media tools for research on social media use in higher education communications and its implications for higher education researchers and institutions.

The *Social Media in International Student Recruiting and Outreach* survey for international admissions asked international admissions staff about the use of social media in international student recruiting and outreach. This exploratory survey sought to clarify which social media tools were being used by university staff, to understand the perceived benefits and drawbacks of social media use, and to identify how universities measured social media use for recruiting purposes. The survey was distributed exclusively online, using new media tools as the primary communication channels and research methodology. The results from the case study reveal new methods in which institutions and researchers can use new communication technologies to gather timely, relevant data to understand trends in social media use in higher education communications. Additionally, the preliminary results of the international student recruiting survey present a snapshot of current trends in international higher education communications.

RESEARCHING ONLINE COMMUNITIES

New communication tools are changing organizational communications across industries. Corporations have adopted new communication channels such as Twitter, Facebook, and YouTube to enhance brand positioning and to listen to their consumers and competitors (Gillin, 2008). Nonprofits are integrating social media into fundraising initiatives while donors are using Twitter to spread news about their favorite cause (Waters et al., 2009). Even the US government has recognized the value of reaching out to constituents and sharing content, with government organizations participating in social networking sites and maintaining blogs (Drapeau, 2009). Higher education is engaged with colleges and universities launching Facebook pages and running Twitter accounts.[1]

Emerging forms of Information and Communications Technologies (ICT) such as social media enable users to create and share relevant content within their virtual communities. User-generated content is produced and distributed in public forums in real time, creating online environments rich in quantitative and qualitative data for the researcher. To capture those data, social science researchers are exploring new methods and adapting traditional methods in the research process (Hine, 2005). In *Virtual Methods: Issues in Social Research on the Internet*, Hine takes the approach that social science research always relies on communication. Regardless of the method, surveys, interviews or observations, social science research involves communication (2005, p. 3). Thus, the author argues, it is "reasonable to ask if changing the mode of communication affects methodological assumptions or practices" (2005, p. 3).

Digital ethnography is among the emerging research methods for understanding and analyzing industry habits in virtual communities such as Facebook, Twitter, and YouTube. Digital ethnography has evolved from traditional methods of ethnography as a methodology to understand the habits and norms of virtual communities (Murthy, 2008). Traditional ethnography is used in the social sciences as a means for gaining insight into a particular culture or community. Researchers focus on a group of people by observing or participating in their communities over a set period of time. Qualitative data is collected through these means and interpreted using "metaphorical, hermeneutic, and analytic" means, using the researcher as a human mediated instrument (Caterall & Maclaran, 2001, p. 230). Ethnography as a method for collecting data on a particular group is considered a flexible and open-ended technique, and one that is well suited to meet the evolving needs in both research areas and of researchers themselves (Caterall & Maclaran, 2001, p. 232).

For the ethnographic researcher, a virtual community can best be understood as "an aggregation of individuals or business partners who interact around a shared interest, where the interaction is at least partially supported and/or mediated by technology and guided by some protocols or norms" (Porter, 2004). This definition, selected from a *Typology of Virtual Communities: A Multi-disciplinary Foundation for Future Research*, takes into consideration the roles and norms of a community as traditionally studied in anthropological disciplines, and applies them to computer-mediated virtual communities. Virtual communities constitute individuals who join a group with shared interests and ideas for the purpose of discussions and exchange. Ethnographic methods, which enable researchers to gain insight and understanding into meanings, habits, and norms of specific communities, are well-suited for adaptation to virtual communities.[2]

Analyzing virtual communities for research is not new, yet research on the subject has only begun to be taken seriously in academic research. Hine argues for more research on virtual communities, addressing skeptics by declaring, "however skeptical we might be of the hype surrounding the new technologies, their self-evident newness and the radical potential which is proposed to them provides a powerful resource to which researchers can hitch their own research agenda" (2005, p. 6). The author makes the case in her book, through a series of case studies, that methodologies in Internet research must be documented, strengthened and not ignored.

For-profit companies have used digital ethnography techniques for market research in the past decade. Marketers analyze consumer habits, monitor brand loyalty, and respond to customer needs and complaints by observing online habits and participating in online communities. In 2002, Robert Kozinets, associate professor at the Kellogg School of Management, published the "The Field Behind the Screen: Using Netnography for Marketing Research in Online Communities," in which he elaborated on ethnographic methods used for harnessing, classifying, and analyzing the data obtained in virtual communities (Kozinets, 2002). He defines "netnography" as "new qualitative research methodology that adapts ethnographic research techniques to the study of cultures and communities emerging through computer-mediated communications" (Kozinets, 2002, p. 2). Though the term itself has since evolved from netnography to digital ethnography, and the communities in which he tested his methods have changed, the methodology remains the same.[3]

Digital ethnographers start with a specific research question and then identify the appropriate online forums that would be most likely to respond to the research question (Kozinets, 2002, pp. 4–5). Relevant communities are chosen based on criteria such as amount of "traffic" as indicated by postings, community interests as related to the research question, access to rich data, and significant member interactions between one another (Kozinets, 2002). Before participating in online communities, researchers should be familiar with the norms and habits of the target communities. After identifying the appropriate online communities, the researcher collects two types of qualitative data during the research period: the data directly from online community participants and the observations of the online community members and interactions (Kozinets, 2002, pp. 4–5). Data are then analyzed to obtain answers to the research question and contextualize information obtained from community participants. Similar to field notes, observations of online community interactions and participant habits contribute to a deeper understanding of the online communities being studied and enhance future research.

In *Digital Ethnography: An Examination of the Use of New Technologies for Social Research*, Murthy advocates strongly for the inclusion of new media technologies into social research methodologies. Despite the proliferation of new communication technologies, Murthy points out the lack of scholarly research on digital ethnography as a valid research method (Murthy, 2008). Building on the only notable previous digital ethnography work in the edited collection of Qualitative Research (2006), Murthy selects four new communication technologies for research methodologies and uses digital ethnography to examine their impact and use in social research. Among his choices are online questionnaires and social networking sites. Murthy describes online questionnaires as a cost-effective, time saving technique to reach a global set of participants and the "ease of implementing structured responses, adaptive questions, and point-and-click" (Murthy, 2008, p. 842). Sites like surveymonkey.com allow users to easily design surveys, access qualitative and quantitative results, and analyze them. Before online services like surveymonkey.com, survey design processes were lengthy. Quantitative stats took longer to calculate and distribution was timely and expensive. According to Murthy, such online services make surveys easier to design, implement, and analyze. Moreover, online survey technologies allow researchers to conduct international, large scale surveys, which before these technologies would have been costly and resource heavy.

Murthy advocates for the inclusion of social networking sites into social research. Taking the position that users network through "existing and compound relations (friends of friends)" (Murthy 2008, p. 844).

Murthy finds social networking sites to be rich in data and useful to ethnographers in a variety of ways. Social networking sites give ethnographers access to potential research respondents, allow researchers to create pages specifically for research, and helps researchers disseminate useful information to their target audiences. Hine (2005) echoes this statement noting that new media offer researchers the possibility of reaching new populations (p. 1). Moreover, online forums help keep the researcher accountable as information is exchanged and presented in public. The ever-changing nature of these tools, in combination with the role of the participant-observer in the research process, Murthy (2008) notes, create challenges for traditional research methodologies (p. 849). Because of the anonymity inherent in digital exchanges, it is difficult to verify respondent's background and qualifications. Furthermore, the researcher must be perceived as authentic to participate in the communities from which they seek information.

Digital ethnography as a flexible social research methodology for analyzing online habits can be applied to examine social media use in higher education communications. Though peer-reviewed academic research in this industry is unavailable, some examples of formal and informal digital ethnographic studies in higher education can be found across the web. Universitiesandcolleges.org released a study on the top 100 colleges on Twitter in October 2009. Researchers used digital ethnography to identify the trends in Twitter account use among the top 100 colleges in the United States. Researchers gleaned information on the account type, number of followers, users following, number of tweets per day, and total number of tweets to understand Twitter usage trends in higher education outreach (UniversitiesAndColleges.org, 2010).

In 2008, Rachel Rueben, an MBA student, conducted a comprehensive-independent study on the use of social media in higher education communications. She created an online survey and distributed it through three higher education list servs (Reuben, 2008). More interestingly, according to the citations in her report, she drew on ethnographic information located in a blog post for an education marketing consultancy website, Academica Group. In a post dated May 2008 and entitled *How Higher Ed Is Using Facebook Pages*, Melissa Cheater reveals the digital ethnographic observations of more than 400 colleges' and universities' Facebook pages (2008a). In November 2008, the same author posted a blog entitled *Facebook Page Best Practices (For Higher Education)*, another post rich in digital ethnographic observations (Cheater, 2008b). Although these results were not part of a larger study, the author used digital ethnography to analyze the rich amount of data available on Facebook to understand higher education best practices. She analyzed the Facebook data to understand and present effective marketing tactics in university profile design, layout, and imagery.

CONTEXT FOR EXPLORATORY STUDY

These informal studies demonstrate the accessibility of data for research using digital ethnographic methods and the richness of data currently available to researchers. With these studies and research tools in mind, GlobalCampus launched the *Social Media in International Student Recruiting and Outreach* survey for international admissions. In the November/December 2009 issue of National Association of International Educators (NAFSA) bi-monthly magazine, *International Educator*, Dessoff (2009) voiced the opinion that internet recruiting is "here to stay" (p. 20). Internet recruiting with social media tools is altering recruiting strategies and teaching traditional PR experts' new ways to communicate with international student populations. Cheryl Darrup-Boychuck, the C.E.O of the U.S. Journal of Academics, emphasized online recruiting as critical to international recruiting methods. However, despite the popularity of Internet recruiting, resources on the methods and practices in international higher education recruiting and outreach are sparse. In NAFSA's *Guide to International Student Recruitment*, 2nd edition, published earlier in 2009, the authors devote three paragraphs to recruiting with social media (Heaney, 2009). In the final paragraph, the author refers readers to the University of Massachusetts Dartmouth longitudinal study on social media use in college admissions, discussed earlier. Moreover, the paragraphs are located in a section entitled "Advertising: What, Where and When to say it," reflecting the classification of social media as a one-way advertising tool, rather than a two-way communication tool (Heaney, 2009, pp. 72–74). In the Internet resources appendix under "Internet Sites – Cyber Recruitment Resources" there are no social media resources (Heaney, 2009, p. 181).

This gap identified an immediate need for information and became the catalyst for the survey by GlobalCampus. Our task was to learn about the current state of international higher education communications. GlobalCampus is an international start up organization with a small team operating across multiple time zones and geographic locations.[4] We created the exploratory survey to close the knowledge gap in current international higher education communication practices. The survey asked which social media tools were being used by university staff, inquired about the perceived benefits and drawbacks of social media use in international recruiting and outreach, and asked how universities measured social media for international recruiting purposes. Working under the time constraints of an exploratory study, we chose social media tools as the most effective tool for information distribution and data collection. Additionally, we sought to learn more about how international higher education institutions were using social media through subjective observations during the research process.

METHOD

On February 8, 2010, we created a blog post hosted on GlobalCampus.com to introduce readers and visitors to GlobalCampus to the survey and link to Surveymonkey.com. The survey was built and administered using Surveymonkey.com. It included 11 close-ended questions, which allowed respondents to check all applicable responses, with the option of adding qualitative information after each question, and 4 open-ended questions. The final question asked for optional contact information.

Social media tools such as Twitter and LinkedIn were used to distribute the survey to an international higher education audience. The GlobalCampus Twitter account (@GlobalCampus) served as the primary distribution channel, with LinkedIn industry forums as the secondary channel.

To reach international admissions staff using social media in international outreach and recruiting, we chose Twitter as a distribution and communication tool. Twitter facilitates information distribution through the unique method of "retweeting." Retweeting gives users an easy option to share relevant information found in the Twitterfeed with their followers.[5] Though the retweet method is subjective and unpredictable, the power of the action is important as it allows for quick information distribution and high visibility of a retweeted link. If a user in the Twitter community sees a post or link of value, the user can retweet the post, giving the link visibility in networks outside of the original user's network. Moreover, researchers can organize information to ensure that target audiences on Twitter are seeing relevant information. By using "hashtags" (#hashtags), Twitter users can organize a post by topic.[6] Hashtags are user-generated organizational tags that categorize information and help information spread through the network. Though hashtags are complex, time sensitive, and changing, through observation of industry leaders on Twitter researchers can identify relevant categories by which they can organize their posts. In the example of international higher education, the hashtags "#highered," "#international," and "#admissions" were identified as relevant tags to categorize the survey. Unfortunately, no specific tag for international higher education exists.

Twitter also facilitates direct interaction between users with a common interest that is not dependent on previous interactions. Thus a researcher can reach out to the head of a university department simply by using the "@reply" feature to ask a question or point out an article of interest. The user contacted can respond publicly to the request, or simply ignore it.

Though the number of followers can vary from day to day, in February, GlobalCampus had an existing Twitter account with approximately 150 followers. The account had been live for three months and we posted information daily related to international student recruiting and international higher education. Through use and observation during those three months, we gained an understanding of the norms of the Twitter community, identified the top influencers in international higher education using Twitter, and gleaned information on the methods for appropriate Twitter posting. Thus as researchers, we first identified the community of interest and sought to understand its habits, roles, and norms before launching the survey.

Using the GlobalCampus Twitter account (@GlobalCampus), we posted the blog link with a message to international higher education professionals to pass it on by using the phrase "Please RT" request. "Please RT" is a phrase used by a variety of Twitter users to ask for users help in spreading information. It is a request to be used lightly and not overused, as overuse is akin to crying wolf. If overused, the poster could be perceived as inauthentic.

Though Twitter is a relevant information distribution tool, the predictability of retweets and information distribution is not exact. To ensure that the survey reached the target audience of international admissions, we chose to utilize LinkedIn as a secondary distribution and communication tool. LinkedIn is a social network for professionals which provides a place where users can exchange ideas and knowledge with an expanded network of other professionals. LinkedIn contains industry forums and groups where users can post relevant discussions, jobs, and news for their target communities. The user-generated content is often monitored by peers and information deemed unnecessary or spam can be removed from the group. Users must request permission and be accepted by community moderators to join groups.

Using the author's existing account on LinkedIn, we identified four groups that would comprise the target audience for the survey: College Counselors: Admissions and Financial Aid; Higher Education Management Group; International Student Recruitment for U.S. Schools & Universities; and NAFSA: Association for International Educators. Many users belong to similar groups. Although we could have posted to more groups, we did not want to be perceived as spam and be expelled from communities.

We posted the original blog post from globalcampus.com into the forums to help promote the survey.

The survey ran from February, 8, 2010 until March 8, 2010. Information gleaned from retweets (RT), direct messages from followers (DM), and contacts from forums in LinkedIn was used to promote the survey to a targeted audience of international higher education professionals. To track and measure the progress of the survey distribution through Twitter and LinkedIn we tracked the number of visits to our GlobalCampus blog post using a common URL shortener at http://j.mp. URL shorteners are a free tool that condenses website addresses into short links to fit into the 140 character-limited field on Twitter. The tool also provides tracking for real time analytics, allowing researchers to view the amount of clicks on a shortened link. We used the analytic tool to count the number of clicks on the GlobalCampus blog link over the course of a month. This measurement helped us to see how many times our blog post about the survey was accessed throughout the day, week, and month. Additionally, we counted the number of retweets about the survey on Twitter to track which type of users were promoting the survey.

RESULTS

Although these results are limited due to the exploratory nature of this study, they illustrate the potential for this approach when used more extensively. We received 30 completed survey responses, measured the progress of survey distribution across social networks, and obtained up-to-date data about the use of social media for international student recruiting and outreach. Respondents were not required to submit contact information. Those that provided voluntary contact information indicated responses from university staffs in the United States, Canada, New Zealand, and Germany. The results from the distribution and data collection methodology are presented first to demonstrate the process and effectiveness of social media as a research distribution tool, followed by a summary of results from the international recruiting survey itself.

Results of Social Media Distribution

On February 8, the first day of the survey launch on Twitter and LinkedIn, 41 people accessed the GlobalCampus blog link via the URL shortener, resulting in two completed surveys by end of the day. The link also received four retweets on the first day from Twitter users in higher education networks, indicating a preliminary interest in the survey among the target audience. On the same day, a member of a shared LinkedIn group messaged us a listserv address specifically for international higher education professionals. The listserv was unknown to us before the survey. Therefore, we distributed the blog post and link on the international education listserv on February 9, further promoting our survey to a target audience. On February 10, David Comp found the survey on the listserv and wrote us for permission to feature it on his industry blog, the International Higher Education Consulting Blog (IHEC).

On February 11, the survey was featured with our permission in a post on the International Higher Education Consulting Blog, encouraging readers to participate in the survey (Comp, 2010). A separate link to the IHEC post was then posted to the GlobalCampus Twitter feed. By being featured in an industry blog, we not only gained new visitors from a target audience, but also more credibility. On February 12, the link featuring the new IHEC blog post, was retweeted four times by Twitter users in higher education, promoting our survey to new networks of followers. By the end of the first week on February 14, the survey link was accessed 108 times, resulting in 10 completed surveys.

Clicks on the GlobalCampus blog link had diminished over the three-day holiday weekend, with zero clicks to our link on February 15. On Tuesday February 16, we reposted the GloblaCampus blog link to our network of Twitter users to bring attention to our survey once more, resulting in 18 more views and 3 more completed surveys. During the second week of Twitter and LinkedIn distribution, there were fewer total clicks than the prior week. At the end of two weeks, there were 140 clicks on the survey link and 18 completed surveys.

We reposted the survey on the GlobalCampus Twitter account again on February 24 to remind users that they had another week to complete it. The post resulted in 30 survey views and two more completed surveys. On February 26, the survey received 14 hits, and two more completed surveys. However, after February 26, survey clicks diminished, despite Twitter posts on March 3 and March 5 reminding GlobalCampus followers that the deadline to complete the survey was March. There were no retweets during that time period. The result of one month of survey distribution on Twitter and LinkedIn was 203 hits to the blog link and 30 completed surveys. This response pattern is illustrated in Fig. 1.

Although the results of the survey itself are limited by the small sample group, they are presented here as an example of the utility of this

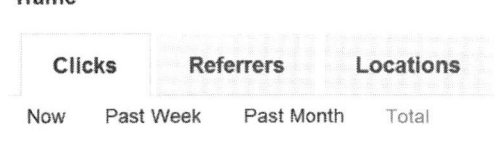

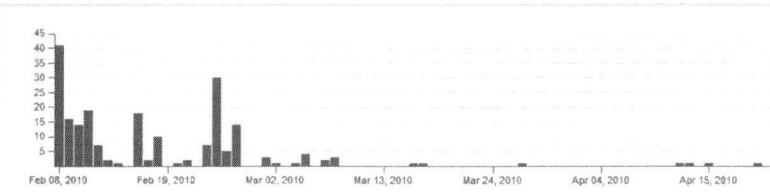

Fig. 1. Snapshot of Link Tracking during Month of Study Using bit.ly.

methodology in an exploratory context. With limited resources and time, we were able to gather timely and relevant data on the social media habits of 30 international education administrators. Furthermore, the data obtained can serve as a starting point for future research in international higher education communications and to promote discussions within the international higher education community.

Results of Exploratory Survey

The survey asked international higher education professionals what types of social media tools they used and who was responsible for their use in international outreach and recruiting. It also sought to clarify the perceived benefits and drawbacks of social media are and how university staffs measure the results. An overview of the results is presented in sections: Logistics, Motivations, and Measurement.

Logistics

The majority of responses overwhelmingly indicated Facebook as the preferred outreach tool, with Twitter also preferred by two-thirds of the respondents (Fig. 2).

These results are in line with the popularity of Twitter and Facebook use among domestic US admissions and outreach staff. YouTube was also

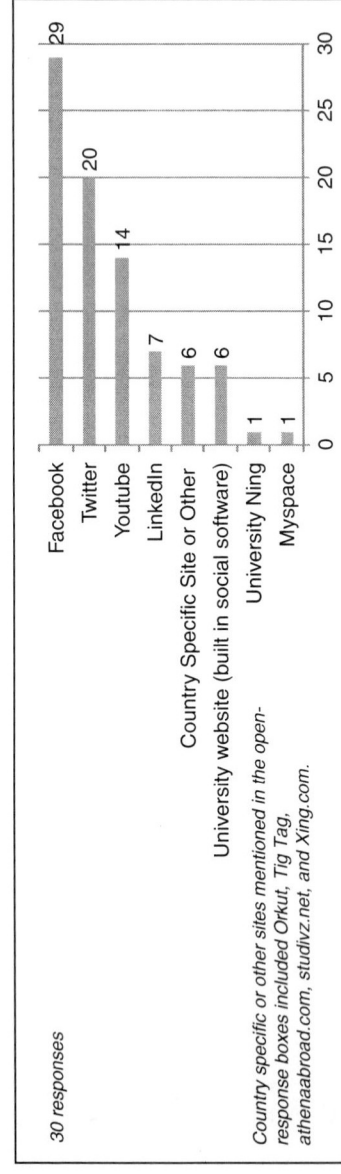

Fig. 2. Results from Question 1 in the Social Media in International Student Recruiting and Outreach Survey: What Social Networking Sites Do You Use for International Outreach and/or Internet Recruiting? (Check All That Apply).

favored by just under half of the responses, possibly reflecting the rise in video use among admissions and outreach staff and by target audiences.

Reflecting the specific needs of international higher education, six respondents indicated they were using different networks to reach students. Although social networks like Twitter and Facebook connect students and staff globally, country-specific sites like Orkut and TigTag can help staff target-specific student populations and ensure their outreach is connecting with a particular demographic.

Responses did not indicate a strong preference for LinkedIn, perhaps because LinkedIn is a community for professionals rather than students. However, for schools looking to recruit and reach out to future graduate students or professionals returning to school, LinkedIn can serve as a useful tool. Interestingly, only one staff indicated using MySpace as an outreach and recruiting tool.

The responsibility of social media outreach activities falls to a variety of staff. The question to determine who is in charge of social media activities elicited the most diverse responses in the survey. Though international admissions representatives primarily handle international outreach and recruiting, respondents were also given the option of choosing and listing another department or staff member, which half of the respondents chose. The variety of these responses, from Marketing and Communications to Business Development, indicate that social media in international outreach and recruitment is shared across departments and roles.

The diversity of staff involved could also reflect the variety of social media use. Social networking sites allow staff to launch online promotional campaigns and promote upcoming university events, responsibilities that are traditionally held by Marketing and Communications departments. These same tools also allow students to ask admissions questions and receive guidance during the application process, which is information normally provided by admissions staff. When a university uses Facebook, these activities occur in one place. As institutions learn more about their online community needs and goals, staff across departments are collaborating and sharing responsibilities to provide relevant information.

Motivations

As international higher education settles into using social media tools, there is a need to understand why institutions are using them. Respondents were asked the reasons why they use social media for international recruiting and about the perceived benefits and drawbacks of their use (Fig. 3).

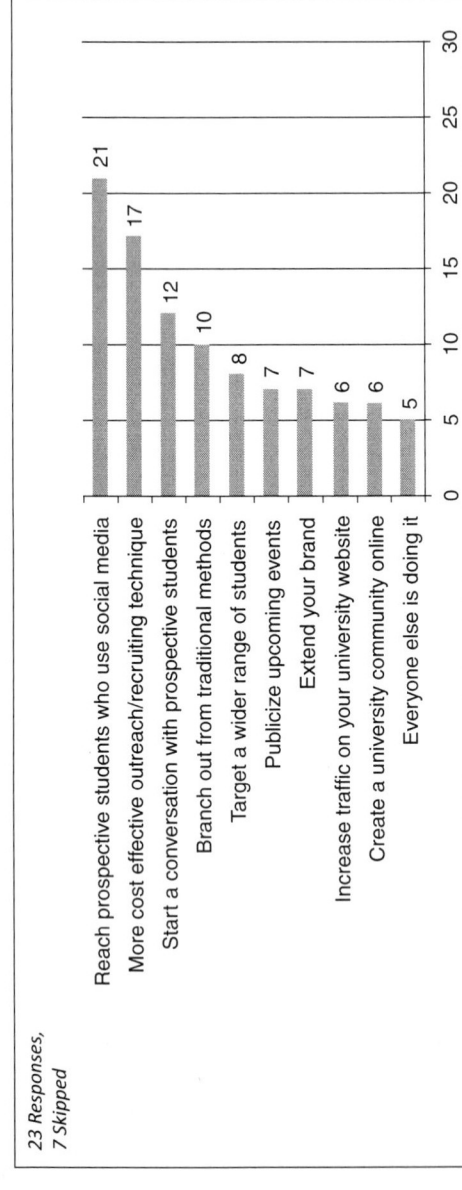

Fig. 3. Results from Question 7 in the Social Media in International Student Recruiting and Outreach Survey: What are the Top 3 Reasons You Use Social Media as Part of Your International Outreach and/or Internet Recruiting Strategy?

The most popular reason for engaging in social media use was to reach students already engaged in social media activities. In an age where students are gathering higher education information outside of university websites, international higher education staffs have noticed and sought to reach these students on familiar ground. Interestingly, respondents indicated that social media offers a more cost-effective recruiting strategy. Compared to traditional methods such as international travel, print and online advertising, social media tools are more cost-effective in international outreach and recruiting. More respondents chose this motivation over extending their brand or driving traffic to their website. Five respondents indicated that they were using social media because "everyone else is doing it."

Two-thirds of respondents selected "direct contact with students" as one of the top benefits of using social networking sites in international student recruiting. Over half agreed that social networking tools allow them more interaction with prospective students, ability to build better relationships, and reach target populations. Only two responses indicated they perceived no benefits to use social media.

According to respondents, the primary drawback of using social media is the ambiguous results garnered from social network recruiting. Ten respondents indicated that having no clear guidelines or information on effective strategies was a downside to use social networking sites. Building on that theme, seven respondents indicated a lack of familiarity with new and changing technologies.

Measurement

Although it is clear university staffs are using social media, many of those surveyed are unclear on how to measure the results of social media use. However, this is a challenge for all social media users across industries. This finding is also reflected in the reduced amount of responses to measurement questions in this section.

When asked if an institutional presence on social networking sites resulted in increased international student enrollment, the majority of respondents indicated that it was too early to tell. However, four indicated they were not measuring results and two indicated they did not see an increase. Five indicated they saw increases, but these increases were either not significant or difficult to attribute solely to social media use.

The three open-ended questions gave respondents an opportunity to elaborate on specific measurement techniques and ideas. However, responses to this section were lower than previous sections. It is unclear whether this is a reflection of normal low response rate to open-ended online questionnaires or a reflection that respondents lack information about measuring social media results.

When asked about quantifying results, Facebook metrics were the most popular way to measure results. Three respondents indicated they measured results by the number of interactions, such as questions, responses, RSVP's to events, within their communities. Respondents also indicated that they would like more participation from fans and more quality conversations as a means to measure results. Additionally, two staff noted the need for more guidance on measurement and a clear strategy for implementing social media outreach, echoing concerns from previous questions about the lack of available data on social media use. Some respondents seem unclear on how to distinguish between "qualified leads" and basic inquiries. This may reflect the lack of a tracking system. As social media use in international recruiting continues, it will be beneficial to understand how leads are identified and how those leads are being tracked from first contact on social networking sites through application and ultimately enrollment.

DISCUSSION

Through use of an online survey and distribution on social networking sites, we received 30 responses and gained insight into social media tools and their communities. The following sections present the discussion of the methodology used and the results of the exploratory study surveying international higher education communications.

Methodology Discussion

Distributing the survey information through Twitter and LinkedIn provided us with a useful methodology to gather survey data. Twitter served as an efficient distribution channel to quickly reach a target audience, and LinkedIn served as a strong tool to ensure our survey reached the right audience. Although distributing the survey, digital ethnographic observations helped us to understand how these tools were used within a target community, allowed us to adapt to new information, and provided us with guidelines for future use in higher education communications research.

Using Twitter as a distribution and communication tool requires adaptability. Information on Twitter moves at a rapid pace. The newsfeed in which users post information and receive information is continuously updating. Thus information posted on Twitter has a short lifespan. Twitter no longer archives tweets after six days, so information must be reposted in order to be seen and accessed during the length of the study. However, overposting can be problematic. The decreased responses to our posts in the last week of the survey, as indicated by fewer clicks on the blog link, may indicate that we had exhausted distribution through our current network. Our followers were no longer retweeting our survey nor clicking on the link. This could indicate that our survey was no longer newsworthy to our followers or simply that the interested people had already participated in the survey. Repeated posts asking users to complete the survey in the last week did not result in an increase in views. Unfortunately, due to the complexity of networks and inability to verify motivations for retweets, this is only speculation on community practices. There seems to be a limited time frame in which researchers can use Twitter to distribute surveys.

User behavior and norms on networks like Twitter change over time and can be hard to predict. We used hashtags such as #highered, #admissons, and #recruit to categorize our survey. However, after the survey was completed, we noticed a useful hashtag that was previously unknown to us: #smcedu. This hashtag consists of social media enthusiasts on Twitter who post and share information about social media trends in education, including higher education. Although we were unaware of this hashtag throughout the month long survey, it was brought to our attention on the last day when we thanked our followers for participating in the survey. A user, who was not a follower of GlobalCampus, retweeted the post to her network, and applied the #smcedu hashtag to categorize it. This act demonstrates how easily information can evolve and change on social networks. Moreover, with the amount of data and information available on Twitter it is hard to predict when information will be noticed, how it will be categorized and what options a researcher has to categorize the information. Research via Twitter requires a flexible approach and a solid understanding of the communities in which the researcher participates.

Because we did not distinguish between clicks to our blog from LinkedIn or Twitter, we do not know how much blog traffic came from the LinkedIn posts. However, we received relevant information from a LinkedIn user that eventually led to a feature in an industry blog. Through a shared connection in a LinkedIn group, we received access to an international education listserv, a community previously unknown to us before the survey launched. From the post on the listserv, we were noticed by a well-known industry blogger, who featured us on his blog and introduced us to his network of professionals in international education. This connection and result not only exposed the survey to more potential respondents, but also gave the survey credibility as it was essentially endorsed by a leading blogger in international education. These intangible connections within loosely connected networks like LinkedIn, give social media their power and require further examination and experimentation by researchers.

Measuring the visits to the blog with the survey link was also difficult. Using a URL shortener will only tell the researcher how many users clicked the link. It does not tell them how long the user stayed on the page to read the link, or if they are a unique or returning visitor. Researchers who are interested in-depth user data would be advised to use better analytic tools, such as Google Analytics. However, to track and gauge the popularity of a link within a network, the URL shortener functioned as a solid assessment tool.

Exploratory Survey Discussion

The data not only obtained from the survey itself gives a snapshot of current trends, but also provides a framework for discussion in future research in international higher education communication. For example, questions to determine how staffs use each social networking site were outside of the scope of this survey. How do university staffs use Twitter to reach out to international students? How do they use LinkedIn? Does YouTube serve as a conversational tool or just a place for international admissions videos? If social media tools combine traditionally separate roles, such as marketing, communications, and recruiting, into one place, who should be responsible for the activities?

The audience also plays a key role in global internet recruiting according to our respondents. Some staffs noted that they used country-specific networks to gain access to students. Sites, such as Orkut, have a more targeted audience than Facebook but did not receive much attention in this survey. However, this may be a function of the lack of international variability in responses. More data from a more focused study, or collected from administrators in specific countries or regions, is needed to understand what specific online communities international students use for social media communication.

Moreover, feedback from international students about their use of social media to obtain timely, relevant information from universities would contribute to a more comprehensive discussion. Social media are two-way communication tools. What information do international students need from online communities? How do they use these same social tools to get information from universities? Answers to these questions would help guide international departments as they reach out to students.

To gauge the effectiveness of social networking sites for international recruitment, international departments need have a clear set of metrics. Facebook metrics were the most popular measurement tool used by respondents, however it remains unclear how staffs use those metrics. What are they measuring? If an international university gains 200 fans in a week, but only three fans ask a question, what is the value of those metrics? Interestingly, when asked about metrics no respondents noted that they count the number of retweets (RT) and mentions (@) on Twitter, yet Twitter was the second most popular tool used by respondents in this survey. Measuring results requires different approaches that are specific to the social tool used.

An equally important question for social media researchers in the international higher education community is how to collect these data for the future and distribute it so university and college staffs have accurate, timely, accessible information at their disposal? To answer these questions and improve on the methods presented in this study, researchers should look to incorporating digital ethnography into their research toolkit. With many respondents acknowledging a lack of information and guidance in social media communications, there is a need for reliable, accessible information. By creating surveys and distributing them through social networks, researchers can gain preliminary data on trends and can share the results in a short timeframe. Moreover, the researcher gains valuable insight into the communities from which he/she seeks information. For example, Facebook was not chosen as a distribution tool for this survey. Though Facebook is a social network, a researcher with a Facebook account is limited in the ability to connect with industry professionals. The GlobalCampus Facebook page is made up of students who like GlobalCampus and were not the target audience for this survey. However, future studies could use digital methodology tools to understand what types of information is exchanged on international admissions Facebook pages and how students interact with university staff.

Researchers could also combine this method with traditional ethnography techniques such as interviews to better understand ambiguous data. Murthy concludes his research by stating that researchers would benefit from including other forms of ethnography alongside digital ethnography. This "multi-modal ethnography" may provide a richer data set from which to draw conclusions (Murthy, 2008, p. 849).

Future Directions

Despite the exploratory nature of the study, we reached 30 international higher education professionals and obtained data about social media habits in international student outreach and recruiting within a month. The response rate to the survey in combination with the useful data obtained from international higher education administrators, suggest that this is a valuable method with great potential for researchers to use and build on when studying social media communication habits. Moreover, digital ethnographic tools can help university staff conduct their own exploratory on communications practices, and thus gain more information to help them navigate new communications technologies.

Returning to Hine (2005), the author argues that "new ways of doing research deserve to be shared, in order to boost the collective stock of models for the research process" (p. 2). This methodological approach and exploratory study contributes to new methods of research, by demonstrating the availability of new research tools, methods, and access to new research participants. Moving forward, we must continue to incorporate these new tools into our research methodologies. We must not expect to report on trends in social media communications without first understanding the tools themselves.

NOTES

1. A website dedicated to guiding students through college process started a list of universities using Twitter and Facebook in October 2009. To understand the pace at which higher education has adopted social media tools, the first list of 50 universities on Twitter was created in December 2009. By April 2010, had five lists of 50 universities using Twitter, totaling 250 universities. Researchers can see the first list here http://mycollegeguide.org/blog/12/2009/big-list-50-colleges-universities-twitter-part-1/

2. Though it is beyond the scope of this chapter to debate definitions, the resource "Community and the Internet" in the Handbook of Internet Studies serves as a comprehensive resource on the many definitions of virtual communities (Kendall, 2010, pp. 309–318).

3. Kozinets identifies five types of online communities for research: boards such as online newsgroups, independent web pages linked by theme in web rings, email lists (listservs), chat rooms, and dugeon rooms. Though these communities still exist, this study focuses on the newest forms of online communities, such as social networking sites.

4. GlobalCampus is a social enterprise dedicated to improve transparency in the international education market. GlobalCampus is a social networking site built for

international education. Users create profiles, add blogs and videos, and exchange relevant admissions information. Universities use the GlobalCampus scouting tool to directly message future international students online, bringing unbiased information directly to interested international students. Students register interest in their preferred universities, create educational profiles, and communicate directly with international admissions staff scouting on GlobalCampus.

5. For an indepth look at retweeting see Mashable's "How to Retweet" guide at http://mashable.com/2009/04/16/retweet-guide/

6. For an indepth look at hashtags see Mashable's "Getting the most out of Twitter #Hashtags" at http://mashable.com/2009/05/17/twitter-hashtags/

REFERENCES

Caterall, M., & Maclaran, P. (2001). Researching consumers in virtual worlds: A cyberspace odyssey. *Journal of Consumer Behaviour, 1*(3), 228–237.

Cheater, M. (2008a). How higher ed is using Facebook pages. Available at http://www.academicagroup.com/node/4598

Cheater, M. (2008b). Best practices (for higher education). Available at http://www.academicagroup.com/node/5971

Comp, D. (2010). Survey on social media in international student recruiting and outreach. Available at http://ihec-djc.blogspot.com/2010/02/survey-on-social-media-in-international.html

Dessoff, A. (2009). Recruiting's brave new world. *International Educator.* Available at http://www.nafsa.org/_/File/_/novdec09_recruiting.pdf

Drapeau, M. (2009). Government 2.0: The rise of the goverati. Available at http://www.readwriteweb.com/archives/government_20_rise_of_the_goverati.php

Ganim Barnes, N., & Mattson, E. (2009). Social media and college admissions: The first longitudinal study. Available at http://www.umassd.edu/cmr/studiesresearch/mediaandadmissions.pdf

Gillin, P. (2008). New media, new influencers and implications for public relations. Available at http://sncr.org/wp-content/uploads/2008/08/new-influencers-study.pdf

Heaney, L. (2009). *Guide to international student recruitment* (2nd ed.). Washington, DC: NAFSA: Association of International Educators.

Hine, C. (2005). *Virtual methods: Issues in social research on the Internet.* Oxford: Berg.

Kendall, L. (2010). Community and the internet. In: M. Consalvo & C. Ess (Eds), *The handbook of internet studies* (pp. 309–325). Malden, MA: Wiley-Blackwell.

Kozinets, R. (2002). The field behind the screen: Using netnography for marketing research in online communities. *Journal of Marketing Research* (36), 61–72.

Murthy, D. (2008). Digital ethnography: An examination of the use of new technologies for social research. *Sociology, 42*(5), 837–855.

National Association for College Admissions Counseling. (2009). Report finds use of social networking tools on the rise in college admission offices. [Press Release]. Available at http://www.nacacnet.org/AboutNACAC/PressRoom/2009/Pages/SocialNetworking.aspx

Porter, C. (2004). A typology of virtual communities: A multi-disciplinary foundation for future research. *Journal of Computer Mediated Communication, 10*(1), n.p.

Reuben, R. (2008). The use of social media in higher education for marketing and communications: A guide for professionals in higher education. Available at http://doteduguru.com/id423-social-media-uses-higher-education-marketing-communication.html

UniversitiesAndColleges.org. (2010). Study: Top colleges embrace Twitter. Harvard, Stanford lead in popularity. Available at http://universitiesandcolleges.org/top-100-colleges-twitter/

Waters, R., Burnett, E., Lamm, A., Lucas, J., Burnett, E., et al. (2009). Engaging stakeholders through social networking: How nonprofit organizations are using facebook. *Public Relations Review*, *35*(2), 102–106.

SOCIAL MEDIA USE BY ENROLLMENT MANAGEMENT

Philip Griffiths and Anthony Wall

ABSTRACT

This chapter investigates two different uses of social networking sites (SNSs) within the same higher education institution. One was used as a means of communicating with students while they were still making their study choices, whereas the other aimed to create a medium for student interaction before they arrived at university. While both attempts had some degree of success in the setting up of the SNSs, dissemination, and control of content were not without their difficulties. Having outlined the theory behind SNSs, the chapter then highlights both the rationale behind the decision to use them and the experience of both users. It then describes how lessons learnt led to changes being made in the following year, before concluding by providing some recommendations for others looking to try similar techniques.

INTRODUCTION

This chapter investigates two different uses of social networking sites (SNSs) within the same higher education institution [the University of Ulster (UU)]. Whilst both were primarily focussed on retention, one SNS attempted to communicate with students whilst they were still making their choices about where and what to study, whereas the second aimed to create a medium for students to interact with one another before arriving at university.

The first recognized SNS was sixdegrees.com, which was established in 1997. Since that time the number of similar sites has proliferated as has the number of users. Some well-known Internet sites began as SNSs and have since become much bigger phenomena (e.g., YouTube and Flickr), whilst other SNSs started out as other forms of interactive online media (e.g., dating sites) before developing into their current formats. SNSs are part of the phenomenon known as Web 2.0 (O'Reilly, 2005), which is a second generation of the web that involves more activity on behalf of users, who are accordingly more responsible for its content.

Whilst SNSs attract a wide range of users, they are primarily utilized by young people (see e.g., Lenhart, Purcell, Smith, & Zickuhr, 2010). It is for this reason that two different departments within the UU chose this medium to either communicate with potential students or set up a mechanism whereby students could communicate with one another. Whilst both attempts had some degree of success the setting up of the SNSs, dissemination, and control of content have not been without their difficulties.

The chapter first outlines the theory behind SNSs before highlighting both the rationale behind the decision to use them and the experience of both users. It then describes how lessons learnt led to changes being made in the following year, both in the way in which the sites were managed and changes to the SNSs used. The chapter concludes by providing some recommendations for others looking to try similar techniques.

SOCIAL NETWORKING SITES

An SNS has been defined as a web-based service that allows individuals to construct a public or semi-public profile within a bounded system, articulate a list of other users with whom they share a connection, and view and traverse their list of connections and those made by others within the system (Boyd & Ellison, 2007). The first part of this definition refers to the fact that there are various access protocols to SNSs, with some giving access to a user's entire list of friends and others allowing the user to hide their lists. Other SNSs would be more exclusive in their nature, and users would need to have certain characteristics to enrol with the site. For example, Facebook, one of the most popular SNSs, started out as an SNS for those with Harvard e-mail addresses only. The second part refers to the user being encouraged to identify others with whom they have a relationship and getting them to join the site. As mentioned earlier, these others are often referred to as friends. This has led to some cynicism in the media (Randerson, 2007), particularly when certain users are seen to be bragging about the number of friends they have. However, as Boyd (2006) indicates, these are not friends in the conventional sense and can be nothing more than a list of contacts, as in an e-mail address book. The other key feature is the building of user profiles: posting photographs, information about their backgrounds and views, and where they live and work. The final part of the definition refers to the interaction between different groups of users within an SNS. As Beer and Burrows (2007) point out SNSs are often used by people who know each other from colleges or workplaces to organize physical meetings and to discuss things that happened that day, but that users also make new, virtual connections. This creates an interesting convergence of physical and virtual worlds.

However, a study carried out by Coyle and Vaughn (2008) on American college students found out that the main purpose of using SNSs was to keep in touch with friends. They also discovered that SNSs were "used for trivial communications (i.e., unimportant message content) with friends, both close and nonclose, and that they are used to maintain friendships, but as a noncentral form of socializing" (p. 15). Therefore SNSs may be convenient for retaining contact when time and distance are issues, but they do not replace voice calls and face-to-face communication. None of the students they surveyed stated that he or she used SNSs to meet new people. Research conducted on American undergraduates by Pempek, Yermolayeva, and Calvert (2009) also discovered that SNSs were used most often for social interaction and mainly with friends with whom the students had a pre-established relationship offline. Only 9% of their sample used social networking to make new friends; this differs from the habits of teenagers, half of whom use SNSs for this purpose (Lenhart & Madden, 2007).

Using their own definition, Boyd and Ellison (2007) believe that the first recognizable SNS was sixdegrees.com, which launched in 1997. The name presumably referring to the theory of six degrees of separation, that is, everyone is no more than six steps away from each person on Earth. Since that time an increasing number of SNSs have launched with varying degrees of success. Whilst some never really take off, others have become hugely popular, leading to commercial success. For example, in 2005 MySpace was purchased by News Corporation for $580 million (BBC, 2005).

There are a number of positive features of SNSs. First, they encourage people to communicate and share ideas and problems with one another. The negative images regarding young people becoming increasingly isolated, spending too much time in front of a computer and avoiding face-to-face contact is not borne out by empirical studies. SNSs form part of a flexible intermixing of multiple forms of communication, with online communication primarily used to sustain local friendships already established offline (Boneva, Quinn, Kraut, Kiesler, & Shklovski, 2006; Ellison, Steinfield, & Lampe, 2007; Gross, 2004; Mesch & Talmud, 2007; Valkenburg & Peter, 2007a, 2007b). Furthermore, the specific affordances of SNSs do appear to facilitate changes in the quantity and, arguably, the quality of communication: these include the ease, speed, and convenience of widespread access and distribution of content and connectivity throughout a near-global network (Boyd & Ellison, 2007; Ito et al., 2008).

Second, some writers feel that the use of SNSs can lead to the development of skills. For example, Perkel (2006) felt that the copy and paste practices used on MySpace was a form of literacy involving social and technical skills. Alexander (2008) also makes the point that dealing with the bounded arena of the lecture theatre (whether physical or online) and the boundary less world of SNSs is a form of double literacy that will accompany learners throughout their lifelong learning. Therefore, educators and advocates of new digital literacies are confident that the use of SNSs encourages the development of transferable technical and social skills of value in formal and informal learning (Crook & Harrison, 2008; Ito et al., 2008).

However, there are a number of risks associated with the use of SNSs, the highest being those associated with bullying and privacy. Cyberbullying is more likely to be a problem for children still at school; however two points are worth mentioning with regard to this serious issue. First, whilst 33% of 10- to 15-year olds contacted in America reported being harassed online in 2007, they were more likely to be intimidated through instant messaging or chatrooms than through SNSs (Ybarra & Mitchell, 2008). Second, according to Hinduja and Patchin (2009) 82% of those bullied online knew their perpetrator and 42% who reported being cyberbullied were also bullied at school. Therefore, more advanced methods of communication in general have led to the rise in cyberbullying and being bullied online by a stranger is rare.

Allied to this risk is the issue of privacy. According to Beer and Burrows (2007) SNS users are willing to detail some of the most private information about themselves in a place where anyone can access it. Hobson (2008) refers to a survey conducted by the Information Commissioner's Office in the United Kingdom (UK), which found that 60% of 17- to 25-year olds posted their date of birth, a quarter put their job title online and almost 1 in 10 gave their home address while two-thirds accepted strangers as friends. Another study was carried out by Taraszow, Aristodemou, Shitta, Laouris, and Arsoy (2010) who looked at the profiles of 131 Facebook users between the ages of 13 and 30. They found that most people, regardless of gender, enter full name (as opposed to a first name only or a nickname), photographs, home, and e-mail addresses in their profiles. However, males are more likely than females to disclose their mobile phone number, home address, and instant messaging screen names. They also found that young people, especially those "between the ages of 18 and 22, seem unaware of the potential dangers they are facing when entering real personal and contact information in their profiles while accepting 'friendship' requests from strangers" (p. 82). However, Livingstone and Brake (2010) make the salient point that since SNSs "are designed for teenagers to provide at least their name, birth date and photograph, such personal disclosures are unsurprising" (p. 78).

Jones and Soltren (2005) give a number of examples of where postings on Facebook have led to student users getting into trouble due to poorly judged entries. Moreover, according to Pavia (2008), Oxford University used Facebook to identify and fine graduating students for disorderly conduct. Therefore, an interesting point was made by Timm and Duven (2008), who felt that "the challenge for professionals in higher education is in engaging in this technology without overstepping their authority" (p. 95).

SNSs in Higher Education

As far as higher education is concerned, SNSs, like much of the Web 2.0 content, can be both a blessing and a curse. As Alexander (2008, p. 156) indicates, "the open nature of Web 2.0 platforms, connected by hyperlinking, lets learners pursue connections across multiple lines of thought." Furthermore, the sharing of information between groups of students can facilitate understanding about a subject. However, the veracity of information available on the Internet, particularly that created by the users themselves is highly questionable; yet it is difficult for teaching staff to constantly monitor exchanges through SNSs to ascertain whether students are passing on erroneous information to one another. Alexander (2008, p. 157) also highlights differences between online course management systems (CMSs), which have become increasingly popular in higher education and SNSs. First, "most CMSs restrict social networking to an individual, discrete class" and "although some CMSs support publication to the open Web, this is not a major adoption point." Second, CMSs support hyperlinking differently than SNSs as "content creators within a CMS can easily link to the outside Web," but "the reverse is not true, because inbound links are blocked by the CMS server." As a result, students increasingly become used to the restricted nature of the CMS and the more worldwide nature of SNSs. However, making a distinction between the factual-based content of the former and the more emotional substance of the latter is not always so straightforward.

According to Collis and Moonen (2008) the mismatch between these two worlds is a source of frustration for students. They are finding that new pedagogical models borne by technology and other forms of innovation in learning have not become part of general higher education practice. This finding was supported by De Boer (2004) who noted that web technology in higher education was being primarily used for support of logistical processes (i.e., content and information provision) rather than for pedagogical change. A survey of UK students (Conole, de Laat, Dillon, & Darby, 2006) reported that they found virtual learning environments (VLEs) disappointing and searched outside them for self-selected learning resources. Collis and Moonen (2008, p. 96) felt that the reasons for this were that "the pedagogies, supported by new technologies, that could lead to innovation are not enough known to instructors, not enough valued, and are perceived by instructors as too difficult to implement." A valid point therefore appears to be that if the use of technology by university personnel does not match the experience and expectations of students, it may not achieve its intended objectives. Notwithstanding, Dunworth (2009) found that SNSs were a good way of keeping in touch with students whilst on placement.

The chapter now turns to the use of SNSs by two different departments within UU. Whilst neither sought to create either a CMS or a VLE and were merely trying to provide a communication medium for either potential or incoming students, some of the problems highlighted in the literature were encountered. The rationale behind the use of an SNS and the experience of the School of the Built Environment and the Department of Accounting will now be respectively outlined.

THE SCHOOL OF THE BUILT ENVIRONMENT

Rationale

The School of the Built Environment is the biggest of its kind on the island of Ireland, and the largest school in UU. It has a comprehensive range of degree disciplines at the undergraduate and postgraduate level, with qualifications ranging from the social sciences to hard engineering. It is a school with a healthy balance sheet, but there are problems. The softer construction disciplines (e.g., Quantity Surveying) attract high numbers of applicants; hence these courses have large cohorts making it difficult to organize enough tutorial sessions, studies advice and dissertation supervision from within the course teaching teams. On the hard engineering end, there exists a course, BEng Energy and Building Services Engineering, which equips graduates to work in the fields of renewable energy and energy efficient building design. These are two areas that could reasonably be expected to attract numerous applications, as climate change and security of energy supply are topical subjects in both the media and secondary education. They are also areas of graduate expertise demanded by employers. Yet this course struggles to attract more than 10 direct applicants per year, with maybe five or six arriving through the UK clearing system that provides a route into university for students who fail to gain their initial choices. The School's aim is to raise numbers on this course to alleviate the overloading of the social science degrees. Each year during the application process some students are given a "change course" offer to Energy and Building Services Engineering if their original application is rejected, which can lead to over 60 extra offers being made. The School, however, wants to attract students to the harder engineering courses initially and whilst open days have been held, they have not been successful in redirecting applicants to this area.

Part of the problem identified was dissemination. UU personnel and industrialists have spent time traveling around schools in Northern Ireland and the border counties of the Republic of Ireland promoting the course and the profession as a suitable and fulfilling career. With the rise in the use of SNSs, it was decided to investigate whether this was a phenomenon that could be employed as a means of attracting students and informally providing them with an opportunity to find out about the course and a career in energy and building services. Such a strategy had been used very successfully by Xavier University in Cincinnati, Ohio (Hayes, Ruschman, & Walker, 2009). Its SNS, which did not use an established provider, "was directed at potential students and included a companion site created for their parents" (p. 117). The objectives therefore were to improve the ratio of those who finally join the course compared to original applications, to improve the visibility of the course amongst its target audience, and to use the SNS to maintain contact with any applicants until they arrive at the university.

Experience

In January 2008, a Bebo site was established with the help of the Office of Lifelong Learning at UU. The site was populated with quizzes, videos of a laboratory tour by students and links to YouTube material of interest. Applicants were encouraged to sign up and use the site to chat with the School from the moment they applied until they registered on the course. The site offered was a place where they could seek help in their studies – especially with mathematics and physics, and prepare for the university experience. A few signed up to the site, but they tended to be those who were already committed to coming on the course. The anticipated flood of "friends" didn't happen. Such an occurrence would be consistent with the experience of Xavier University, where it was found that the SNS was very good for engaging those students who have already expressed an interest in a course, but less effective in creating the interest in the first place (Hayes et al., 2009).

Why was it not the success that had been hoped? Feedback from the first year students who joined the course in September 2008 showed that they saw the site as trying to break into their territory – youth culture, and it was not considered "cool." The project manager does admit to not having much experience with these sites and, having since seen Facebook in action, is now aware of the time and energy required to maintain an active site to which "friends" return often. The mistake was seeing it as a site that people would actively register with, whilst SNSs work by reaching out to others. In the site's first 14 months, it only had just over 100 page views with few comments. To find a way out of this, the course director invited the views of the first year course representatives. This led to them being offered the opportunity to run the site.

A Way Forward

Handing the site over to the students led to some immediate changes of content; moreover, the rest of the first years joined (15 in total) and the number of page views rose to 232. The first change was to move the site from Bebo to Facebook. When asked to explain this, course management was informed that "this is where young people now meet; Bebo is no longer where the youth 'congregate'." Moreover, they now run it as a site for existing and potential students with a section for forthcoming events. The students are creating new material, for example, photos of site visits and a "home video" in the style of *The Blair Witch Project*. One potential avenue being explored is to "advertise" on school Facebook sites, by posting comments and links back to the course site. At the time of writing, the recruitment cycle for 2010 is nearing the end and plans are being put into place for 2011. Being able to reach students before they choose their 16+ options as well as those making their final choice A2-level subjects (A2s being the final examinations pupils sit in the UK before leaving school) is essential if students who might be interested in the course are encouraged to continue studying mathematics and physics to the highest level. Being pro-active in how the site reaches potential applicants is the new focus.

The School has also utilized SNS to aid with the transition from school to the university. Retention of students commencing courses at UU has become a major concern of senior management as it affects the capital grant given by the regional government. The School has therefore developed a substantial induction program to aid in this transition. This involved the use of the Ning SNS (2009). This particular SNS was chosen as it provided a closed site to which members had to be invited and hence limited access to students arriving at the university to commence their studies. The school-wide course induction programs were supplemented in 2009 by a virtual induction (Millar, Tierney, & Eadie, 2010). The Jordanstown campus of UU is large, 114 hectares, and the layout and room notation can be confusing to those unfamiliar with the building. Videos and interactive maps were used to aid student preparation for the commencement of the first semester. Previous visits to the campus for open days would have introduced students solely to the "Mall" that connects the various blocks in which teaching, administration and laboratories are situated. They would then, on arrival, be expected to quickly gain an orientation of the campus as they moved between lecture rooms, laboratories, seminar rooms, and other facilities. The other theme of the site was student interaction. This was used by incoming students for a range of reasons, primarily in preparation for their arrival at the start of semester, for example accommodation, travel, clarification regarding the registration process, timetable hours, and general university experience. Apprehension and excitement about the new stage in their educational experiences also emerged from the discussions.

Millar et al. (2010) reported that students enjoyed using the SNS in preparation for commencing their studies and found it helpful. They showed support for all aspects provided (e.g., maps, tours, discussion boards) and did not suggest anything new that the course team considered worthy of including for the 2010 intake. Like the Bebo website initially used by Energy and Building Services, a majority of the Ning users stopped visiting after a couple of weeks of the semester; those that did were just "dipping" to see if there was anything new. The authors concluded that any process that lowers student anxieties around the transition process is of value whatever the long term outcomes.

Overall, therefore, the original objectives were achieved: the ratio of those finally joining the course when compared with the original applicants improved; the visibility of the course was eventually enhanced, having moved the site to Facebook; and the SNS enabled regular contact with applicants until they arrived at the university and now plays an important role in the induction process.

THE DEPARTMENT OF ACCOUNTING

Rationale

The Department of Accounting is responsible for two of the most popular business-related courses within UU, the BSc in Business Studies and the BSc in Accounting. Like most universities, UU has problems retaining students, especially in their first year of study. The aforementioned courses having large numbers would lose a larger proportion than other courses and thus a number of initiatives were suggested to try and address this problem for the 2008/2009 intake. Another problem more particular to UU is that it attracts a high proportion of local students. The vast majority of these students commute to the university to attend lectures or seminars and then travel home afterwards. Beyond the use of the library and canteen facilities there is very little interaction with the university, that is, few avail of the large amount of social and sporting clubs. As well as not interacting with the university students tend not to interact with one another. Small groups arrive from local schools and have a habit of staying together; furthermore, the courses would only provide limited opportunities for meeting other students. Therefore some students are left fairly isolated and see the university as simply a less social form of secondary school. This becomes a problem whenever such a student runs into difficulties with assessments; with no real anchor to the university and no real friends with whom to discuss their anxieties they can drop out of courses. By the time the university realizes this, it is normally too late.

It was felt that by giving students some method of communicating with others before arriving on the course, some of these problems could be addressed. It was decided that when students were sent confirmation of their acceptance into either the Business Studies or Accounting degree, they would also be sent a postcard containing details of the SNS. The objective, therefore, was to get students communicating with one another before their arrival; with the hope that some friendships may form, reducing any feelings of awkwardness when the cohort eventually met up for the first time. An SNS site was used as it was seen to be a medium with which people of that age were familiar; furthermore, it can lead to the development of skills (Alexander, 2008; Crook & Harrison, 2008; Ito et al., 2008; Perkel, 2006). A similar strategy had been used at Harrisburg University of Science and Technology, which set up a single sign-on web portal allowing new students to situate themselves as part of the Harrisburg University community (Sevier, 2007). Other colleges that had successfully used SNSs for this purpose include Saint Michael's College in Vermont and Marietta College in Ohio (Sevier, 2007). The chosen site was Bebo, as although this had fallen out of popularity in other parts of the United Kingdom, it was thought still to be popular in Northern Ireland.

Experience

The construction of the site involved considerable planning with several meetings being held between members of the Department of Accounting to discuss what content should go on the SNS. Initially it was felt a number of talking head type videos would be a good idea, with introductions from the head of the department, the course director, and the head of first year studies. It was also felt that a video giving a quick tour of the campus would be of benefit. Coordinating the content of these videos over the summer period turned out to be too time consuming, therefore only the video of the campus tour was eventually made. As will be seen later any university generated content is almost certainly underutilized, and thus it was probably advantageous that these introductory videos were not made. One possible reason for this is that staged videos are not the content the users of SNSs are expecting and such sites are visited to get access to immediate, raw, and somewhat unfiltered information. The filming of the campus however still turned out to be problematic. As previously mentioned it was summer, and so the normally busy corridors were virtually empty. There was some footage available, but areas such as a new sports centre still needed to be filmed. What turned out to be a 12-second clip on the final product took over 4 hours to film and involved gym users having to sign permission slips, the constant moving of those who did not want to be filmed and a lot of assistance from the sports centre staff. The main point here is despite the large amount of assistance received from other departments the person in charge of the project must still devote a significant amount of time to it and can never assume a task will be carried out unless it is directly overseen by them.

This point became very poignant for the dissemination phase. It was assumed that the staff responsible for posting the confirmation material would be fully aware that the postcards would need to be included in the envelopes being sent to students that contained details of their acceptance into the degree program and all of the normal joining instructions. However, there was some form of communication breakdown and with the project manager not checking that this had been done the envelopes went out without the postcard containing details of the SNS. It was only when the project manager began to check the sites for usage after several days had passed, and found no entries on either of them, that the mistake was discovered and rectified.

Once students did receive notification of the dedicated SNSs, several of them began to use the sites. Gradually the numbers grew with 33 accounting students (32% of those enrolled for the course) and a more disappointing 15 business studies students (11% of the intake) eventually joining the sites. Immediately a number of points became clear. First, the students appeared to have no real interest in making any connections with their future cohort. The initial messages were all about self-promotion; photographs were posted (often showing the student with a partner) along with details of their social habits and links to other sites, particularly music pages. Later on students posted their own videos, usually links from YouTube and more photographs of nights out or similar events. Interestingly, Buffardi and Campbell (2008) who investigated such acts of narcissism on SNSs found that these narcissistic traits reflected the offline behavior of the individuals; therefore, the more immediate nature of the Internet was not making them behave any differently. Second, the students had no interest in any of the university content. Although it is not known if any of them looked at the campus tour video, there were no entries for one of the blogs set up by the project manager, or for a very brief poll set up by another member of the project team. The blog was entitled "getting started" and encouraged students to discuss how they were planning to travel to the university, the idea being to initiate car sharing. The poll asked the students how they felt about starting university and gave them five options ranging from excited to apathetic. Third, attempts to monitor and police the site turned out to be more difficult than envisaged. With so many links going from the SNS to other websites, it was impractical to follow them all to ensure all the content was suitable. However, even when some of the content was perceived to be less than desirable, it was felt that any early attempts to step in would be counterproductive. For example, one of the very early users of the accounting SNS used a mild expletive in their initial entry. Whilst the word would not have been acceptable in an assessed piece of work, it is used in everyday language and had the project manager attempted to chastise this student, it would have been incompatible with the general message being portrayed that UU was a vibrant, dynamic, forward thinking institution.

Another aspect regarding the use of the SNSs that the planning team underestimated was its continued use. It was incorrectly assumed that once the students arrived at the university, they would stop using them and either form conventional relationships or invite new acquaintances onto their regular SNSs. However, students continued to use the sites as one of their regular methods of communication. Whilst this was encouraging it also meant that any monitoring of the site was not up to date, and therefore, any content that could be considered undesirable or inflammatory may have been input onto the site in previous communications or uploads. This meant that it might have been months since it was originally posted making any chastisement futile. Furthermore, it could be argued that if no other user has complained about the format then it had not upset any particular party; although such an argument would not stand up to any real scrutiny. It is interesting to compare this continued usage with the abandonment of the SNS by the students of the School of the Built Environment. The reason for the different engagement strategies is probably due to the different natures of the SNSs; the Department of Accounting's focused on student retention and therefore was encouraging students to communicate, whilst that of the School of the Built Environment was primarily a recruitment tool with the communication being between it and the applicant, not between the students themselves. Finally, as with the School of the Built Environment, the use of Bebo might have immediately cast UU as an institution that was out of touch with its target audience. One early user had made the comment that using Bebo "was a trip down memory lane."

Despite these setbacks the use of SNSs was definitely seen as an overall success. Those students that had joined the university SNSs felt they had achieved their purpose in that students who would not have normally associated with one another had interacted via the SNSs and over the course of the academic year more students signed up for them. It was decided therefore to repeat the exercise with the intake for 2009/2010. Nevertheless lessons had been learnt. First, it was decided to make use of Facebook as opposed to Bebo, which was seen in Northern Ireland as mainly a site for much younger people. Whilst the video containing a quick tour of the campus was left on the sites, all other course- or university-related material was removed. To prevent any repeat of the dissemination problems, one of the project team sent out the postcards directly to the incoming students. The results of these actions proved to be fairly mixed. Out of a possible 90 students, 27 (30%) joined the accounting SNS, whereas for the business studies SNS 36 out of possible 136 (26%) signed up. Therefore, the numbers joining the accounting SNS were down slightly but the number of business studies students joining had more than doubled when compared to the respective 32% and 11% uptake for the 2008/2009 cohort.

CONCLUSIONS AND RECOMMENDATIONS

Since their conception in 1997 the number of SNSs has grown exponentially, as has the number of users. Like other forms of Web 2.0, SNSs require action on behalf of the user including the creation of a profile, the identification of friends who are then invited to join the site and the interaction with both actual and virtual acquaintances. It was because SNSs are seen as a communication medium mainly used by young people and having some educational benefits that two departments in UU decided to create their own profile within a well-known SNS in order to boost the recruitment and retention of students. Whilst both these original sites and latter ones created for the following year's entry continue to be used, there are a number of lessons that both departments have learnt, and these may be of use to other higher education institutions looking to go down a similar route.

First, the creation of a dedicated SNS, even within an established provider such as Bebo or Facebook, is not something that happens overnight. The site needs to be carefully planned, designed, implemented, and disseminated. Whilst both departments received an enormous amount of assistance, the perception that it can all be left to the IT department is misleading and any person in charge of such a project will find that it is very time consuming. Furthermore, the project manager needs to keep abreast of activities at all stages. This was highlighted for the Department of Accounting when there was a failure to disseminate information about the SNS at the most appropriate time. Had the project manager overseen this vital stage rather than letting go too early, the usage levels for both of the Department's original sites might have been greater. Second, it is essential to be constantly aware of the generation gap. The project managers were either part of the baby boomer generation (born between 1945 and 1960) or generation X (born between 1961 and 1979), whereas the target audience were all generation Y (born between 1980 and 1997). Any university content on the SNSs was ignored and students communicated with each other in a way that seemed strange to both project managers. For example, the initial communication was all one-way, "look at me" type messages, with no mention of how students felt about going to university or the course of study they were about to undertake. Hayes et al. (2009) make the interesting point that when one creates an SNS, "it is not unusual for those participating in it to take unintended directions" (p. 121). Therefore, higher education institutions are going to have to be prepared to yield some level of control.

This point is of interest as it would appear to contradict the findings of writers such as Collis and Moonen (2008) and Conole et al. (2006) who felt that students were disappointed at the efforts higher education has made to utilize the Internet and that they had to go outside the bounded world of CMSs or VLEs for self-selected learning resources. The impression gained by both project managers was that the students want SNSs for themselves and do not want university staff entering this world to provide what they see as relevant information. Whilst neither SNS was a VLE or CMS, the impression gathered was that students were quite comfortable in their own worlds, and whilst they made use of the sites, they saw them as quite separate to their higher education. It is possible that students see any adult connected to the university as part of an older generation and have no real desire to communicate with them. In their aforementioned study of American undergraduates, Pempek et al. (2009) found that students did not use an SNS to keep in touch with their parents and these findings might explain why the students joining the UU sites did not want to use them to interact with university personnel. However, the fact that neither of the sites had the participation that was hoped for may be due to the fact that they did not match the experience and expectation of the future students and thus, for this point, a similar conclusion to writers such as Collis and Moonen (2008) and Conole et al. (2006) could be made. Once the sites were up and running the project managers more or less left them as they were and apart from the occasional course announcement, nothing new or innovative was ever added. As with the CMSs and VLEs, the students may have perceived the establishment of the SNSs as a half-hearted measure.

Finally, the monitoring of the sites is a task that must be carefully thought through. The most feasible option is that the creators of the SNS set out guidelines about what is deemed acceptable with regard to language, topics of conversation and content (e.g., video clips and photographs) and then as far as possible constantly monitor the sites to ensure no entries are falling outside these parameters. This will mean that either the project manager, or one of their team, must set aside time every working day to check that the guidelines are being followed; occasional browsing of the site is of little use as any offensive material may have been posted too long ago for any form of chastisement to be effective. Another possible option would be to have someone fully dedicated to the monitoring of such a site. However, one common trait associated with generation Y according to Kane (2010) is that they are "tech-savvy" and therefore grew up with technology and rely on it to perform their jobs better, as a result they are plugged-in 24 hours a day, 7 days a week. Therefore, trying to constantly monitor an SNS would be highly impractical as students communicate at all hours of the day. Moreover, regardless of the effectiveness of such monitoring, it could be seen as waste of taxpayer's money. As before, it is essential to be aware that what may seem unacceptable to an older person might be everyday exchanges of information for generation Y. One major issue is the legal ramifications of who is actually responsible for distasteful content; the person who posted it, those responsible for setting up the sites or the SNS provider (e.g., Facebook). Discussions with UU's legal team have assured the authors that they are not responsible, but it is, like many issues with regard to the internet, a grey area; partly due to the international boundaries that are crossed in dealing with websites. Nevertheless, whilst not wishing to encroach on students' privacy or be seen to overstep any authority, the monitoring of SNSs is an important activity; any cyberbullying must be dealt with swiftly and the image of the university must not be tarnished due to undesirable content.

Timm and Duven (2008) felt that most higher education institutions did not have "standards of conduct specifically related to activity on social networking sites" (p. 99) in their current policies. The implication therefore is that there should be an overall, institution-wide policy on how students use university SNSs. Individual departments and schools could then refer any potential users to this policy and then, as with most websites, students could confirm that they have read and understood the terms and conditions before use. Whilst this makes it easier for individual departments to set up their own SNSs without having to create parameters for use, it does not solve the problem of monitoring the site for instances of undesirable content. Moreover, universities will only feel it is worthwhile creating such a policy if there is a widespread use of SNSs for student interaction throughout the institution.

The use of SNSs in higher education is interesting. Oradini and Saunders (2008) saw a role for SNSs within universities but a "wider acceptance and precise definition" of its role is required before the potential is realized. A noteworthy conclusion from their work was the desire of both staff and students for the SNS to be integrated with the VLE. Is an SNS the new e-mail? It certainly provides an instant messaging service of greater speed and wider dissemination than phone text messages. The growth of smart phones with SNS applications ("apps") will widen the accessibility of these sites and increase user interaction and engagement time. Whether students band together and use them to devise group assignment submissions outside of VLEs is unknown. They undoubtedly provide a good record of asynchronous multi-way communication, which should be encouraged as a learning/reflecting tool. However, whether students will adopt "official" SNSs as a means to find, and prepare themselves for, a course at university is a question that has not yet been fully answered.

REFERENCES

Alexander, B. (2008). Web 2.0 and emergent multiliteracies. *Theory into Practice, 47*(2), 150–160.

BBC. (2005). News Corp in $580m Internet buy. Available at http://news.bbc.co.uk/2/hi/business/4695495.stm. Retrieved on June 9, 2009.

Beer, D., & Burrows, R. (2007). Sociology and, of and in Web 2.0: Some initial considerations. *Sociological Research Online, 12*(5). Available at http://www.socresonline.org.uk/12/5/17.html. Retrieved on June 9, 2009.

De Boer, W. (2004). *Flexibility support for a changing university.* PhD dissertation, Faculty of Behavioural Sciences, University of Twente, Enschede, The Netherlands. Available at http://www.wimdeboer.nl/work.htm. Retrieved on June 18, 2009.

Boneva, B., Quinn, A., Kraut, R., Kiesler, S., & Shklovski, I. (2006). Teenage communication in the instant messaging era. In: R. Kraut, M. Brynin & S. Kiesler (Eds), *Computers, phones, and the internet: Domesticating information technology* (pp. 201–218). Oxford: Oxford University Press.

Boyd, D. M., & Ellison, N. B. (2007). Social network sites: Definition, history, and scholarship. *Journal of Computer-Mediated Communication, 13*(1), 210–230.

Boyd, D. (2006). Friends, friendsters, and top 8: Writing community into being on social network sites. *First Monday, 11*(12). Available at http://firstmonday.org/htbin/cgiwrap/bin/ojs/index.php/fm/article/view/1418/1336

Buffardi, L. E., & Campbell, W. K. (2008). Narcissism and social networking web sites. *Personality and Social Psychology Bulletin, 34*(10), 1303–1314.

Collis, B., & Moonen, J. (2008). Web 2.0 tools and processes in higher education: Quality perspectives. *Educational Media International, 45*(2), 93–106.

Conole, G., de Laat, M., Dillon, T., & Darby, J. (2006). JISC LXP: Student experience of technologies: Final report. Available at http://www.jisc.ac.uk/whatwedo/programmes/elearning_pedagogy/elp_learneroutcomes.aspx. Retrieved on June 18, 2009.

Coyle, C., & Vaughn, H. (2008). Social networking: Communication revolution or evolution? *Bell Labs Technical Journal, 13*(2), 13–18.

Crook, C., & Harrison, C. (2008). *Web 2.0 technologies for learning at key stages 3 and 4.* Coventry, England: Becta.

Dunworth, M. (2009). Supporting students through social networking. *Journal of Practice Teaching & Learning, 9*(1), 64–80.

Ellison, N., Steinfield, C., & Lampe, C. (2007). The benefits of Facebook 'friends:' Social capital and college students' use of online social network sites. *Journal of Computer-Mediated Communication, 12*, 1143–1168.

Gross, E. F. (2004). Adolescent internet use: What we expect, what teens report. *Applied Developmental Psychology, 25*, 633–649.

Hayes, T. J., Ruschman, D., & Walker, M. M. (2009). Social networking as an admission tool: A case study in success. *Journal of Marketing for Higher Education, 19*, 109–124.

Hinduja, S., & Patchin, J. (2009). *Bullying beyond the schoolyard: Preventing and responding to cyberbullying.* Thousand Oaks, CA: Corwin Press.

Hobson, D. (2008). Social networking – not always friendly. *Computer Fraud & Security, 20*, 20.

Ito, M., Horst, H. A., Bittanti, M., Boyd, D., Herr-Stephenson, B., Lange, P. G., Pascoe, C. J., & Robinson, L. (2008). *Living and learning with new media: Summary of findings from the Digital Youth Project.* Chicago: The John D. and Catherine T. MacArthur Foundation.

Jones, H., & Soltren, J. H. (2005). Facebook: Threats to privacy. Project MAC: MIT Project on Mathematics and Computing. Available at http://www-swiss.ai.mit.edu/6.805/student-papers/fall05-papers/facebook.pdf. Retrieved on June 3, 2009.

Kane, S. (2010). Generation Y. Available at http://legalcareers.about.com/od/practicetips/a/GenerationY.htm. Retrieved on March 18, 2010.

Lenhart, A., & Madden, M. (2007). *Teens, privacy & online social networks: How teens manage their online identities and personal information in the age of MySpace.* Washington, DC: Pew Internet & American Life Project.

Lenhart, A., Purcell, K., Smith, A., & Zickuhr, K. (2010). Social media and mobile internet use among teens and young adults. Available at http://pewinternet.org/Reports/2010/Social-Media-and-Young-Adults.aspx. Retrieved on June 24, 2010.

Livingstone, S., & Brake, D. R. (2010). On the rapid rise of social networking sites: New findings and policy implications. *Children & Society, 24*, 75–83.

Mesch, G. S., & Talmud, I. (2007). Similarity and the quality of online and offline social relationships among adolescents in Israel. *Journal of Research on Adolescence, 17*, 455–466.

Millar, P., Tierney, C., & Eadie, R. (2010). Use of virtual networking to facilitate transition to tertiary education. Available at http://eprints.ulster.ac.uk/10149/1/11_Millar_Tierney_Eadie.pdf. Retrieved on June 24, 2010.

Ning (2009). About Ning. Available at http://about.ning.com/. Retrieved on December 15, 2009.

Oradini, F., & Saunders, G. (2008). The use of social networking by students and staff in higher education. In: *Proceedings (papers and abstracts) of iLearning Forum 2008 conference and plugfest* (pp. 236–242). Champlost, France: European Institute for E-Learning (EIfEL). Available at http://www.eife-l.org/publications/proceedings/ilf08/ilearning-forum-2008. Retrieved on December 15, 2009.

O'Reilly, T. (2005). What is Web 2.0: Design patterns and business models for the next generation of software. Available at http://oreillynet.com/1pt/a/6228. Retrieved on June 9, 2009.

Pavia, W. (2008). Oxford University fines students with the aid of Facebook. *The Times*, 9. Available at http://www.timesonline.co.uk/tol/life_and_style/education/article3768282.ece. Retrieved on March 26, 2009.

Pempek, T. A., Yermolayeva, Y. A., & Calvert, S. L. (2009). College students' social networking experiences on Facebook™. *Journal of Applied Developmental Psychology*, *30*, 227–238.

Perkel, D. (2006). Copy and paste literacy: Literacy practices in the production of a MySpace profile. Available at http://people.ischool.berkeley.edu/~dperkel/media/dperkel_literacy-myspace.pdf. Retrieved on June 18, 2009.

Randerson, J. (2007). Social networking sites don't deepen friendships. *The Guardian*, September 10.

Sevier, R. A. (2007). Using social networking to its fullest potential: Learn how colleges and universities can benefit from using these communities in marketing efforts. *University Business*. Available at http://www.universitybusiness.com/viewarticle.aspx?articleid=764. Retrieved on June 24, 2010.

Taraszow, T., Aristodemou, E., Shitta, G., Laouris, Y., & Arsoy, A. (2010). Disclosure of personal and contact information by young people in social networking sites: An analysis using Facebook™ profiles as an example. *International Journal of Media and Cultural Politics*, *6*(1), 81–101.

Timm, D. M., & Duven, C. J. (2008). Privacy and social networking sites. *New Directions for Student Services*, *124*(Winter), 89–102.

Valkenburg, P. M., & Peter, J. (2007a). Internet communication and its relation to well-being: Identifying some underlying mechanisms. *Media Psychology*, *9*, 43–58.

Valkenburg, P. M., & Peter, J. (2007b). Preadolescents' and adolescents' online communication and their closeness to friends. *Developmental Psychology*, *43*, 267–277.

Ybarra, M. L., & Mitchell, K. J. (2008). How risky are social networking sites? A comparison of places online where youth sexual solicitation and harassment occurs. *Pediatrics*, *121*, e350–e357.

PART II
SOCIAL MEDIA IN ADVISING AND MENTORING

SECOND LIFE: THE FUTURE OF EDUCATION IS HERE TODAY

P. Charles Livermore

ABSTRACT

Participation in online courses in both traditional universities and newer for-profit organizations is burgeoning. Indeed, students entering higher education increasingly have experienced online education at the secondary and even primary levels. Students have immense wherewithal with digital media use through messaging, gaming and mobile platforms. Reference librarians in the epoch of Wikipedia and Google are experiencing a steady decline in the number of in-person reference questions. However, disruptive innovations in teaching technologies such as multiuser-virtual-environments (MUVEs) now enable quasi-face-to-face consultations by librarians with students. The use of virtual environments might well be bolstered by the unsustainability of the traditional brick-and-mortar based educational facility grounded interaction due to the new financial strictures on many educational institutions and their stakeholders. In many ways libraries and other elements of higher education are evolving away from physical onsite usage to an online interface that in many ways reflects gaming interfaces. That is, geographically separated learners can meet with librarians together as teams to get informational and technical support through a variety of platforms and interfaces. This chapter is a report on providing the support of an experienced reference librarian through the Second Life virtual world interface. Included are descriptions of Second Life sites and resources and how they might be utilized for library functions. Educational venues in Second Life are describes and explained, as are learner avatar use and Second Life educational experiences. Second Life is a technology that invites experimentation and growth for those in higher education.

INTRODUCTION

Second Life (SL) is one of a number of virtual worlds. It is, arguably, the one most open to educators. At this point, it is too early to tell if SL is going to be the killer-app virtual world that will come to dominate the field of education. But it is the belief of this author that as virtual worlds mature and technologies improve virtual world environments will be increasingly utilized for the education of all students from kindergarten through the university.

When discussing SL one of the questions that is frequently asked is WHY? This chapter is designed to serve two purposes. The first is to review the reasons for the author's belief in the future of virtual worlds. Here is a brief summary of these reasons.

1. An increase in online and distance education classes in both high school and higher education. An increasing number of high school students are leaving high school with experiences with distance education classes and the accompanying opportunities for choice in their education.
2. The relationship between SL and games or gaming. The intellectual challenges of education and the problem-solving nature of games are similar. College students are spending considerable amounts of time and energy playing games. Higher education would be foolish not to develop online classes that take advantage of the features of games and gaming that are enticing college students (Gee, 2003).
3. The development of the computer as more than simply another tool. Computers are becoming more sophisticated and are being accepted as team members rather than as simple tools (Nass, Fogg, & Moon, 1996).
4. The increase of online databases and a corresponding decline in in-person usage of the library building. Like it or not, in-building use of libraries is declining and the use of the libraries' materials from outside is increasing.

Although SL has been around since the early 2000s there are still many who are uncertain as to what it is and how it works. The virtual world called SL exists on a server or computer that is owned by Linden Labs, the company that developed SL. It can be accessed via the internet from any computer that has the SL program installed (free). An individual can create an account (free) that gives that individual access to SL. Upon entering SL an individual can search for sites (or "islands") that have been created by other individuals.

Second, the chapter reviews but a few of the many sites available to educators and to discuss other opportunities available in SL.

Third, to discuss the classroom in which the author conducts library sessions with students.

Fourth, to expand on the reasons for the author's belief in virtual worlds.

SECOND LIFE SITES

Following are but a few of the exciting sites available in SL which would be appropriate to explore as a part of the curricula for many college courses:

United States Holocaust Museum-Kristallnacht display: Here you can explore the streets of a German city in the late 1930s to see and visually experience the beginning of the Nazi's final solution.
http://slurl.com/secondlife/US%20Holocaust%20Museum1/13/56/26

Vassar College's impressive reproduction of the Sistine Chapel: Although students may never get to the actual Sistine Chapel, Vassar's recreation in SL can offer an approximation of that experience.
http://slurl.com/secondlife/Vassar/202/91/25

Genome Island: Containing a comprehensive overview of genetics and the path to discovering DNA.
http://slurl.com/secondlife/Genome/111/98/86

New York City, Harlem: Offers opportunities to explore this historic neighborhood including the Apollo Theater, Cotton Club, and more.
http://slurl.com/secondlife/Virtual%20Harlem%202/172/193/30

The SL Globe Theater: Plays are performed at the Globe quite regularly and allow audience and class participation.
http://slurl.com/secondlife/sLiterary/23/15/24

These sites, and many others, allow students to explore these events and locales in ways many of them may never experience.

The above listing of sites represents a small portion of what can be explored in SL. A search in SL allows both students and instructors to search for other areas of interest. It should be noted that searching in SL relies on a site's creator's to provide accurate descriptive terms. The lack of inadequate indexing of sites has made it difficult to find sites that are known to exist.

For the interest areas that do exist individuals can enter and explore via their avatar (an electronic creation that can take the form of a human, an animal, or a fantastic object). Avatars can meet and interact with other avatars. Using keyboard controls the avatar can walk, run, and even fly. An avatar can communicate with other avatars using the keyboard to "chat" or a headset and microphone to actually talk to other avatars.

In addition to the above more educational sites there are opportunities to shop for fashionable clothing so your avatar can have the latest styles, amusement parks with rides and other activities, and, just as we have seamier neighborhoods in real life so there are individuals who have created seamier places in SL. There are the "adult" sites for those with more exotic tastes. As in real life you have a choice of moving in these neighborhoods as you wish. However, in my three years exploring SL I have only once accidentally found myself in a neighborhood which could be considered "adult" in nature. If one is not interested in staying in such sites the teleport function will facilitate a quick and easy exit.

One of the advantages for students is that there is no cost to establish an account. Included with the free download of the SL software is an individual's avatar. It comes fully formed and dressed; however, it can be modified to an individual's personal tastes. None of the sessions I have held for students required them to spend any money. And I have spent a total of about 50 dollars in the 3 years I have been active. This has been for uploading images I have used in my demonstration slide shows for the databases I discuss. I have also purchased a slide viewer to facilitate the presentation of my slides; and I have purchased a building, fountains and some clothing. There are a number of sites in SL which will make arrangements to allow instructors to teach classes with little or no money. If one wishes to own an island the cost can be considerable. The approximate 2010 educational prices are about $900.00 to purchase an island plus an additional monthly maintenance cost of $90. Given the cost of a real life classroom these prices are inexpensive and present a wise investment for college and universities to explore this relatively new educational experience.

CLASSROOM

Several years ago a faculty member here at St. John's University (NY) mentioned he was able to acquire an SL island as part of a technology grant.

As part of several of his business courses he was assigning students to explore some of the businesses that had been established in SL. His, goal, in part, was to have students explore these businesses in light of business theory and practice. There were also research assignments accompanying these practicum.

In some cases the courses being offered would be distance education courses. I suggested that his students would benefit from having a library presence on his island. Since distance education students there might not have an opportunity to visit any of the St. John's University Libraries, the goal was to create a library on the island that contained instructional guides for locating the research information required for the completion of assignments.

Having no money to hire a builder for the library's needs, several primitive instructional guides were created. This involved simply creating screen shots of databases illustrating search techniques and posting them on the island. Over the years this has evolved (through the purchase of an inexpensive slide viewer) into more complex presentations. Along with slide presentations there are also links on the island which take the students outside SL to the databases required.

As my SL building skills have improved so has the realization that SL, while having some first life similarities, has the possibilities of the most wonderful fantasy movies. In SL one can fly and Scottie can "beam me up" – SL buildings do not need to be designed with elevators. So my present library classrooms are located on pods with no walls and no ceilings – even if it rains in SL one does not get wet. These pods are connected with ramps. At first the ramps had no railings and some students (not having developed appropriate movement skills) kept walking off the edge. Students new to SL are frequently movement challenged and require a few sessions before they become comfortable in the control of their walking and flying. Ramps now have railings to guide students from one level to the next.

In the classroom there are several presentations which outline the steps involved in different databases. Presentations are available to students 24/7 and consist of a PowerPoint like showing of screen shots demonstrating the steps necessary for searching databases. Each slide in the tutorial is accompanied by captioning to offer further explanations of what is being shown. This information can be captured by the student and downloaded for further review. During appointments with students, singly or in groups, I am able to add additional comments as questions arise.

Many of the students attending the tutorials work full-time, go to school part-time, and have families requiring care. The tutorials have been scheduled to accommodate a student's busy schedule. They have been held as early as 6:00 am and as late as 1:00 am. This also meets the needs of many of the students who attend these classes as distance learners in locations around the globe spanning many time zones.

The largest group that has met to date is 10, although attendance by 40 could easily be accommodated. When students have met in a group, there have been discussions of the assignment, difficulties encountered and information that has been found. I hope to find ways of increasing this interaction with a goal of having the SL area as a meeting point for students who might not be able to get together any other way.

WHY SECOND LIFE

An Increase in Online/Distance Education

In 2008 over 300 colleges and universities world-wide were involved in SL (Michels, 2008). The *Statistical Abstract of the United States 2010* lists 4,352 institutions involved in higher education as of 2007, in the United States alone – so that's 300 colleges and universities in the United States of 4,352 world-wide involved in SL. However, individuals such as the author are not reflected in this statistic as St. John's University (New York) does not have a site and is not part of the 300. I suspect that the universities of many other individuals are not included in the 300 figure as well. Although St. John's itself does not have a presence in SL one of its professors does own an island. I participate on his island. Emgeetee Island is owned by Dr. Charles Wankel, a professor in the management department at the University, who has granted me ownership privileges allowing me to build and create a library presence on his island. The Second Life URL of the island is http://slurl.com/secondlife/Emgeetee/131/111/24. A more optimistic view of participation in SL's educational opportunities is the membership of the SL education listserver. Christine Lagorio of the *New York Times* reported in 2007 that "subscribers to its (Linden Lab) education listserver number more than 1,000."

Over the past 2 years I have met with about 50 students from Dr. Wankel's classes and offered advice and narrated slide presentations of how to search and use the various business databases available at the university. By and large my impression (based on the limited number of positive comments received) is that the sessions were useful – not a bad thing to say about any class. In fact, some even said "very useful."

As to the question WHY? "Why is anyone involved in Second Life?" The question I ask is, "Why aren't more educators involved in Second

Life?" My reason for being involved in MUVEs (multiuser–virtual–environments – that's what SL is) is that I am experimenting with what may likely be the way distance education classes are taught in the future. We are moving in that direction.

Many educational institutions are already involved in Online/Distance Education.

> During the 12-month 2000–2001 academic year, 56 percent (2,320) of all 2-year and 4-year Title IV-eligible, degree-granting institutions offered distance education courses ... Twelve percent of all institutions indicated that they planned to start offering distance education courses in the next 3 years ...
>
> In 2000–2001, 90 percent of public 2-year and 89 percent of public 4-year institutions offered distance education courses, compared with 16 percent of private 2-year and 40 percent of private 4-year institutions.
>
> College-level, credit-granting distance education courses at either the undergraduate or graduate/first-professional level were offered by 55 percent of all 2-year and 4-year institutions. College-level, credit-granting distance education courses were offered at the undergraduate level by 48 percent of all institutions, and at the graduate level by 22 percent of all institutions (Waits, National Center for, & Westat, Inc., Rockville, M.D., 2003).

My own institution, St. John's University (New York), has announced an increased commitment to distance education and lists it as a priority. And, this year, 2010, the University of California announced it was starting a pilot program to

> offer online undergraduate degrees and push distance learning further into the mainstream ... Yet plenty of universities have offered online options for years, and more than 4.6 million students were taking at least one online course during the fall-2008 term, notes A. Frank Mayadas, a senior adviser at the Alfred P. Sloan Foundation who is considered one of the fathers of online learning. 'It's like doing experiments to see if the car is really better than the horse in 1925, when everyone else is out there driving cars,' he said. (Keller & Parry, 2010)

And we are already involved in virtual worlds of a sort. In 2005, 150 of the 229 schools on the *U.S. News & World Report* (2005) ranking of top colleges and universities used Blackboard to "create a networked learning environment. SL is a more sophisticated extension of what we are already doing.

But regardless of what universities and colleges are doing, elementary and high school students, our future customers, are already taking online and distance education classes.

In the late 1990s, Paul Allen of Microsoft founded Apex Learning to provide online courses for high schools. In three years the enrollment for these classes grew 300% – from 8,400 in 2003 to 30,200 in 2006. Apex Learning, in 2008, served 4,000 school districts and now offers *core* courses for these same schools. Twenty-five states have similar programs (Christensen, Horn, & Johnson, 2008). Students in high school are growing up with online courses. They are online natives, their experiences are that online courses are in the main stream – online classes are part of the norm. Since 1999 Apex Learning has served:

660,000 students
2.8 million enrollments
4,500 school districts
50 states
72 countries (Apex Learning, 2010)

Based on the current levels of adoption by high schools it is predicted that by 2019, 50% of high school courses will be delivered online. "In other words, within a few years, after a long period of incubation, the world is likely to begin flipping rapidly to student-centric online technology" (Christensen et al., 2008).

So what does SL have that makes it worth exploring.

Here are two possible explanations.

> Instructors say the Second Life class experience is particularly enhanced for distance learners. In Second Life, classmates and instructor don't just communicate in chat rooms; they can actually see one another – or, at least, digital alter egos – on screen.

And,

> Rebecca Nesson, a Ph.D. candidate in computer science, brought her class at Harvard Extension School to Second Life last semester. 'Normally, no matter how good a distance-learning class is, an inherent distance does still exist between you and your students,' she says. 'Second Life has really bridged that gap. There is just more unofficial time that we spend together outside of the typical class session' (Lagorio, 2007).

It is the present "inherent distance" between students themselves and between student and faculty that exists in distance-learning classes that SL overcomes.

Christensen further points out,

> First, computer-based learning will keep improving, as all successful disruptions do. It will become more enjoyable and take full advantage of the online medium by layering in enhanced video, audio, and interactive elements (2008).

Games and Gaming

On the SLed listserver there have been discussions about SL's relationship to games, including whether SL is a game or not. A more fruitful discussion, for me, would have revolved around how to introduce more games into the educational activities that are possible in SL.

In the mid-1970s many of us sat in front of our television sets mesmerized by a tennis-like game called Pong. It was black and white – a small white circle was batted back and forth across the television screen – each player had control of a white line, paddle if you will, that could be moved up and down on the extreme left and right of the screen. The goal was to move the paddle up or down to "hit" the ball and bounce it back to the other side of the screen to your opponent who was waiting to return it to you. The ball moved faster and faster as the game progressed and the paddles became smaller and smaller. Played today, Pong might not be as exciting as the earlier description. But at the time it was revolutionary. It was inter-active television, it was the crudest MUVE (multi user virtual environment) and it was addictive – everybody in the room wanted to play "My turn! My turn!"

I want to see educators and educational institutions tap into the positive aspect of addiction to games and see games developed to enhance the educational experience. I want to see these games in my SL classroom. In 2003, "Seventy percent (70%) of college students reported playing video, computer or online games at least once in a while, and 65% of college students reported being regular or occasional game players" (Jones, 2003). My grandson, in California, at the age of seven, is playing games with his cousins, in Pennsylvania, and is quite experienced in these MUVEs. He moves his avatar around the environments in his X-Box just as I move my avatar in SL. SL will not be a foreign place to the next generation of college students – it may be a different town, county or state – but it will require only simple adjustments. Many of the students who have attended my classes in SL come to it for the first time. They find the learning curve an easy one to overcome.

> Computers let us make models that work the way some part of the world does. These simulated models make it easier for us to get things done in the real world by letting the computer do some of the work we otherwise would have to do for ourselves. ... Computer and video games can change education because computers now make it possible to learn on a massive scale by doing the things that people do in the world outside of school. They make it possible for students to learn to think in innovative and creative ways just as innovators in the real world learn to think creatively. (Shaffer, 2006)
>
> we have to move away from thinking about education in terms of the traditional organizations in schools. The academic disciplines of history, English, math and science

are not the only way to divide up the world of things worth knowing. The work of creative professionals is organized around what I call *epistemic frames:* collections of skills, knowledge, identities, values, and epistemology that professionals use to think in innovate ways. (Shaffer, 2006)

Computers are Acceptable Teammates
A few paragraphs ago there was discussion about how SL bridges the gap that exists in current distance education classes, gaps between students themselves and between the students and faculty. I suggest that this gap reduction results from the relationship that develops between the human owner and the electronic avatar. When attending my first conference in SL I found myself experiencing similar personal space emotions that I experience in real life. Strangers are welcomed in a circle that is further from me than are my friends. Hayduk (1994) calls this one's "personal space". Using myself as an example, if someone I know approaches me I welcome them within 3 or 4 ft, strangers are welcome but I am more comfortable if they are beyond the 3 or 4ft circle. In SL I found myself transferring these privacy barriers to my avatar. It surprised me. Having experienced this transference I started paying attention to it and found it paralleled my reactions in other situations. At a crowded SL event my privacy circle mirrored the circle I have when on a crowded subway train. People could come much closer – even touching me. As the crowds thinned out I wanted the greater degree of separation (Ferl & Millsap, 1992).

> Clifford Nass of Stanford University has explored the relationship dynamics that can exist between a human and a computer. "In short, recent thinking about computers implies that computers are no longer mere tools; in some ways, they are more like human counterparts."
>
> Nass' "manipulated identify and interdependence to create team affiliation in a human-computer interaction ... In sum, the results of this study suggest that humans interact with computers by using similar social rules and dynamics as when interacting with other humans." (Nass et al., 1996)

Based on my own reactions to relationships with other avatars in SL and the implications offered by Nass' research, I suggest that a closeness not possible in present online/distance education classes can be achieved should these same classes be developed in a SL or other MUVE situation.

Decline in Library Reference
As a librarian at St. John's University (NY) I see the trend toward online classes, an increase in distance education, the reduction of print resources, and the increased availability of library research material online. That

coupled with the fact that all students receive a computer on enrollment that provides them with access to the online library from where ever they happen to be has resulted in a decreased use of the physical library.

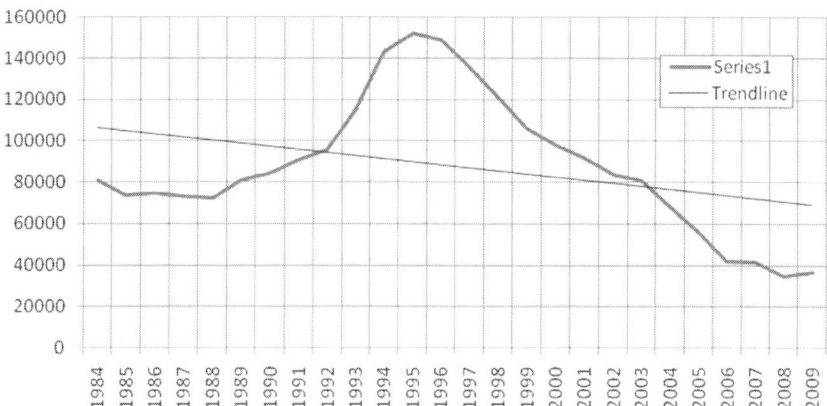

Echoing my observation of a decrease in the use of the reference desk and librarians over the past few years is an article that recently appeared in the *Journal of Library Administration*

> many academic libraries are finding that their reference statistics are plummeting as more students find their own information, unassisted, online. (Lippincott, 2010)

That same article discusses students' time-shifting from the hours the traditional library is open.

> College students of the millennial generation often do their academic work either with or around their friends or classmates, make ample use of technology and digital content, and focus on their academic work late in the day and into early morning.

The decrease in attendance in the actual library building has resulted in fewer contacts with a library staff that is uniquely placed to assist them with their research problems. As the University moved from print to online resources librarians noticed an increased need to assist students in these new resources. As I assisted students in their online research and watched how they went about their searches I realized that students had little conception of how indexes worked. Previously, when students requested the *Reader's guide to periodical literature,* perhaps the most commonly used periodical index in the United States, I would frequently direct them to *Reader's Guide* – and offer assistance if they asked. But, in part, my assumption was that they could read and would easily see the organization of an index.

After assisting students with online searches and noting their lack of awareness of how indexes worked I began to pay more attention to how students used our remaining print indexes. I discovered that the clear organization of material that I saw was not apparent to our students. By spending a few more moments with a student and showing them how indexes were organized with regard to their research, I was usually rewarded with the dawn of comprehension on the part of the student. I suspect that knowing a student could read and pointing them to the indexes in the library has led many librarians to the assumption that all was well with a students' research. Having visited numerous libraries and observed student's behavior at the index tables I suspect that I am not the only librarian who has noted this confusion about how indexes, and the library in general, worked.

As libraries have moved to online indexes they have allowed students greater access to the libraries' content but this has resulted in less contact with the librarians able to provide the instruction necessary for creating the best possible search. It is my belief that MUVEs, such as SL will offer the most real-life like opportunity for librarians to interact with students and other researchers in a most effective manner and continue to offer the needed instruction for research.

As the liaison person between the library and distance education faculty and, being aware that one of the stated goals of the University is to make our materials and services equally available to both campus and distance students, I see SL as an additional way of bridging the distance gap and providing a "face-to-face" experience to students who might never visit the real-life campus. SL fits with our goal of seamless service to distance students.

CONCLUSION

The City of Rochester, New York is filled with empty lots on which formerly sat manufacturing and processing facilities for the film that filled the cameras in the United States and around the world. Digital cameras changed the photographic industry and left Kodak the victim of what has been called a disruptive innovation. The irony of this is that Kodak invented digital photography and produced the first digital camera back in 1975 (Dobbin, Sep 9 2005).

Today there are:

- Increasing conversions from printed to online indexes, books, journals etc.; increasing abilities for students and researchers to conduct their

research from the comfort of the home, dorm room or simply at tables in the piazza in front of the library;
- increasing acceptance of computers as team members and people interacting with them as extension of themselves;
- predictions that by 2019 50% of high school classes will be taught online; and
- companies such as Apex (discussed earlier) which are potentially in a position to provide competition to traditional institutions of higher education.

Universities today are increasing their commitment to online/distance education. The methods today for offering these courses is certain to improve as new technologies and techniques are found. SL appears to offer advantages that present means of providing online/distance education do not. Whether SL or another company provides the service, multiuser–virtual–environments are likely to become more prevalent in the provision of online education. SL offers an excellent opportunity for today's educator to experiment with the future.

REFERENCES

Apex Learning (2010). *About us.* Available at http://www.apexlearning.com/Company/About.htm

Christensen, C. M., Horn, M. B., & Johnson, C. W. (2008). *Disrupting class: How disruptive innovation will change the way the world learns.* New York: McGraw-Hill.

Dobbin, B. (2005). Digital Camera Turns 30-Sort of. Available at http://www.msnbc.msn.com/id/9261340/. Retrieved on July 22, 2009.

Ferl, T. E., & Millsap, L. (1992). Remote use of the University of California MELVYL library system: An online survey. *Information Technology and Libraries, 11*(3), 285. Available at http://proquest.umi.com/pqdweb?did=907115&Fmt=7&clientId=9216&RQT=309&VName=PQD

Gee, J. P. (2003). *What video games have to teach us about learning and literacy* (1st ed.). New York: Palgrave Macmillan.

Hayduk, L. A. (1994). Personal space: Understanding the simplex model. *Journal of Nonverbal Behavior, 18*(3), 245. Available at http://proquest.umi.com/pqdweb?did=6136109&Fmt=7&clientId=9216&RQT=309&VName=PQD

Jones, S. (2003). Let the games begin. Available at http://www.pewinternet.org/Reports/2003/Let-the-games-begin-Gaming-technology-and-college-students.aspx

Keller, J., & Parry, M. (2010). University of California considers online courses, or even degrees. *The Chronicle of Higher Education,* Available at http://chronicle.com/article/In-Crisis-U-of-California/65445/?sid=at&utm_source=at&utm_medium=en

Lagorio, C. (2007). Pepperdine in a treehouse. *New York Times,* p. 4A.22. Available at http://proquest.umi.com/pqdweb?did = 1190461541&Fmt = 7&clientId = 9216&RQT = 309&VName = PQD

Lippincott, J. K. (2010). Information commons: Meeting millennials' needs. *Journal of Library Administration, 50*(1), 27. Available at http://www.informaworld.com/10.1080/01930820903422156

Michels, P. (2008). Universities use second life to teach complex concepts. Available at http://www.govtech.com/gt/252550

Nass, C., Fogg, B. J., & Moon, Y. (1996). Can computers be teammates? *International Journal of Human–Computer Studies, 45*(6), 669–678. doi: 10.1006/ijh.01996.0073.

Shaffer, D. W. (2006). *How computer games help children learn.* New York: Palgrave Macmillan.

U.S. news & world report's top ranked colleges and universities use blackboard. (2005). Available at http://www.prnewswire.com/cgi-bin/stories.pl?ACCT = 109&STORY = /www/story/10-19-2004/0002287294. Retrieved on May 27, 2009.

Waits, T., National Center for, E. S., & Westat, Inc., Rockville, M. D. (2003). *Distance education at degree-granting postsecondary institutions: 2000–2001. E.D. tabs.* Available at http://search.ebscohost.com/login.aspx?direct = true&db = eric&AN = ED481027&site = ehost-live

MENTORING 2.0 – HIGH TECH/HIGH TOUCH APPROACHES TO FOSTER STUDENT SUPPORT AND DEVELOPMENT IN HIGHER EDUCATION

Melanie Booth and Arthur Esposito

ABSTRACT

Web 2.0 technologies are resulting in great shifts: "from institutions to networks, from vertical structures to horizontal systems, from hierarchies to heterarchies, from bureaucracies to individuals, from centre to periphery, from bordered territories to virtual cyberspace" (Fraser & Dutta, 2008, p. 2). When we think about how these shifts apply to our experiences advising and mentoring our students in higher education, we do not think it is a stretch to say that when these technologies are employed thoughtfully, these eruptions likely do occur in particular ways that can, in fact, facilitate student support, development, and learning in new ways. Though we use a variety of social media applications to facilitate our practice as mentors and advisors, we acknowledge Daloz's (1999) concern about technology: "More, faster, and farther seem to be the driving values. Thus entangled in the Internet, spun about at hyperspeed, drowning in information, starved by virtual reality, should we wonder that we hunger for real *reality? Can such technology nourish our need for community, intimacy, contemplative time, wisdom?" (p. xxv). Daloz sincerely questioned if technology could in fact support "good mentoring."* A mere eleven years later, we two advisors/mentors (one from a large public university in the East; one from a small private university in the West) answer with a resounding "Yes!" In fact, in our experiences, social media technologies can extend *the possibilities of good educational mentoring and advising in higher education.*

INTRODUCTION

In their book *Throwing Sheep in the Boardroom: How Online Social Networking Will Transform Your Life, Work, and World,* Fraser and Dutta (2008) captured the phenomenon of the power shift that Web 2.0 technologies are facilitating: "from institutions to networks, from vertical structures to horizontal systems, from hierarchies to heterarchies, from bureaucracies to individuals, from centre to periphery, from bordered territories to virtual cyberspace" (p. 2). When we consider how this applies to our experiences advising and mentoring our college students, we do not think it is a stretch to say that when these technologies are employed thoughtfully and strategically, these shifts likely do occur and can, in fact, facilitate student support, development, and learning in new and potentially enhanced ways.

WE ARE MENTORS, FIRST

Before we delve into how we use social media to engage and connect with our students, let us tell you about what we do and who our students are. Art is the Director of Discovery Advising at Virginia Commonwealth University (VCU) in Richmond, Virginia. His students are primarily in their first year of college study and have not declared a major of study yet, though his program also serves continuing students who have not yet declared a major. His students are primarily in their first year of college and have not declared a major of study, and his program also serves continuing students who have not declared a major. Melanie is the Director of the Center for Experiential Learning and Assessment and the Prior Learning Assessment (PLA) program at Marylhurst University in Portland, Oregon. Her students are all returning adult undergraduates, many of whom are in the midst of or seeking personal or professional transition and/or transformation. She primarily teaches courses in the Prior Learning Assessment program; as an adjunct, she also teaches in the Communications and Education departments. Though our roles, responsibilities, and student populations are significantly different, as are our institutions (one large public university in the East; one small private university in the West) we both approach our work as educational mentors. We are both teachers in the formal sense, but the term "mentoring" extends our reach to our students beyond "teaching" – beyond content, instruction, and assessment – to a place of support, challenge, guidance, and dialogue. As Daloz (1999) described, mentors are first and foremost guides in that "they lead us along the journey of our lives" (p. 18).

As mentors, we operate by a few key tenets. First, we believe that good mentoring is good teaching in that it facilitates learning. So whether we are formally teaching students in our courses or less formally teaching as advisors, we work from the perspective that the best guide is a teacher; the best teacher a guide. With this kind of relationship, mentors support their students through stages of their education, just as professors and instructors support students' learning in the classroom (Koring, Killian, Owen, & Todd, 2004). The second tenet that defines our work is that good teaching and thus good mentoring can facilitate development and growth in the learner; more specifically, it can foster the conditions for transformative learning to occur. In this way, our work extends beyond the instrumental details of advising – what courses to register for, what degree requirements need to be met, how to focus one's time better to ensure learning, etc. Daloz (1999) reminded us that one of the best possible outcomes of an education is this possibility for significant and transformative learning in which the student engages in "successively asking broader and deeper questions of the relationship between oneself and the world ... To imagine otherwise, to act as though learning were simply a matter of stacking facts on top of one another, makes as much sense as thinking one can learn a language by memorizing a dictionary" (p. 243).

We see transformation in our students. Art's students are transforming from primary and secondary teacher-centered students to critical thinking, self-directed college learners as they enter adulthood. Melanie's students, while already adults in age, are also experiencing changes in themselves and their relationships to learning, their instructors, other students, course content, and to the worlds in which they live (Booth, 2007). As mentors, we walk beside our students during this process. We strive to be the mentors that Daloz (1999) described: mentors can be trusted because they "have been there before. They embody our hopes, cast light on the way ahead, interpret arcane signs, warn us of lurking dangers, and point out unexpected delights along the way" (p. 18).

Finally, we understand and enact the idea that trust between people is the key to learning and development. Our students need to trust us – to know that we are present to support their growth and not to play "gotcha"; that we will push them, many times, to places that are uncomfortable, but that we will be there to support them as well. With great intention we strive to engender trust with our students, see their movement, give them a voice, carefully introduce conflict, challenge their taken-for-granted ideas, watch for their growth, and emphasize their positive movements (Daloz, 1999, pp. 123–124). In doing so, we are also careful, as Daloz suggested, to monitor and reflect on our relationships with students. As we have gradually implemented Web 2.0 tools into our daily work, we have been even more highly reflective about our practices.

MENTORING 2.0

To enact all of these principles of mentoring, we supplement (and in many cases, supplant) our face-to-face, email, or phone-based meetings with students with a variety of social media applications. Among other tools, Art uses Facebook as his primary advising tool, intentionally "friending" all of his students the first week of the school year (we discuss this implication later in the chapter). Melanie connects with many of her students on Facebook, is a member of their networks on LinkedIn, and also interacts with several of her students through her own and their blogs. YouTube, wikis, social bookmarking, and Ning are other social media applications that we use in order to connect – to *be engaged with* the lives of – our students. Though we use many social media tools on a daily basis with our students, we acknowledge Daloz's (1999) concern about technology: "More, faster, and farther seem to be the driving values. Thus entangled in the Internet, spun about at hyperspeed, drowning in information, starved by virtual reality, should we wonder that we hunger for *real* reality? Can such technology nourish our need for community, intimacy, contemplative time, wisdom?" (p. xxv). Daloz sincerely questioned if technology could in fact support "good mentoring." A mere 11 years later, we answer with a resounding "Yes!"

For instructional purposes, the use of social media has been coined "Pedagogy 2.0" (McLoughlin & Lee, 2008). This refers to the use of social media to "enable the development of dynamic communities of learning through connectivity, communication, and participation" (p. 3). Pedagogy 2.0 is situated in connectivism (Siemens, 2004), by which learning is a process "of creating a network of personal knowledge, a view that is congruent with the ways in which people engage in socialization and interaction in the Web 2.0 world – a world that links minds, communities, and ideas while promoting personalization, collaboration, and creativity" (McLoughlin & Lee, 2008, p. 2). The possibilities that social media offer us to connect to and engage with and among our students as mentors prompt us to use the term "Mentoring 2.0" – an educational approach that we also ground in connectivism.

Leslie and Landon (2008) contended that when Web 2.0 technologies work, "it is often because the right conditions that allow networks to grow exist" (p. 4). We propose that many of the conditions that allow these technologies to work and grow are similar conditions that allow good learning to work and students to "grow" in higher educational settings. Conditions such as trust, dialogue, motivation, collaboration, input, guidance, and a sense of connectedness and community that support learning and growth for students in higher education are conditions that social media can enable and, in fact, promote. In essence, these are the conditions provided by good educational mentors (Daloz, 1999; Nakamura & Shernoff, 2009). Reichelt's (2007) concept of ambient intimacy – "being able to keep in touch with people with a level of regularity and intimacy that you wouldn't usually have access to, because time and space conspire to make it impossible" (para 3) – comes into play in our practice as well. Social media provides us new and particular ways, which we will demonstrate herein, to have "regularity and intimacy" with our learners, to be conversational and dialogical with them, to engage in collaboration, to have openness, connectedness, and community with and among them. These tools can extend our face-to-face relationships and can make them more meaningful and impactful. These tools also help us shift the power relationship that is typically found between instructors or advisors and students in higher education, just as Fraser and Dutta (2008) proposed. Let us share a few examples.

READING BETWEEN THE LINES: WHAT A STATUS UPDATE CAN TELL YOU

As aforementioned, one of the key components to mentoring – to supporting students in the way that we do – is trust. When relationships with students are built on trust, we can make great strides in supporting their growth and development. To build trust we first listen and then ask questions to help students reveal to us what we need to know or to facilitate their own reflective thinking. In order to be good mentors, we have to earn students' trust, and we do that as Daloz (1999) suggested: suspending our own agendas and attempting to enter our students' worlds (p. 122). We have found that social media tools have helped us do this even better, whether by reading students' blog posts or by following their posts on Facebook. Case in point: Art's student Emily.

One Monday, Art logged onto Facebook and saw that Emily had updated her relationship status: "Emily has gone from being 'in a relationship' to being 'single.'" The following Wednesday Art received an email from Emily requesting an appointment as she was considering transferring to a different school closer to home. He remembered her Facebook update and considered a possible connection. When she came in that Friday, he asked her how life was treating her (not intimating that he had read her Facebook update but rather allowing her to introduce that topic if she so chose). She responded to this and quickly identified her new status as the primary reason she wanted to leave ("he's just there, every time I turn around, everywhere I go").

In Emily's case, Art was able to begin engendering trust from the minute he requested her friendship on Facebook (he requests this of all his advisees as soon as they enter his caseload each fall, an important consideration that we will address later in this chapter). His note that he includes in all such friendship requests reads this way: "Just your academic advisor, making himself accessible ... go read the 'About Me' blurb on my profile so you can rest assured I'm not here to spy on or stalk you." When students read his "About Me," they read that he is not there to list prohibitive behavior or police them, but rather to foster a mutually trust-based relationship. His students routinely accept his friend requests and see that he is comfortable entering their Facebook world. When students accept Facebook friend requests, they have chosen to allow us into their personal, though not necessarily private, space. They knowingly give us access to the extent that they are comfortable; if desired, they can restrict access through use of their privacy settings.

Art was comfortable discussing the extra-curricular topics that were affecting Emily's decision given that she had not chosen to restrict his access to these topics on her Facebook profile. Emily opened up about her personal life in such a way as to allow Art to ask her questions that guided her to see the causal relationship between her recent break up and her desire to transfer. Facebook, in this case, allowed Art to "peek" into her life, and because they were already "friends," allowed him to delve into it a bit more deeply than had this trust-based relationship not been established in the first place. After a long conversation, Emily made the decision that although her ex-boyfriend's presence on campus might be troubling for a little while, transferring was really not in her best long-term academic interest.

Facebook is, of course, not the only social media tool that allows connected people to learn about each other's daily experiences and thoughts. Melanie's students often post similar updates on LinkedIn; moreover, many of the updates in both LinkedIn and Facebook are posted by her students through Twitter. By being connected with many of her students through these technologies, Melanie is able to read how her students are experiencing their courses and help out when she sees an appropriate opportunity. Carla, a PLA student, regularly posted to her Facebook status line about struggles that she was having writing her essays. On one particular post, she wrote, "Ok, I have writer's block. Totally stuck! How will I ever get this essay done?" By adding a comment, Melanie shared a tip to that post: "Have you tried turning the topic into a question and then brainstorming answers to it?" Carla's comment back was, "That worked! Thank you!" Lana, another PLA student, frequently posted progress updates about her essays and her overall academic progress on LinkedIn, and many of her network members, including Melanie, offered their congratulations. In one example, Lana shared, "Three subtopics down; one to go. Paper due Monday; I know I will make it!" Melanie wrote back, "Congrats! I am looking forward to reading it as I am sure it will be one of your best yet!" Lana commented back, "I think you might be right! It's pretty good!"

Two important aspects about these examples stand out to us related to building and maintaining trust in social media spaces. First, it is important, in our experience, that accepting friend or network requests is a choice that students get to make instead of a requirement for the relationship; choice represents trust. Art intentionally "friends" students, and when he does he lets them know the invitation is entirely optional, and they usually accept. Melanie's practice is not to "friend" students proactively but to accept their friend requests as she feels warranted. (See our discussion about power and "creepy treehouses" later in the chapter).

The second important aspect about these examples is that Art's ability to see Emily's status change on Facebook was potentially accidental. Given that he now has more than 1,000 friends on Facebook, Art would need to police his "news feed" (the application on Facebook that reports activities of your friends) on a perpetual basis. Further, no one but Facebook insiders really know what algorithms are used and what indicators lead to certain friends' posts showing up and others not. For these reasons, and because we appreciate that that supplemental contact in online spaces cannot replace interpersonal interactions in advising/mentoring relationships, we do not rely solely upon social media to forge trust-based, civic friendships (Rawlins & Rawlins, 2005) with our students. Social media simply allows us to extend our praxis into additional environments, but not (necessarily) better environments.

A NEW WAY TO HAVE A VOICE: STUDENTS JOIN A FACEBOOK GROUP

Anyone who hopes to guide students through developmental phases needs to understand where the journey begins for the person they hope to support. Hearing students and understanding where "point A" is on the "point-A-to-point-B" journey upon which mentors serve as guides is an essential first step in any mentoring relationship. By identifying the student's "opening position in the dialogue" (Daloz, 1999, p. 123), we can connect future learning more directly to the lives and experiences of each student, and social media tools allow us to better know the lives and experiences of each student. We contend that we accomplish this aspect of mentoring more effectively by giving students a voice in their education in the spaces where the "rest of their life" resides – in social media. In the case that follows, Facebook allowed students a public, digital way to have a voice, and also assisted their advisors who wished to help students understand the intentions of a program as well as some implications of their actions.

Not long after VCU implemented its new first-year seminar course, Focused Inquiry, many students voiced their dissatisfaction and frustrations with the course through Facebook, one of their primary means of self-expression. In one of Art's routine sweeps through the items in his Facebook feed, he saw that a few of his students had joined a group called "Focused Inquiry is a Waste of My Time." Seeing the teachable moment inherent in this scenario, he immediately joined the open group in an attempt to identify the disconnect between the students' expectations and those of the program's designers and instructors. The dialogues that followed, both in Facebook and in his office, were some of the most productive in his advising career.

One of Art's advisee/friends from the group, Claire, sent him a private Facebook message within a week of his joining the group: "Mr. Esposito, what are you doing in this group, won't you get fired?" Art explained to

Claire that he was not concerned about that, as VCU does not make it a policy to police social networks for these sorts of things (see our discussion later in this chapter about institutional policy), nor was it his intention to tell group members that he agreed or disagreed with their premise. Art began an advising dialogue with Claire by asking why she really felt the course to be a waste of her time. By encouraging her to dig deeper into her own experiences of the course and her feelings, and to go beyond the edgy, sound-bite comments most students had written on the Facebook group's wall, Art gently challenged some of her statements, shared a different perspective that she had not considered, and was able to recommend specific strategies and a way forward in the course that allowed her to better understand and meet the desired outcomes of the program.

Mark was another of Art's advisees in the group. Art engaged him in a conversation about Focused Inquiry in the next face-to-face appointment they shared after Art joined the group. Art asked "So, Focused Inquiry is a waste of your time – define 'waste' for me?" Mark grinned and said, "Oh, the Facebook group; are you pissed at me for joining?" Art confirmed that he was not: "I didn't join to fight with you guys about your opinions. I just want to understand your frustrations to see if I can guide you through what could be a potentially damaging obstacle to your academic success." In a conversation similar to the one he shared with Claire, Art again gave Mark an opportunity to more deeply understand the purpose of the course and help chart out an action plan.

Though it is true that both of these conversations might have taken place with or without Facebook, by joining the group to learn more about it and showing support to these students in the social network environment, Art met them on their terms and in their "space" rather than his own. In this way, Facebook has become "the new commons" (Schwartz, 2009). Art did not post any disagreements to the group site; he instead took inventory of the students who joined, and identified ways to connect with them individually about their frustrations. The trust that this engendered in his students, in turn, allowed Art to guide them through this academic turbulence in a way that the students voluntarily accepted and over which they took ownership.

One fear we hear from our colleagues about such groups established and then joined by students – on Facebook and in other social media spaces – is that the institution is "losing control." Indeed, control is exactly what is changing, as we cited earlier by Fraser and Dutta (2008). We propose that an alternative perspective to this is that students' concerns and challenges are simply being organized and communicated in a new way, a way that now often lets us "in" instead of keeping us "out" of the conversation. We can thus use social media tools to help us better understand students' perspectives and address them as individuals.

REFLECTIONS ON GROWTH: USING SOCIAL MEDIA TOOLS TO ACKNOWLEDGE AND SUPPORT SUCCESS

Another key element of our mentoring practice is acknowledging students when they are successful; we believe positive feedback that is specific, along with sharing our words of encouragement, is key in helping students continue to grow and learn. As cited earlier, by being Facebook and LinkedIn friends with students, and by subscribing to their blogs if they have them, Melanie has first-row access to understanding how her students are experiencing their essay writing and can accordingly use the tools in return to support their success. With several of her PLA students, Melanie can respond to a student's Facebook status update that shares an accomplishment quickly and simply by clicking the "Like" button. This simple message to students lets them know she is happy that they succeeded or are making progress – a great way to acknowledge students' positive movement (Daloz, 1999). Though Daloz wrote about such movements from a developmental standpoint, connecting with students in these key ways helps foster their own sense of movement and provides them with personal acknowledgment, as well as a sense of individual care. Though this could be done by email or in person, Facebook allows the interaction to occur quickly and in the norm of the particular communication tool and space that students are using anyway.

Similarly, Art regularly uses Facebook to congratulate his students on successful semesters or making the Dean's List. When such a congratulatory note is posted to a student's Facebook wall, the student not only benefits from Art's acknowledgement of positive movement, but from additional congratulations of fellow students, friends, and family members in their social network who have seen Art's post. Further, when students receive Art's congratulations on Facebook, given that "blind copies" are not possible in the network, they know his messages are more personal and sincere than those automatically generated through ".edu" email programs.

Again, Facebook is not the only tool that Art or Melanie uses to support student success. Melanie's student Sarah is a blogger who posts regularly about her life as an adult returning to college. Some of Sarah's posts are about her daughter who is stationed overseas, some are about her community-based activities, or her other two children, but most are about school, and several are about her PLA writing. By subscribing to Sarah's blog through an RSS reader, Melanie can read and, if needed, comment on Sarah's posts. Melanie also re-posts some of Sarah's posts in her own blog, which sends the message to Sarah that she is "listening" to her and that she values her ideas enough to share with others.

Similarly, Melanie uses her own blog (PrattleNog) to share ideas, strategies, and success stories with her students. When students complete their PLA portfolios, Melanie video tapes a 4–5 minute session of the student (with permission) talking about his or her experience of the program, its benefits and challenges. These videos are posted to the university's YouTube channel, and then Melanie embeds the video into a blog post that congratulates the student and shares a bit more context about his or her success story. Melanie then emails the link out to all current students, several faculty, and staff, and also posts it on Facebook and LinkedIn. Students often share the link with friends and family. Not only do students have acknowledged their accomplishments publicly ("Look mom-I'm on the web!" said one, when she posted the link back to her own Facebook wall), but current students are supported by knowing – by hearing and seeing! – that the challenging task they are undertaking can be accomplished.

We cannot emphasize enough how making public the positive feedback we want to share with students – in these virtual spaces – supports our work as mentors (we also cannot emphasize enough that we would never publicly post constructive or negative feedback for fear of embarrassing students and losing their trust, as well as fear of violating privacy policy). If we are already "friends" with students in these spaces, these announcements, notes, or re-posts are more often than not welcoming and encouraging. Students are in these spaces, just like we are, to share parts of their lives with others; we continually hear from them that our public recognition means a lot to them. After hundreds, possibly thousands, of such posts or re-posts collectively, neither of us has had one student request that we not do so.

IMPLICATIONS OF MENTORING 2.0

What these examples reveal is that using these tools that allow us to enact Mentoring 2.0 – Facebook, blogs, YouTube, LinkedIn, etc. – provides us with new ways to meaningfully connect with our students. However, the use of these tools also reveals implications for traditional models and practices of mentoring and advising. As Fraser and Dutta (2008) warn us, social media tools can be threatening because they "challenge core assumptions" (p. 2), in this case, our tried-and-true ideas about advising and mentoring in higher education. Perhaps there is no greater implication than the diffusion of what has often been a power relationship. Social media has been called an "equalizer," and as Fraser and Dutta (2008) described, we no longer have direct control over the spaces in which communication between us and our students occurs. What we *can* control is how we engage with students in these spaces and how we manage our own participation. Four specific implications have influenced and shaped our Mentoring 2.0 practices accordingly.

Creepy Treehouses Become Welcoming Treehouses

We have aforementioned (and it bears repeating) that trust is the key element to our mentoring approach. Trust comes about when we are authentic as ourselves – as individuals, not institutions – and when we are invitational with our students instead of demanding or prescriptive. In the last couple of years, much has been revealed about how social media tools are being adopted for higher educational purposes: from recruiting prospective students to engaging alumni, many institutions and individuals within our hallowed halls and ivory towers are turning to social media to foster a sense of community and connectedness and this quality called "engagement." Aleman and Wartman (2009), focusing their work on Facebook specifically, reveal that for the current generation of college students (Art's students), computer-mediated communication is in part how they live their lives, and for this reason colleges and universities are attempting to reach out and engage students using these technologies. At the same time, one of the fastest growing segments of social media users is women over the age of 55 on Facebook (Smith, 2009) and 75% of business employees are using social media technologies for business purposes (MacManus, 2008). The adult-learner population of Melanie's student body thus is also becoming one of the most frequent users of these technologies.

So, we know our students are "there," but how can we ensure that we do not barge our way into their personal and potentially private social media spaces? One of the critiques and significant concerns about the educational uses of these tools is the notion of "creepy treehouses," what Stein (2008) defined as "a situation in which an authority figure or an institutional power forces those below him/her into social or quasi-social situations" (para 7). This is, in part, why it is critical that the requests we make to our students to participate with us in these spaces are optional, are, in fact, invitational. Art's invitation to students to be his Facebook "friend" reads as follows: "I am not here to spy on you or police your behavior. I send you this invitation to be friends as a way for you to have access to me through this space; you may contact me here, and I can share information with you here as well. There are many other ways we can communicate, so accepting this invitation is entirely optional." We do not know if our students feel pressured to accept our requests, but once they accept (as most do), we enact this promise. It is important to note, as well, that we are not using these spaces as formal instructional or assessment spaces (we use our learning management systems for such); we *are* using these spaces to extend our access to students (and their access to us) and to build more personal, mentoring-based relationships on the existing institutional relationship.

For students who elect not to join us, we use other means to engage them as individuals and to build that trusting relationship. However, for students who do elect to have us join them, we carefully use the tools to extend our reach, to get to know students more personally, and to share more of ourselves with them. We propose that a careful, considered use of these kinds of tools can create *positive* shifts in power (toward a more learner-centered support system), what we might call "welcoming treehouses," places and spaces where our students feel invited, comfortable, and well-supported.

Daloz (1999) indicated that "an important way in which some mentors establish a trusting bond is through mirroring the language and even the movements of their students" (p. 210). We can do no better job mirroring our students than by maintaining profiles in the same social media spaces in which they are spending time and communicating. Our personal pages and profiles look personal; they do not look like an institutional page or represent the "voice of the institution." As Robbins (2008) suggested, "social media creates new ways to learn without the communities and structures provided by institutions" (slide 25). We thus provide not an authoritative institutional presence, but a personal presence, one in which we can encourage students to embrace their own educational decisions with guidance from us within the social spaces that they and we co-exist. We also take it upon ourselves, at key times, to not mirror but to model appropriate use.

Teachable Spaces for Teachable Moments

A second implication of using these tools that has become clear from our experience is that, as we shared previously, existing in these spaces provides us with new and unique opportunities for teachable moments, quite often about the spaces themselves. We discussed above the choice-based approach that Art takes to "friend" requests for his students; simply the fact that we can call it an honest request with no assumption that students will accept and no requirement that they do is, in a way, attaining permission or approval from each student individually. However, when students open their social media spaces to us and either accept or invite us to them, we also gain glimpses into some actions that we fear are not in their best interest. Our experiences echo Alexander's (2008) notion that while students may come to higher education with highly developed technological skills, they may not have yet developed the intellectual skills to carefully or critically consider how they are using them (p. 200). At least one time each term, each of us reaches out to students to help them understand the consequences of their actions in social media environments. Whether it is one of Art's students arranging a "10-kegger party" with friends, or one of Melanie's posting complaints about her boss or co-workers, when students post such messages in public, online environments, we propose a magnificent opportunity to embrace "the teachable moment." We have found that more than one approach can be effective in response to this moment of opportunity: a personal message or the posting of a universal note.

In many cases, Art will send a private Facebook message to one of his advisees who may have been a bit reckless in sharing her or his escapades. Some examples of the sort of message Art sends include the following: "I realize you're trying to get the word out to all your friends how fun your party was, but the picture of you with the beer in your under-aged hand might not go over so well with the authorities if it falls into the wrong hands." Or, "while you're considering the most effective and efficient ways to get the word out about your party, don't forget that university officials also have access to this space. And though you can trust your own security settings, are you sure you can trust those of any friend to whom you've sent this invitation?" Likewise, Melanie has cautioned her students in private messages to them about the information they reveal in public, online spaces, including the student who posted in LinkedIn, "I can't take this job anymore-get me out of here." Not only is that information accessible to her current and potential future employers, but the digital trail she leaves with that one seemingly innocent comment may haunt her in years to come.

In some cases, when it seems a better idea to make a general statement to a broader audience, Art will post a "Facebook Note" on his profile page. A Facebook Note is similar to a blog post, can be sent to specific friends or groups of friends and/or simply posted to your profile page. In the note he typically titles "Poor Choices," he reminds students that his intention in requesting their friendship on Facebook is not to list prohibitive behavior or to report them to authorities, but rather to encourage them to make wise choices about both their actions in the real world and those they choose to share with uncontrolled viewers in social media spaces. Other reminders in the note include the ever-increasing number of employers who access social media sites when screening potential new hires, how educational institutions react to certain types of cyber-bullying of students and faculty, and how one can never take the "Facebook friend" label too seriously, noting the number of vindictive students who have reported other students in these spaces.

Again, our goal is not to police our students in these spaces, but to connect with students therein and help them understand the choices they make. In so doing, we show students that we are committed to their academic success, the common goal of our civic friendship (Rawlins & Rawlins, 2005). Nonetheless, social media technologies have caused institutions to reconsider existing or create new policies to, in fact, police student and faculty use.

The Changing Landscape: Policy 2.0

Alexander (2008) pointed out that not only when it comes to Web 2.0 and a sense of "losing control" but also needing to support new technologies, a higher educational institution might be best served to get "out of the way of users" (p. 199). This is a significantly uncomfortable stance for academic institutions, given concerns about privacy with which student services professionals and faculty at universities across the country have grappled with ever since the Family Educational Rights Protection Act (FERPA) was written in 1974. This date is significant in that it places the creation of academia's arguably most important privacy policy well before the advent of the internet. Until relatively recently, our biggest concern was how to identify whether we were really talking to the student on the other end of the telephone line. As we sit here in 2010, we can see that situation really has not changed that much.

In regard to the "Wait-what about student privacy?" question that we usually receive from colleagues, our answer is abrupt: We ask back, "What about it?" We always act as professionals in our conversations with students, just as we would by email or in the hallway, and we are still in control of what information we share publicly and what we do not. We also argue that if university employees do not understand how social media tools work, they should not be using them professionally. One simply needs to understand both the provisions of FERPA and their own institution's compliance policies to ensure no inappropriate conversations are conducted and no protected information is shared in the social spaces. Indeed, as institutions struggle to understand the privacy implications inherent in occupying social media environments, they often fail to see that the statutes they already have in place, such as computer use policies, are sufficient for online communications and information sharing in social media environments.

Additionally, organizations such as the National Academic Advising Association are, at the time of this writing, developing best practices for the use of social media in collegial advising scenarios that can provide useful guidelines as well (assuming the guidelines can keep up with the changes in technologies). In the end, we believe that for the ways in which we mentor and advise students, social media environments are no more than delivery tools, arguably similar to the telephone – an incredibly engaging and information-rich telephone that allows multiple conversations at once, but a telephone nonetheless.

Our Workloads and Our Caseloads

A final implication of Mentoring 2.0 is related to both workload and caseload. Colleagues frequently ask us how we manage to do one more thing, to use one more technology. Where do we find the time? Neither of us has felt that we have quantitatively more work using these tools; what we have found is that the work is qualitatively different. When we are actively using these tools, we are often not using others, such as email or the phone. For Melanie, a blog post that is published to all of her students takes as much time to write as an email to one or all of her students, though the message is exactly the same. For Art, using Facebook to work with advisees has virtually eliminated phone appointments, and Facebook allows him to post and push reminders to his students as a group through the technology they are using instead of to individuals through a technology they are not (their ".edu" email addresses). Though we still actively use email for certain kinds of communications, it seems that increasingly, as Carnevale contended, "email is for old people" (Carnevale, 2006).

Finally, we believe that the concept of ambient intimacy (Reichelt, 2007) referred to previously helps us work with more students, more effectively. Social media allows us ambient intimacy with many *more* of our students (and alumni) than we would otherwise be able to be and stay connected with through our universities' formal communication tools. It may not always be a direct connection; but for our work, an ongoing indirect connection is better than no connection at all. Melanie has more than 200 student and alumni "friends" on Facebook and in LinkedIn; Art's students on Facebook alone exceed 1000 from multiple years of advising. We both maintain relationships with students – sometimes formal, sometimes casual – after they have left our programs or graduated. Using these tools has allowed us to stay *connected* with them all.

IN CONCLUSION – YES, IT IS PERSONAL

On April 16, 2007, a colleague of Art's invited him to a Facebook event called "National Poke Someone On Facebook Day." The intention of the event was to get as many users as possible to engage in the network's "poke" feature, an application that Facebook created to allow you to nudge someone into thinking about you, to let someone know you were thinking about them, or both. Art accepted the invitation and proceeded to poke most of his student and colleague Facebook friends that morning, not thinking much else would come of the event but some light-hearted cyber-interaction designed to put smiles on their faces and let them know he was playing along with them in their space, as their peer.

As the morning wore on, a troubled young man at Virginia Tech (a sister institution to Virginia Commonwealth University) embarked on the most deadly university shooting spree in our nation's history. All thoughts of "poke day" were jostled out of mind, but as Art logged back into Facebook, eager to see if any of his Virginia Tech student/friends or colleagues were posting updates about their well-being, he found that one student had returned his poke. In fact, he was the only one who did that day. The student also sent Art a Facebook message letting him know how much he appreciated all his help that year as his advisor and that it was really good, "today of all days," to know someone at the university was thinking about him. The student wrote, "Thank you for poking me Art; thank you for just thinking of me and being there for me."

As social media tools and technologies make their way into our professional work as mentors, advisors, and instructors, as well as into our daily personal lives, we see that by having the power shift in ways that it is, by creating welcoming treehouses for our learners, and by being "friends" with students in these spaces, we can invite a new kind of engagement with them as well. In our minds, there is no longer an either/or proposition between high tech and high touch; these tools allow the high tech to foster and facilitate our "high touch" practices. These tools complement and support our mentoring work. For us, and for our students, these tools allow us to *be personal*, because being personal, we think, is how we can best be professional.

REFERENCES

Aleman, A. M., & Wartman, K. L. (2009). *Online social networking on campus: Understanding what matters in student culture*. New York: Routledge.

Alexander, B. (2008). Social networking in higher education. In: R. N. Katz (Ed.), *The tower and the cloud: Higher education in the age of cloud computing* (pp. 197–201). Washington, DC: Educause.

Booth, M. (2007). *A study of adult undergraduate learners' experiences of becoming and being self-directed learners*. Ed.D. dissertation, Fielding Graduate University, California (Publication No. AAT 3279462).

Carnevale, D. (2006). E-Mail is for old people. *The Chronicle of Higher Education*. Available at http://chronicle.com/article/E-Mail-is-for-Old-People/4169

Daloz, L. A. (1999). *Mentor: Guiding the journey of adult learners*. San Francisco, CA: Jossey-Bass.

Fraser, M., & Dutta, S. (2008). *Throwing sheep in the boardroom: How online social networking will transform your life, work, and world*. Hoboken, NJ: Wiley.

Koring, H., Killian, E., Owen, J. L., & Todd, C. (2004). Advising and teaching: Synergistic praxis for student and faculty development. *The Mentor: An Academic Advising Journal*. Retrieved from Pennsylvania State University Website: http://www.psu.edu/dus/mentor/040728hk.htm

Leslie, S., & Landon, B. (2008). *Social software for learning: What is it, why use it?* Report for the Observatory on Borderless Higher Education, OBHE, London.

MacManus, R. (2008). Report: Nearly 70% of businesses allow social media usage. *ReadWriteWeb*. Available at http://www.readwriteweb.com/archives/report_businesses_social_media_usage.php

McLoughlin, C., & Lee, M. J. W. (2008). Future learning landscapes: Transforming pedagogy through social software. *Innovate Online*, 4. Available at http://www.innovateonline.info/pdf/vol4_issue5/Future_Learning_Landscapes__Transforming_Pedagogy_through_Social_Software.pdf

Nakamura, J., & Shernoff, D. J. (2009). *Good mentoring: Fostering excellent practice in higher education*. San Francisco, CA: Jossey-Bass.

Rawlins, W. K., & Rawlins, S. P. (2005). Academic advising as friendship. *NACADA Journal*, 25(2), 10–19.

Reichelt, L. (2007). Ambient intimacy. *Disambiguity* blog. Available at http://www.disambiguity.com/ambient-intimacy/

Robbins, S. (2008). *Social media in education: The conflict between technology and institutional education, and the future* [PowerPoint slides]. Presented at Educause 08. Available at http://www.slideshare.net/intellagirl/educause08-social-mediaand-education-presentation?type=powerpoint

Schwartz, H. (2009). Facebook: The new classroom commons? *The Chronicle of Higher Education*. Available at http://gradstudies.carlow.edu/pdf/schwartz-chronicle_9-28-09.pdf

Siemens, G. (2004). *Connectivism: A learning theory for the digital age*. Available at http://www.elearnspace.org/Articles/connectivism.htm

Smith, J. (2009). Fastest growing demographic on Facebook: Women over 55. *Inside Facebook*. Available at http://www.insidefacebook.com/2009/02/02/fastest-growing-demographic-on-facebook-women-over-55/

Stein, J. (2008). Defining "creepy treehouse". *Flexknowlogy* blog. Available at http://flexknowlogy.learningfield.org/2008/04/09/defining-creepy-tree-house/

LEARNING TOGETHER: USING SOCIAL MEDIA TO FOSTER COLLABORATION IN HIGHER EDUCATION

Neil Ford, Melissa Bowden and Jill Beard

ABSTRACT

This chapter focuses on how social media tools can be used to enhance collaboration in higher education and the benefits and challenges that this can bring. We investigate how two social media tools, social bookmarking, and microblogging, can be utilized to foster collaboration and determine why this is important in contemporary higher education. Case studies of social media use at Bournemouth University show how social bookmarking and microblogging have already yielded benefits. The case studies are grounded in the challenges facing higher education in 2010. We explore how social media has been used in the context of a need to enhance academic excellence and drive efficiencies in the face of funding constraints and changing demographics.

The case studies illustrate, first, how social bookmarking has been used to foster group cohesion, reflective practice, and evaluative skills in students, as well as being used at an institutional level to drive professional and administrative efficiencies; and second, how microblogging has made a difference in promoting reflective learning, group cohesion, and professional awareness in students and how this style of social networking has contributed to enhancing academic and professional networks.

Whilst the tools, uses, and stakeholders vary, the case studies show how social media has enabled collaboration between, students, academics, librarians, learning technologists, and even professional groups beyond the institution. We conclude that, when used appropriately, social media can facilitate the collaboration that will be essential to overcome the challenges facing higher education.

INTRODUCTION

This chapter was written shortly after the UK Government published its vision entitled *Higher Ambitions: The Future of Universities in a Knowledge Economy* (2009), providing a context where the challenge of driving up excellence must happen amid funding constraints and there is a clear need to "focus … resources where they can have the greatest return" (Department for Business, Innovation and Skills, p. 4). This context is well understood by Bradwell in his work *The Edgeless University* (2009) where he states, "technology can help universities move from where they are now to where they need to be" (p. 11). Bradwell also discusses the challenge of an increasingly diverse higher education demographic with a need "[to] include students with caring responsibilities, students with disabilities, students learning in the workplace; and students from different ethnic and religious backgrounds" (p. 18).

In this context, collaboration is central to learning and service delivery in our universities. As well as driving the efficiencies needed to improve academic excellence in a climate of funding constraints, collaboration offers new ways to teach and learn in the face of changing demographics. In UK higher education, where "two out of five higher education students are currently studying part-time; 59 per cent are mature and almost 15 per cent come from overseas" (Bradwell, 2009, p. 18), the phrase "distance learning" extends beyond a description of physical distance to incorporate the "psychological aspects of distance" (So & Brush, 2008, p. 319). Students may feel a sense of remoteness from their cohort for various reasons such as age, gender, ethnicity, and pressure of family or work commitments. This sense of distance can be overcome by collaborative learning where students "engage in class activities, interact with others and solve problems or complete tasks, think and talk about their thinking, and explore answers to the problems or tasks" (Wang, 2007, p. 150).

Much has been said about the way students of different generations and backgrounds interact with technology. Prensky (2001) and Oblinger and Oblinger (2005) were pivotal with their discussions of digital natives, digital immigrants, and Net-Gen students when describing the changes and challenges for education. How can social networking tools foster collaboration to make a difference to academic excellence and to the effective and efficient use of resources? How, in the wireless, increasingly mobile and ubiquitous world of technology "fading into the foreground" (Ipsos MORI, 2007, p. 15) can the academic library support the academic community with this rapid change? Brabazon (2007) advocated a new partnership between academics and librarians to "support new modes of reading, writing and communicating, integrating discovery, searches, navigation and the appropriateness of diverse resource" (p. 39).

In this chapter we look at the potential contribution of two social media tools, social bookmarking, and microblogging, to develop learning communities, build partnerships between academics, librarians, and learning technologists, and contribute to the much sought efficiencies. A description of social bookmarking and its potential to aid collaboration is followed by two case studies of social bookmarking use at Bournemouth University. The first describes an externally funded UK Higher Education Academy project entitled e-Res (2008) that looked at the use of social bookmarking to help resolve the difficulty of distance learners being able to discuss and share resources they had found. Our second case study describes how librarians have used social bookmarking to collaborate on the discovery and evaluation of Internet resources and how this has created efficiencies, reducing both duplication of effort and administrative tasks.

Next, we describe microblogging, and in particular Twitter, as a tool with the potential to develop collaborative academic and professional networks. Our third case study looks at the use of Twitter with students on a healthcare programme, a discipline in which "professionals are expected to work collaboratively in multiprofessional teams, sharing knowledge and skills in delivering quality care and support to service users" (Miers, Rickaby, & Clarke, 2009, p. 673). Our final case study explores how microblogging can be used to foster professional networks and continuing professional developments in libraries.

SOCIAL BOOKMARKING

What is Social Bookmarking?

In the early days of the Internet, web browsers built in tools that (depending on your preferred brand of browser) allowed you to "bookmark" or "favourite" links to webpages. The links were stored on the user's computer, which meant that the bookmarks were only of use to the person who had created them, and only then if they were using that same computer. Social bookmarking is an evolution of this functionality, where, instead of the bookmarks being stored on an individual user's computer, they are stored on the Internet.

Whilst the term "social bookmarking" is still relatively new (Redden, 2010), sites that enable users to share their bookmarks have been around since the mid-1990s, for example, a paper from 1998 described itList and MURL as two simple services that allow users to record and share bookmarks (Balas, 1998).

The personal benefits of social bookmarking are obvious to anyone who works on more than one computer. By storing bookmarks on the Internet (or in "the cloud"), social bookmarking services like Diigo, StumbleUpon or Delicious, to name but a few, enable users to access their favourite links from wherever they are (Secker, 2008).

Adding a bookmark is very simple, essentially users create an account with a social bookmarking service (such as Delicious), then save the web address and other information about sites they want to bookmark to that account. Social bookmarking services also allow users to share their bookmarks with others and augment the bookmarks with their own content. One example of this is by adding tags – short keywords or phrases that help users to organize and retrieve their bookmarks (e.g., a user researching holidays might tag all of the sites they find with the word "holiday"). Users can also add longer descriptions, as well as being able to search for resources that have been bookmarked by others.

It is being able to share bookmarks with others and add user-generated content that really sets social bookmarking apart from maintaining private, individual lists of bookmarks. How do these functions benefit collaborative working though, and how can they be utilized in higher education?

How Can Social Bookmarking Enable Collaborative Working?

Social bookmarking sites offer a very different source for finding web resources than traditional search engines. Search engines use web robots to scour the Internet and add sites to databases according to programmed algorithms whereas web pages only get added to social bookmarking sites if, even on a very basic level, they have been judged by a human to have some *value*. By adding bookmarks to the system, a user increases the data stored in that system and improves it for all the other users.

With this in mind, the population of users on a particular social bookmarking site influences not only the amount but also the type and quality of bookmarks in the system. Blackboard Scholar is one of a number of social bookmarking tools specifically tailored for use in education. Whilst it can be used independently, it is commonly embedded within the blackboard virtual learning environment (VLE).

Its user-base consists of those who are currently involved in education, and this is reflected in the resources bookmarked. In early 2010, popular bookmarks on Scholar included a guide for writing research papers in the APA style, human anatomy sites, and a link to an online medical dictionary. Comparing these to popular bookmarks on Delicious during the same period (websites on how to make money from Twitter and the latest iPhone apps) shows that different social bookmarking sites cater for different communities and give very different search results.

As well as Scholar, Connotea and CiteULike have been designed specifically for bookmarking academic sources, and a number of bespoke systems have been developed for specific institutions, for example, Unalog has been customized at Yale (Chudnov, Barnett, Prasad, & Wilcox, 2005), and RISAL (at the University of Hong Kong) embeds social bookmarking technology in a repository of learning and teaching material (Churchill, Wong, Law, Salter, & Tai, 2009). In all these examples, the community of users is an important factor in ensuring the quality of the resources bookmarked in the system.

Social bookmarking tools allow users to classify their bookmarks by assigning tags (short keywords that describe the sites) to them. These user-defined tags form what is known as a folksonomy, described by Guy and Tonkin (2006) as a "type of distributed classification system. It is usually created by a group of individuals, typically the resource users. Users add tags to online items, such as images, videos, bookmarks and text." (p. 1).

Whereas search engines retrieve results on the basis of matching strings of text, tagging allows users to retrieve results based on the meaning others have attached to them. Research by Al-Khalifa and Davis (2007) suggests that tags in folksonomies are semantically richer than keywords generated by automatic keyword extraction tools and, in terms of effectiveness of information retrieval, there is evidence to suggest that social bookmarking tools are comparable to search engines (Morrison, 2008).

Whilst folksonomies arise from an informal use of tagging, the tool can be used in a more formal way to label resources as being for a particular group or activity. Some argue that this use is not in the spirit of using tags to create folksonomies, but tagging in a more formal way certainly has its uses in education (Secker, 2008). With regard to information literacy instruction, Luo (2010) found evidence that librarians are using tags to present course-specific resources to students. Beyond using tags to present resources to students, they can also be used to engage students in resource discovery. Inviting students to tag resources to share in a group activity encourages them to evaluate the resource and judge whether it is appropriate for academic study.

Social bookmarking also allows users to add information other than tags that may help others to evaluate the resource or facilitate retrieval. Most social bookmarking tools allow users to add a description of the site they are bookmarking and some allow users to rate sites, commonly by adding stars. If a web page has been favourably described or starred by another user, it is more likely to be worth clicking on. Whereas finding and evaluating a web page with Web 1.0 was a solitary affair, with Web 2.0 the results are shared so that all those who come after can also benefit.

The ability for users to add descriptions to bookmarks has a particular significance in higher education. Bradwell (2009) identifies information literacy as particular skills need, "[t]he skills that students lack when they arrive at university are much the same as those students have always needed to develop: the capacity to filter and analyse sources and to assess the validity and authority of material" (p. 57). Adding a description to a resource requires a certain degree of evaluation and reflection and the capability to do this with social bookmarking makes it a powerful tool in information literacy instruction.

Saeed, Yang, and Sinnappan (2009) conclude that a student's learning style can influence their technology preferences and hence the academic performance gains associated with different social media. Similarly, Godwin (forthcoming) highlights a number of studies suggesting that social media use in education needs to be both appropriate to the group of students and used in the right way to be effective. So and Brush (2008) observed, it is "important to employ pedagogically sound strategies" as instructing "learners to work on a group project does not necessarily mean they will work collaboratively" (p. 320).

The features of social bookmarking described above (sharing resources with a like-minded community of users, classifying and retrieving bookmarks using tags, and value-add in the form of user-generated content such as descriptions) all provide opportunities to use social bookmarking in higher education – as long as it is used for the right reasons.

Social Bookmarking at Bournemouth University

Bournemouth University Case Study 1: Exploring and Sharing Evidence in Learning

At Bournemouth University, academic, library, and learning technology staff used social bookmarking to enhance collaborative learning in a cohort of midwifery students (Taylor, 2008). Whilst the group are not distance learners in the strictest sense, the time they spend together as a group is limited. They spend much of their time in placements across the South of England, and they are taught across two geographically distant campuses.

Evidence suggests that "learning is enhanced when knowledge is shaped by the activities and perspectives of the group" (Wang, 2007, pp. 151–152). Indeed, group interaction "has been recognised as one of the most important components of learning experiences both in conventional education and distance education" (Jung, Choi, Lim, & Leem, 2002, p. 153). In the past, first year students had carried out an activity to find, evaluate, and share evidence to support the UNICEF 10 steps to successful breastfeeding. However conducting this as a classroom-based activity was not always practicable due to the distributed nature of the cohort (Taylor, 2008).

The social bookmarking tool, Scholar, was introduced to the students as an alternative way for them to find, evaluate, and share evidence. In this case study, the learning exercise was not driven by a wish to use the technology per se, rather social bookmarking overcame the practical problem of how to bring geographically diverse students into a room to conduct a group exercise. In fact, the use of social bookmarking enhanced the student learning experience, as knowing that the resources they added would be seen by the group encouraged students to reflect on the appropriateness of the resource to the situation and evaluate the resource, perhaps more critically than they otherwise would have done. As So and Brush (2008) observe, collaborative learning can encourage students "to develop critical thinking skills through the process of judging, valuing, supporting or opposing viewpoints" (p. 320).

Scholar was chosen as the social bookmarking tool because it is embedded within Bournemouth University's VLE (Dale & Cheshir, 2009), and this may have been significant in its successful use with Bournemouth University students. Burhanna, Seeholzer, and Salem Jr.'s (2009) study of student perceptions of Web 2.0 used focus groups to show that students are acutely aware of issues such as authority and privacy. One of the conclusions of the study is that, rather than infiltrating what students consider to be social spaces (such as Facebook), social media should be brought within learning environments (such as VLEs) for effective educational use.

Several features of social bookmarking made it appropriate for this purpose. Agreeing on a common tag for the exercise allowed the students to share resources that they had found with their cohort and academic staff. Kamel Boulos and Wheeler (2007) point out that tags can be utilized to make social bookmarking a "community-based tool." Interestingly, one of the learning points from this case study was the need for guidance on tagging to be clear and for standard conventions to be followed. For the academic to easily retrieve the students' bookmarks, it was essential that the resources were tagged consistently. This problem was also identified by the LASSIE case study on social bookmarking (Secker, 2008). Being able to add a description to their bookmarks was important for the students to demonstrate how they had evaluated the resource.

Finally, being an online tool meant that the students could complete their activity from anywhere, "[even] on placement in the wards ... it enabled a sharing of information that ... couldn't fit into the classroom sessions" (Taylor, 2008). Despite their geographic spread, the academic using the tool felt that the students worked together (Dale & Cheshir, 2009). An additional benefit was that students stated that they enjoyed being able to share bookmarks and intended to continue to use the tool beyond the exercise (Taylor, 2008).

Bournemouth University Case Study 2: Collaborative Working on Subject Resource Guides

Librarians at Bournemouth University have recently begun to use social bookmarking for producing subject guides to multimedia resources on the Internet. A need was identified after a number of enquiries from academics regarding the copyright implications of using sources such as YouTube in their teaching materials. Images and film are increasingly available on the Internet, but the copyright implications of using them in education are sometimes complex and vary from source to source. A pilot study to develop subject guides to suitable multimedia resources linking to appropriate copyright guidance at the point of use was undertaken to determine the work involved in producing such a resource, and its potential benefits.

In the pilot study, librarians from the schools of Services Management and Health and Social Care both collected resources relevant to their subject areas. A number of features of Scholar suggested that it was suitable for cataloguing resources for the project. As Scholar is embedded in Bournemouth University's VLE, both librarians had already had some experience of using it. On a very simple level it allowed URLs to be stored very easily; however, other features of social bookmarking also lent themselves to the project. Scholar allows tagging, which allowed the librarians to classify and organize the resources at the point of discovery. By using multiple tags, the librarians were able to: specify that the webpage had been bookmarked for this project, denote which school it had been bookmarked for and, also, classify the resource in a sub-category (e.g., TV and film resources).

As well as being able to find each other's resources using the project tag, the librarians connected their accounts using the social networking tool built into Scholar. Being able to see each other's bookmarks was particularly useful for sharing sites relevant to both schools, for example user friendly guides on copyright. One finding from this pilot that is consistent with our first case study is that, for these kinds of uses of social bookmarking, it is very important for tagging conventions to be agreed upon right at the start of the project. In this case, a minor difference in the tags used by each librarian meant that some of the materials bookmarked had to be re-tagged.

The ability to add user-generated content enabled the librarians to add descriptions containing information such as the authority or size of the resource. This librarian value-add facilitates end users evaluating the resources. Links to the copyright policies of the resources bookmarked were also included in the descriptions and this informs end users, at a glance, which resources are cleared for their intended use (e.g., to tell lecturers if images from a particular source are copyright cleared for use in lecture slides).

This use of social bookmarking initiated from a need to simply collect and share resources but has yielded other benefits. Traditionally in projects of this type, librarians collate lists of resources that are then passed on to the web developer to turn into a web page. This is fairly labour intensive for the web developer and means that any time subject librarians want to add or edit links they have to submit the changes to the web developer. Scholar includes a tool that allows RSS feeds to be created from searches of Scholar tags. In this case, the web developer just created links to the Scholar feeds – rather than manually creating lists of links and descriptions in HTML. As well as saving the initial job of manually creating HTML pages, it allows the page to be dynamic. If a subject librarian wants to add a web resource to the page, all they have to do is to bookmark that page with the appropriate tags in Scholar. The new webpage is automatically added to the feed without the need for the intervention of the web developer.

Another major benefit of using social bookmarking for this type of task is that librarians can share each other's discoveries. One finding from the pilot phase of the project is that many of the resources were useful additions to the lists for both schools (e.g., Flickr's creative commons search is a useful source of photos regardless of your subject area). Because the bookmarks are available to all to see, and can be retrieved using the project tag, it is possible for librarians to quickly and easily reuse the resources that have already been found by their colleagues.

It is perhaps important to stress at this point that this project was a pilot designed to determine in principle the most effective way for a team of librarians to collaboratively collect and evaluate resources. Changes to Scholar's search functionality during the pilot phase and limitations of the RSS feeds produced have driven the librarians to investigate other social bookmarking tools (such as Delicious) for the next phase of the project. One of the benefits of piloting the project on a small scale was that, whilst proving the concept of social bookmarking for collaborative resource discovery and evaluation, it also provided the opportunity to carefully evaluate the specific social bookmarking tools before wider implementation.

In both of these social bookmarking case studies, the drivers for using social bookmarking were different, in the former it was an appropriate tool because it facilitated collaborative resource discovery and evaluation among geographically distant learners, in the latter it allowed librarians to avoid replicating work by capitalizing on the discoveries of their colleagues. This latter point is perhaps particularly significant in the current context of UK higher education, where costs are rising faster than funding, and it is essential that universities change their business model to harness the efficiencies that disruptive technologies, such as social media, offer (Bradwell, 2009).

MICROBLOGGING

What is Microblogging?

Microblogs enable users to send and receive short messages (typically 140 characters, including spaces) through the web, mobile phones, and third-party applications. Indeed, the 140 character limit was originally set so messages could be sent as texts from mobile phones, which have a 160 character limit. Examples of services include Plurk and Jaiku, but Twitter is the most popular microblogging service, made famous by celebrity users and "its very effective use in the political arena" (Fernandez, 2009, p. 35), notably the Obama presidential campaign.

Twitter describes itself as "a real-time information network powered by people all around the world that lets you share and discover what's happening now" (Twitter, 2010). The use of "what's happening now" is significant; originally Twitter asked users to post in response to the question "what are you doing?" but this changed recently to "what's happening?" Social media observers suggest this reflects a change in how the service is being used. "[T]weets have evolved to more than everyday experiences" (Mashable, 2010) and now involve sharing links to web content, photos, videos, music and "most importantly, real-time accounts from people who are in the midst of a newsworthy event, crisis, or natural disaster" (Mashable, 2010).

In essence, microblogging is a social experience. Users can choose to follow (receive updates from) people who interest them and can be followed in turn by other users. Unlike Facebook, users do not need to give each other permission to view tweets (unless a user has set their account as private). Twitter users can converse through @replies (public messages) and direct messages (private messaging). Information can be widely shared by re-tweeting (re-posting) tweets from other users. Hashtags, for example, #followfriday, are user-generated tags to organize tweets; popular subjects appear in "Trending Topics." Finally, users can create lists of their favourite Tweeters, for example, "librarians."

The statistics from the first Twitter conference, "Chirp," in San Francisco revealed that the service has (at the time of reporting) over 105 million users (Arthur, 2010). It receives around 19 million queries a day (about 600 million queries per month) which, as Bradley observes, potentially makes Twitter the second largest search engine following Google (Bradley, 2010a). Add to this "the current spam volume is now down to about 1% of the total volume of tweets per day" (Dybwad, 2010) and the power of Twitter as an information source becomes apparent.

Teenagers have been enthusiastic adopters of social networking sites such as Facebook, so it was initially assumed by social media commentators that they would be the main user group on Twitter. However, research by Lenhart, Purcell, Smith, and Zickuhr (2010) for the Pew Internet & American Life Project found data suggesting "that [American] teens do not use Twitter in large numbers" (p. 39). Lenhart et al. conducted surveys in September 2009 with both teens and adults in the United States, which showed that "19% of adult internet users ages 18 and older use Twitter" but "only 8% of online

American teens ages 12–17 use Twitter" (p. 39). These data are confirmed by the anecdotal evidence in a report for Morgan Stanley (Robson, 2009) on teenagers and media written by a 15-year-old summer intern, Matthew Robson. He comments that "teenagers do not use twitter" (p. 2).

Why is this? For Matthew Robson, cost is a disincentive for teenagers, "texting twitter uses up credit, and they would rather text friends with that credit" (Robson, 2009, p. 2). Dybwad offers an alternative perspective, commenting that "a teenager's social circle is far smaller and more closely defined than an adult's network" (cited by Parr, 2010). She observes this may be "why more closed networks like Facebook are more appealing to teenagers than Twitter, which is a completely public experience" (Dybwad cited by Parr, 2010). Furthermore, Parr contends that teenagers "haven't had the time to build up expertise, life experiences or a career that would merit content creation" (2010), although this seems to narrowly define "content" as text-based, whereas many teenagers routinely upload photographs to Facebook and videos to YouTube.

Interestingly, the majority of users are not posting updates using the Twitter website itself; statistics from Chirp show that "75% of Twitter traffic comes from third-party apps" (Arthur, 2010) and "37% of active Twitter users use their phone to tweet" (Arthur, 2010), as Matthew Robson described, earlier. There are "more than 100,000 Twitter applications" (Arthur, 2010) running on web services and mobile devices using Twitter's open application programming interface (API). Furthermore, the development of Twitter's new "@anywhere" service will allow "[o]perators of third-party websites to ... integrate some basic Twitter functionality" into their pages (Axon, 2010); as with Facebook Connect, @anywhere will enable users to login to supporting websites with their Twitter account details.

How Can Twitter Enable Collaborative Working?

As Stuart (2010) comments, "[o]ne of the reasons social media sites are popular is because they have relatively low barriers to entry" (p. 47). It is free to set up a Twitter account and accounts with third-party applications, such as Tweetdeck, Twitterrific, and Twhirl are also freely available. For many users, there will be no need to purchase new equipment to access the service thanks to "the ubiquity of laptops and smartphones" (Ferenstein, 2010a). This section explores how higher education institutions have been using Twitter – attracted in part by low start-up costs-to enhance teaching and library support.

Studies have shown that the benefits of increased student discussion and collaboration are "better academic performance, motivation, and a likelihood of adopting different points of view" (Ferenstein, 2010a) leading to more meaningful learning. In focus groups conducted by Burhanna et al. (2009), they found that undergraduate students were "more open to educational experiences that involved peer interaction, as opposed to traditional instructor-student communication" (p. 527). Wang (2007) comments that in "this learning environment, independent and reflective thinking skills will be improved" (p. 150). Accordingly, academics in the United States and the United Kingdom have been using Twitter to encourage greater student participation in and out of the classroom.

Some universities have been using Twitter successfully as a tool to encourage in-class discussion. Purdue University has developed a new application called "Hotseat," "that integrates Facebook, Twitter, and text messaging to help students 'backchannel' during class" (Dybwad, 2009). Students' comments are projected onto a screen "with everyone in the class including the professor able to see the messaging as it happens" (Dybwad, 2009). Dr Monica Rankin of the University of Texas at Dallas invited her students to comment or ask questions during lectures using their laptop or mobile phone and found that "her experiment with Twitter began pulling more students into discussion" (Ferenstein, 2010a).

Twitter has also been used to encourage student collaboration outside of lectures and seminars. Students at Leicester University "were provided with an iPod touch, given instructional materials, and told they had to make a few academic-related tweets a day" (Ferenstein, 2010b). The result was "a thriving community" of students, tutors, and "even members outside of the program" (Ferenstein, 2010b). The experiment was so successful the university is investigating extending use of Twitter throughout the whole campus.

Academic libraries in the United States and the United Kingdom have implemented Twitter as a communication tool to post news, promote events, raise awareness of resources, and share photos or videos. As Godwin (forthcoming) observes, to be successful, academic libraries must go to the students, wherever they are. Twitter allows libraries to communicate information to users quickly and cheaply, and the "return on investment (of time and skills) is huge" (Fernandez, 2009, p. 37). This kind of "quick win" is particularly important in the context of funding constraints in the HE sector.

However, to get the maximum benefit from Twitter, it is not enough for libraries to simply broadcast information; micro-blogging must be used collaboratively. Twitter can enable libraries to develop stronger relationships with users by facilitating conversation. Users could make comments (both good and bad), ask questions, and suggest resources. In turn, libraries could respond to feedback, which can be fed into service development processes. Using social media in libraries "has the potential to pay great dividends in the form of user loyalty," as it creates "an atmosphere in which library users are connected with librarians" (Fernandez, 2009, p. 37).

The use of Twitter in education generally is not without challenges. Do students actually *want* to use social media tools, such as Twitter, to communicate with lecturers or librarians? As mentioned earlier in this chapter, undergraduate students in a focus group expressed a "clear sense of separation between educational and social spaces in the online environment" (Burhanna et al., 2009, p. 527). They stated a preference for using an institution's VLE for course-related matters, seeing the use of social media in education as an encroachment into their personal space (Burhanna et al., 2009, p. 527). Can students be expected to use an external tool and will they be disadvantaged if they choose not to participate?

Time is also a consideration. If Twitter is used to encourage in-class discussion, a lecturer will realistically need the support of a teaching assistant to monitor the backchannel. In many institutions, this support will not be available. If Twitter is used outside of class, the lecturer will need to establish boundaries about when they are available to respond to student tweets. Libraries using Twitter must post regularly and respond in a timely way to user comments or questions. As Stuart (2010) observes, "users have an expectation of a constant flow of new information" and "it quickly becomes obvious when institutions are not fully partaking in the community" (p. 46).

Microblogging at Bournemouth University

Bournemouth University Case Study 3: Using Twitter to Support Teaching
A lecturer on a healthcare programme at Bournemouth University introduced Twitter into a unit for first year students in January 2010. The lecturer had observed that students were not using the tools in the institutional VLE (such as discussion boards and wikis) to engage in post-session discussion. This could be because students "have to login and navigate to ... the course to engage in discussion, collaboration and sharing," which means "the communication is sometimes forced and out of the context of the day-to-day, hour-to-hour, and minute-to-minute experience" (Dunlap & Lowenthal, 2009, p. 130).

The lecturer selected Twitter as a synchronous communication tool with potential to encourage students to engage in discussions outside the classroom. Furthermore, it was thought that Twitter might encourage quieter students who did not feel comfortable asking questions in class to contribute. Jung et al's study (2002) found that "students who were able to express themselves freely during the online peer interactions ... may have become more involved in the learning process" (p. 160). The lecturer planned to participate by posting course announcements, sharing news items of professional interest, and engaging in discussions with students. By interacting with learners in an online environment, a teacher can act "as a motivator to encourage divergent answers and develop critical thinking" (Wang, 2007, p. 150).

Twitter was introduced to the students towards the end of the unit. The lecturer was fully aware it would have been preferable to incorporate Twitter from the beginning. However, the nature of social media meant it was important to grasp the moment; as Widdows (2009) observed, "Web 2.0 moves quickly and so should we" (p. 58). This was intended as an informal pilot with a small cohort of students to explore the potential of microblogging to enhance student learning on healthcare programmes.

The lecturer gave an in-class presentation about Twitter, followed by a live demonstration of how to use the Twitter website and selected third-party applications. The students were asked to complete a short, informal questionnaire to gauge their prior experience of using Twitter. This revealed mixed knowledge amongst the group, but the majority of students had some understanding of how it could be used to benefit their learning through encouraging group discussion. The lecturer created a Twitter account for the unit, and the students were given the option to create an account themselves.

It was important to establish boundaries around use from the beginning. The lecturer had clearly stated times when they could be expected to be available to students on Twitter. The unit account was intended for professional communications only, but some of the students also used their Twitter account for personal communications. In practice, this was not a problem, but the students were all informed of the importance of presenting an appropriate image when participating in a professionally orientated online community.

The lecturer made the unit account private, as this was a pilot, but one consequence of this was that the students missed out on potential engagements with users outside the university, such as practicing healthcare professionals or members of professional bodies. The lecturer will consider making the unit account public (ensuring compliance with university policy on social media use) when it is introduced to the next cohort of students.

Studies have shown that interprofessional communication is "particularly important for students graduating from health and social care professional programmes" (Miers, Rickaby, & Clarke, 2009, p. 673).

In practice, more students expressed an interest in using Twitter than actually participated. In the cohort of 31 students, 13 created (or already had) a Twitter account and followed the unit account. The majority of these tweeted at least once. The tweets included reflections on teaching sessions, asking the lecturer questions, tweeting from a professional conference and peer to peer tutoring on using Twitter effectively.

The lecturer asked the students to complete the short, informal questionnaire about Twitter again at the end of the unit to evaluate the student learning experience and assess the outcomes of the pilot. Some students who did not participate commented they wanted to use Twitter but time constraints were a barrier, due to the introduction of the tool at the end of the unit. The lecturer intends to use Twitter with the next cohort of students, but it will be introduced from the beginning of the unit.

In addition to timing, two main lessons will be taken forward from the pilot. First, the lecturer intends to use Group Tweet, a function that allows a group member to post an update to all other members using a direct message. This circumvents the issue experienced by students in the pilot of making sure all the students were following each other, as well as the unit account, in order to receive all updates.

Second, the use of Twitter was not a compulsory element of the unit. Many students take a strategic approach to their studies, spending time on compulsory or assessed elements only due to work or family commitments. The lecturer is considering possibilities for integrating Twitter into the unit more effectively. For example, it could be used as a method of formative assessment to evaluate students' participation in discussion or students could be required to create an account and post a specified number of tweets in order to meet the attendance requirement of the unit. However, it is essential the use of social media in teaching is closely linked to learning outcomes and "expectations for participation have to be clearly articulated" (Dunlap & Lowenthal, 2009, p. 133).

Bournemouth University Case Study 4: Using Twitter in an Academic Library

In law, it is particularly important that staff and students are up to date with legal news and developments. To address this, the subject support librarian for law created a pilot current awareness service for this user group using the start page service, PageFlakes. However, this was not popular with the law academic staff with whom it was trialed. They found checking through a page of automatically generated links for items of relevance was too time-consuming.

Instead, they wanted a current awareness service where information was filtered and bite-sized. The law librarian had a personal Twitter account, and thought it was a tool with potential to meet their requirements. Also, it was hoped Twitter would enrich the student learning experience by encouraging the law cohort to engage in discussion with each other and with the law librarian. Studies on collaborative learning have found that "a feeling of connection positively affect[s] students' self-motivation" (So & Brush, 2008, p. 329).

The law librarian created a Twitter account, @bulawlibrary, in June 2009. The first step was to find people to follow. Various information professionals, news services, legal publications, law database providers, government organizations and local colleagues were selected, many of whom followed @bulawlibrary in return. At the time of writing, the account is following 66 Twitter users, has 156 followers, and is on 12 user-generated lists of tweeting librarians.

The content for the account was generated in two ways. If a follower posted a tweet of interest, it was re-tweeted to @bulawlibrary's followers. Also, an RSS aggregator (Google Reader) was used to gather feeds from relevant websites, such as law blogs. The feeds were evaluated by the law librarian and items of interest were tweeted. The main challenge was information overload; there is a lot of daily information to evaluate in tweets and RSS feeds. However, using the tools described has ensured the management of the Twitter account has not been too time-consuming.

Another strategy that has streamlined the professional Twitter experience has been using a third party tool, instead of the Twitter website, to post updates. After using the Twitter website for a short time, its' inability the automatically shorten URLs and the frequency with which the "fail whale" appeared (indicating the website is overloaded) became frustrating. So, a third party application, Tweetdeck, was trialed. This tool can be down-loaded free to a computer desktop or smartphone. The user can monitor tweets from followers, mentions, and direct messages on one screen, plus it automatically shortens URLs.

The @bulawlibrary account was promoted to law students (under-graduate, postgraduate, and professional) in library training sessions and a link to the account was placed in the law librarian's email signature. The promotion was deliberately low-key; this was not a formal case study, but an informal trial of a tool that could have potential to add value – simply and cost effectively – to the services already provided by the law librarian.

There are some Bournemouth University law students following @bulawlibrary, although it can be difficult to establish a user's identity as people tend to adopt a pseudonym as their user name on Twitter (whereas they are more likely to use their real name on Facebook). However, the majority of followers are external. They are legal professionals, individuals from the finance and law sectors, legal publishers, and law firms. The law librarian plans to promote @bulawlibrary to the next cohort of law students, hoping that more will be interested in the service.

One of the challenges has been that @bulawlibrary is identifiable with the university and any online activity will reflect on the institution. This has meant that the account has been, of necessity, more of a broadcast medium than a tool to facilitate conversation. This is a possible disadvantage, as although "personal asides are not the primary purpose of an institutional presence on Twitter" they do "help build relationships, encourage interaction and put a human face on the library" (Stuart, 2010, p. 47).

The Twitter account has not succeeded in achieving the proposed outcome of encouraging law students to engage with each other using this medium. However, Jung et al. (2002) suggest that participation "can be measured in several ways" (p. 160) and "[r]eading others' messages" as well as "posting one's own messages" and "responding to others' opinions" can also be "used to indicate participation level" (p. 160). The extent to which students were reading tweets is not measurable in an informal trial of this type.

However, an unforeseen outcome is that the account has become a useful extension of the law librarian's professional network. It allows the law librarian to keep up to date with legal information professionals and the legal sector as a whole, which in turn informs skills teaching and student appointments. The law librarian joined a committee of the British and Irish Association of Law Librarians (BIALL) recently through professional contacts made on Twitter. The account was added to a list of British Librarians on Twitter (Bradley, 2010b) which attracted new followers for @bulawlibrary from all sectors of the information profession, enabling the law librarian to engage with the wider professional community. Twitter has become a valuable tool in facilitating continuing professional development with little effort and no cost implications.

CONCLUSION

Social media, such as social bookmarking or microblogging, offers those in higher education the opportunity to expand their personal networks and to collaborate and learn within those networks. At its best, social media can foster collaboration between students, academic staff, librarians and learning technologists. In this chapter, we have shown examples of collaboration, enabled by social media, yielding benefits. By facilitating collaborative learning, social bookmarking allows users to benefit from the discoveries of their peers. For students, this can encourage reflection and evaluation when selecting information. For universities, it can drive efficiencies in service delivery and enhance professional practice.

We have also seen how microblogging can be used to promote discussion between groups of students and academics. This can encourage reflective learning, group cohesiveness, and professional awareness, as well as providing new channels for student feedback. Finally, microblogging can be used to extend an institution's existing communication mediums and to create opportunities for continuing professional development.

Although the low costs and popularity of social media make it an attractive prospect for educators, it is important to use it only where pedagogically appropriate. As Bradwell comments, "[w]hile technology opens up many new possibilities, matching these possibilities with a vision for teaching and learning is the real challenge" (Bradwell, 2009, p. 58).

Although there is no direct discussion in the chapter about supporting the underpinning literacies needed for the student to work effectively with social media tools, Beetham, McGill, and Littlejohn (2009) attest to the ongoing and recognized partnerships between academics and librarians when delivering information literacy and this remains pivotal to academic success in the increasingly blended and digital world of learning.

REFERENCES

Al-Khalifa, H. S., & Davis, H. C. (2007). Exploring the value of folksonomies for creating semantic metadata. *International Journal on Semantic Web and Information Systems*, *3*, 12–38.

Arthur, C. (2010). Twitter has 105m registered users, 600m searches per day and more numbers from chirp. *The Guardian*, April 14. Available at http://www.guardian.co.uk/technology/blog/2010/apr/14/twitter-users-chirp-details. Retrieved on April 14, 2010.

Axon, S. (2010, March 15). Details: Twitter's new @anywhere platform. Available at http://mashable.com/2010/03/15/twitter-at-anywhere/. Retrieved on March 31, 2010.

Balas, J. L. (1998). It's the little things that count. *Computers in Libraries*, *18*, 35–39.

Beetham, H., McGill, L. & Littlejohn, A. (2009). *Thriving in the 21st century: Learning literacies for the digital age (LLiDA project)*. A JISC funded study. Available at http://www.jisc.ac.uk/media/documents/projects/llidareportjune2009.pdf. Retrieved on March 14, 2010.

Brabazon, T. (2007). *The University of Google: Education in the (post) information age*. Aldershot: Ashgate.

Bradley, P. (2010a, April 15). Twitter second largest search engine? Perhaps. Available at http://philbradley.typepad.com/phil_bradleys_weblog/2010/04/twitter-second-largest-search-engine-perhaps.html?utm_source=twitterfeed&utm_medium=twitter. Retrieved on April 15, 2010.

Bradley, P. (2010b). British librarians on Twitter. Available at http://tweepml.org/100-British-Librarians-on-Twitter/. Retrieved on July 9, 2010.

Bradwell, P. (2009). *The edgeless University: Why higher education must embrace technology* (Available at http://www.demos.co.uk/files/Edgeless_University_web.pdf?1245715615. Retrieved on April 23, 2010). London: Demos.

Burhanna, K., Seeholzer, J., & Salem, J., Jr. (2009). No natives here: a focus group study of student perceptions of Web 2.0 and the academic library. *Journal of Academic Librarianship*, *35*, 523–532.

Chudnov, D., Barnett, J., Prasad, R., & Wilcox, M. (2005). Experiments in academic social book marking with Unalog. *Library Hi Tech*, *23*, 469–480.

Churchill, D., Wong, W., Law, N., Salter, D., & Tai, B. (2009). Social bookmarking–repository–networking: Possibilities for support of teaching and learning in higher education. *Serials Review*, *35*, 142–148.

Dale, P., & Cheshir, K. (2009). Collaboration between librarians and learning technologists to enhance the learning of health sciences students. *New Review of Academic Librarianship*, *15*, 206–218.

Department for Business, Innovation & Skills. (2009). Higher ambitions: The future of universities in a knowledge economy. Available at http://www.bis.gov.uk/assets/biscore/corporate/docs/h/09-1447-higher-ambitions.pdf. Retrieved on April 28, 2010.

Dunlap, J., & Lowenthal, P. R. (2009). Tweeting the night away: Using Twitter to enhance social presence. *Journal of Information Systems Education*, *20*, 129–135.

Dybwad, B. (2009, November 3). Purdue University adds Twitter and Facebook to class participation. Available at http://mashable.com/2009/11/03/hotseat/. Retrieved on April 28, 2010.

Dybwad, B. (2010, March 23). Twitter reduces spam to 1% of tweets. Available at http://mashable.com/2010/03/23/twitter-spam-1-percent/. Retrieved on March 31, 2010.

Ferenstein, G. (2010a, March 1). How Twitter in the classroom is changing social engagement. Available at http://mashable.com/2010/03/01/twitter-classroom/. Retrieved on March 31, 2010.

Ferenstein, G. (2010b, January 10). 3 ways educators are embracing social technology. Available at http://mashable.com/2010/01/10/educators-social-technology/. Retrieved on March 31, 2010.

Fernandez, J. (2009). A SWOT analysis for social media in libraries. *Online*, *3*, 35–37.

Godwin, P. (Forthcoming). It's all about social media, stupid! In: P. Dale, M. Holland, & J. Beard (Eds), *University libraries and digital learning environments*. Aldershot: Ashgate.

Guy, M., & Tonkin, E. (2006). Folksonomies: Tidying up tags? *D-Lib Magazine, 12*. Available at http://www.dlib.org/dlib/january06/guy/01guy.html. Retrieved on April 23, 2010. doi:10.1045/january2006-guy

Ipsos MORI. (2007). Student expectations study: Key findings from online research and discussion evenings held in June 2007 for the Joint Information Systems Committee. Available at http://www.jisc.ac.uk/publications/publications/studentexpectations. Retrieved on July 24, 2008.

Jung, I., Choi, S., Lim, C., & Leem, J. (2002). Effects of different types of interaction on learning achievement, satisfaction and participation in web-based instruction. *Innovations in Education and Teaching International, 39*, 153–162.

Kamel Boulos, M. N., & Wheeler, S. (2007). The emerging Web 2.0 social software: An enabling suite of sociable technologies in health and health care education. *Health Information & Libraries Journal, 24*, 2–23.

Lenhart, A., Purcell, K., Smith A., & Zickuhr, K. (2010). Social media and mobile internet use amongst teens and young adults. Available at http://pewinternet.org/Reports/2010/Social-Media-and-Young-Adults.aspx. Retrieved on July 6, 2010.

Luo, L. (2010). Web 2.0 integration in information literacy instruction: An overview. *Journal of Academic Librarianship, 36*, 32–40.

Mashable. (2010). The Twitter guide book. Available at http://mashable.com/what-is-twitter/. Retrieved on March 31, 2010.

Miers, M. E., Rickaby, C. E., & Clarke, B. A. (2009). Learning to work together: health and social care students' learning from interprofessional modules. *Assessment & Evaluation in Higher Education, 34*, 673–691.

Morrison, P. J. (2008). Tagging of and searching: Search retrieval effectiveness folksonomies on the World Wide Web. *Information Processing & Management, 44*, 1562–1579.

Oblinger, D. G., & Oblinger, J. L. (Eds). (2005). *Educating the net generation*. Boulder, CO: Educause.

Parr, B. (2010). Teens just don't blog or tweet. Available at http://mashable.com/2010/02/03/teens-dont-tweet-or-blog/. Retrieved on July 7, 2010.

Prensky, M. (2001). Digital natives, digital immigrants. *On the Horizon, 9*, 1–6.

Redden, C. S. (2010). Social bookmarking in academic libraries: Trends and applications. *Journal of Academic Librarianship, 36*, 219–227.

Robson, M. (2009). How teenagers consume media, *Morgan Stanley Research* (July 10), n.p. Available at http://media.ft.com/cms/c3852b2e-6f9a-11de-bfc5-00144feabdc0.pdf

Saeed, N., Yang, Y., & Sinnappan, S. (2009). Emerging web technologies in higher education: A case of incorporating blogs, podcasts and social bookmarks in a web programming course based on students' learning styles and technology preferences. *Educational Technology & Society, 12*, 98–109.

Secker, J. (2008). Case study 2: resource sharing and social software. London School of Economics, Centre for Learning Technology. Available at http://clt.lse.ac.uk/Projects/Case_Study_Two_report.pdf. Retrieved on April 6, 2010.

So, H.-J., & Brush, T. A. (2008). Student perceptions of collaborative learning, social presence and satisfaction in a blended learning environment: Relationships and critical factors. *Computers & Education, 51*, 318–336.

Stuart, D. (2010). What are libraries doing on Twitter? *Online, 34,* 45–47.
Taylor, A. (2008). The UNICEF UK baby-friendly initiative-exploring and sharing the evidence: Case study 8. In: B. Newland (Ed.), *eRes: Innovative e-learning with e-resources.* Bournemouth: Bournemouth University.
Twitter. (2010). About Twitter. Available at http://twitter.com/about. Retrieved on April 14, 2010.
Wang, L. (2007). Sociocultural learning theories and information literacy teaching activities in higher education. *Reference & User Services Quarterly, 47,* 149–158.
Widdows, K. (2009). Web 2.0 moves 2.0 quickly to wait: Setting up a library Facebook presence at the University of Warwick. *SCONUL Focus, 46,* 54–59. Available at http://www.sconul.ac.uk/publications/newsletter/46/14.pdf. Retrieved on May 4, 2010.

USING SOCIAL MEDIA IN STUDY ABROAD

Penny Schouten

ABSTRACT

In November 2009 NAFSA conducted an online survey, the results analyzed by the Education Abroad Technology Task Force. Respondents included associate colleges, baccalaureate colleges, research universities, program providers, and specialized institutions of all sizes. It examined the current use of communication technologies such as social networking sites, within the Education Abroad field, as tools for marketing programs, orientation, advising, community building, and alumni networking. The survey also examined staffing and the training needs of education abroad professionals to identify and use appropriate forms of social networking technology that are available.

INTRODUCTION

Whether it is staffing issues, or college administrators reluctant to adapt to social networking, or from a lack of understanding of how social media tools can support their mission and goals, study abroad professionals have not yet embraced social media. By developing a set of behaviors and best practices, international educators will be empowered to persuade administrators and to adapt social media technology to help them reach their objectives.

In the past, study abroad was about going to a foreign country, disconnecting from all that was familiar and safe-your family, your routine, your language, your mental and physical comfort zones. Personal growth and enlightenment occurred when you were on your own, independently solving problems, and dealing with difficult situations in a strange environment. A student might find themselves in a location where the culture, food, language, and living conditions were unfamiliar. Some intrepid travelers might end up in areas where electrical service, telephone service, and mail delivery were sporadic at best. These usually become the richest living abroad experiences because of the isolation from all that is safe and commonplace.

Today, thanks to mobile phones, students can blog, tweet, and update their Facebook page from just about any location as long as they can get a signal. Parents, friends, and advisors located in the student's home country are 10 seconds away by mobile phone application. If the student is having a problem abroad, friends and family at home know about it before the on-site program advisor, who is better located and prepared to deal with it.

So, how could the ability to stay in touch 24/7 across time zones and continents possibly enhance this experience? There are some who will say it does not, that by staying constantly connected to their home life inhibits their abilities to connect with the local community in which they are studying. Perhaps this is true, but the reality is that technology will continue to evolve and be integrated into a student's experience abroad. The institution needs to accept this and integrate it into the abroad program's pedagogy. Rather than an enemy to the purity of an abroad experience, it can enhance the program, improve communication flow and prevent small problems becoming a full-blown crisis (Table 1).

USAGE

Until recently, no official research has been conducted into social media use in international education. In 2009 NAFSA: The Association for International Educators surveyed 515 education abroad office directors and assistant directors on their use of social media. The results revealed that most study abroad offices were not using social media technologies, (Reinig, Schouten, & Bova, 2010). For those that said they were using social media,

Table 1. Types of Technology Used by Study Abroad Offices.

	Facebook	Twitter	Instant Messaging	Blogs	Wikis	Live Chat	YouTube Video	Webinar	Flickr	LinkedIn	Ning	Second Life	Customized	Other
Yes	378	114	92	189	26	56	126	64	50	41	12	0	21	93
No	137	401	423	326	459	459	389	451	465	474	503	515	494	422

Notes: The NAFSA Technology Taskforce results show a majority of respondents use Facebook, but do not take advantage of other complimentary social media tools. One administrator said they used it "because students, after they graduate, do not use our university website, Facebook is a great way to keep in touch with study abroad alumni-a place where they can post photos, answer questions to prospective study abroad students, and blog about international and global topics." Another noted that "staggering proportions of undergrads are on Facebook, so our presence there brings us to their level, in their world, to meet them where they are."

One study abroad professional found that "videos and blogs have become increasingly important recruitment tools. We are undergoing a web restructuring, and the student focus groups all requested more photos, videos and blogs. When we started adding these, students responded very well. Our students participating on faculty led programs without fail set up their own Facebook pages, in addition to our office Facebook page, which is rather dull" (Reinig, Schouten, & Bova, 2010).

some indicated in the comment section that "using" meant they had an inactive profile. Going by the comments, those using social media actively and effectively were in the minority.

That is not their fault. Usually, an education abroad office is understaffed and overburdened by paperwork, program issues, or student problems. One program abroad requires a large amount of documentation for each student. There are home campus application forms, support documentation, health/medical forms, insurance forms, and release agreements. Once accepted, a student has to submit applications and all required forms required by the host institution. Forms may be duplicated, but because the host country's legal language requirements are different, a seemingly identical form is necessary. If a visa is required, it adds more documentation and forms. Additional tasks such as logistical planning, academic planning, advising, crisis management, keeping up-to-date on issues within the industry and general office maintenance leaves staff no time for professional development/training or creating and maintaining social networks.

Besides time management issues, study abroad administrators seem to lack an understanding of what types of social media are available and the benefits of using them to reach their communication and marketing goals. As indicated in Table 1, the majority of institutions surveyed by NAFSA indicated they were using Facebook, but they were not using complementary social media like YouTube, Twitter, or blogs.

The NAFSA survey also asked how study abroad administrators are using social media. The majority (70.5%) are using it to engage and recruit students. 65% are using social networking for alumni outreach and 60% are building a virtual community. These numbers are fairly consistent, and it would make sense that marketing to prospective students and reaching out to alumni who could help recruit students would also lead to community building.

Just half of all respondents were using social media to advise students. In such cases, when recruiting students, they are answering general questions regarding the experience and the program. However, some international educators might not be comfortable advising in the informal atmosphere of social media. Issues of privacy and sensitivity, like an individual's learning disabilities and medical conditions, are not appropriate discussions for an open forum.

Less than 50% of those surveyed are using the technology to network with colleagues, monitor their institution's reputation or for pre-departure advising. This demonstrates the inability to see social networking as the opportunity for a sustainable community of prospective students, current students, alumni, faculty and colleagues. Alumni, current students, home campus faculty, and colleagues from the campus abroad can advise prospective students and promote programming. Home campus faculty and host campus faculty and staff can network, share ideas, research and discuss faculty-exchange opportunities. Colleagues can keep each other up to date with program or student-related issues, as well as current issues within the field of international education.

WHY USE SOCIAL MEDIA?

The health, safety, and security of their students are major concerns for international educators. Although many arguments for using social media revolve around marketing, advising, and relationship development, the strongest motivation is keeping up-to-date with events around the world. News on social media is sometimes only seconds old, faster than radio and television. When US Airways flight 1549 crash landed on the Hudson River in 2009, tweets, photos, and videos were instantly available. In May 2008, as China was being hit with a major earthquake, Robert Scoble, a technology blogger based in the United States, tweeted about it. In a comment on a story on the BBC News website, Scoble states: "I reported the earthquake WHILE IT WAS STILL HAPPENING and minutes before the USGS web site reported it and about 30 minutes before any mainstream news reports came out (most didn't come out until after an hour). Please look into it. This was the first Tweet I did: http://twitter.com/Scobleizer/statuses/809121152" (Cellan-Jones, 2008).

In April 2008, James Buck, a University of California-Berkeley student was arrested in Egypt at an anti-government rally. He tweeted "Arrested" using his cell phone and as the message spread among his contacts, his school hired a lawyer, and he was released the next day, (Simon, 2008).

Being aware of an emergency situation so quickly allows the study abroad advisor to react faster and activate their crisis management plan. Social media not only brings that awareness but also gives the advisor multiple channels to share with their stakeholders what is being done to handle the crisis.

Social media gives study abroad administrators the ability to exchange information with colleagues and experts they usually would not have access to on a daily basis. Unique situations with regard to travel or visas can be quickly remedied by tapping into a network of people who either have a solution or know someone who can help.

Social media provides an inexpensive way to promote study abroad programs to the widest possible audience. In the past, study abroad program promotion consisted of print advertisements, Internet banner ads, free program listings either in printed directories like Peterson's Study Abroad Guide or the IIE Study Abroad Guide, on websites like StudyAbroad.com and iie.org, and in-person promotion at study abroad fairs and conferences. With social media there are many more options. Besides having their own blogs, LinkedIn groups, Facebook, Twitter, YouTube, and Flickr profiles, by participating in conversations on other blogs, profiles and groups they raise awareness of their brand identity. On a tight budget targeted ads through Facebook or Google pay-per-click ads can reach very specific groups of people.

COMMUNICATION/MARKETING PLAN

If you are an institution or a study abroad service provider, you should review your business and marketing plans. Analysis of your audience, goals, and strategies will help focus your communications plan. If employed correctly, social media can be very effective for a small organization with a limited budget because it is cost effective, reaching many people over various channels for little cost. Most applications are free with minor fees for service upgrades or advertising opportunities. It is a useful outreach tool for the usually tight budgeted study abroad office.

To know how to effectively reach your target audiences, you must first find what tools they are using to communicate. Determine the communication culture at your institution and those you wish to reach. Chances are your marketing department has already done a study and can tell you where students get their information from, how they prefer to communicate, as well as what channels they are using with each other. As a study abroad office you may also need to consider alumni, parents, colleagues, current and potential partner universities, international organizations, and government institutions. These entities may not be using the same channels as your students, but must also be integrated into your plan.

Once you find the appropriate networks, a communication plan should be developed. Social media should be one of the tools you are using to achieve your goals. Obviously, if you want to internationalize your campus, you are not just going to set up a Facebook page as the sole internationalization tool. You will have partnerships with institutions abroad, you will integrate international faculty and scholars into the college community, sponsor relevant events, etc.

All communication channels should be similarly branded and identifiable as an official channel of our organization so when students move from one channel to another, it is instantly recognized as belonging to the organization. Someone intent on wreaking havoc can use your institutional logo and name to create a fake, but official looking account. If given proof that someone is using your name and logo in a detrimental manner, you can ask the managers of the service to shut down the fraudulent account.

USING SOCIAL MEDIA

Social networking is more than marketing and recruitment. When social media leaders like Chris Brogan, Robert Scoble, and Paul Gillin speak about the field, they emphasize relationship building, open, honest communication, community building, and transparency.

> It's okay to want an audience. When we're trying to build awareness, we want an audience. We create things to get people's attention. For some, the creation is advertising. For others, it's face to face events. For others, it's content (like this blog post). If you're clever, you create in a variety of formats.
>
> This builds audience. Audiences are those folks who gather to hear what you have to say. But that's not a community.
>
> A community looks to each other to sustain the relationship and some of the interactions. Communities don't gather without a purpose, and so building an audience that you then convert into a community is certainly one method to get that experience going, but it doesn't just happen.
>
> Community happens when people feel they're among like-minded others and when they feel their contributions matter. (Brogan, 2009)

International educators can use social media in tandem with other communication methods for:

1. *News/information feed*: Follow media, governments, host schools, industry leaders on Twitter and Facebook to keep up to date with world events, policy changes, and developments significant to your students and their abroad programs. Do regular key word searches, set up Google Alerts for relevant subjects. Share news and discuss implications with colleagues.
2. *Marketing/promotion/recruitment*: Use a Facebook group or fan page to answer questions from prospective students/parents, run photo contests

that the group members judge. Use a Twitter search to find students asking questions about study abroad, then answer with link to website resources. Use a social media aggregator to collect Facebook updates, Twitter feeds, Flickr and YouTube posts on one site to see collectively what your community is doing. Use YouTube and Flickr to show your program and students in action.
3. *Advising*: Use real-time services like UStream, Skype, or BlogTalk Radio to conduct live interactive program advising or orientation programming. Produce instructional YouTube videos demonstrating the application process, explaining culture shock or dealing with other study abroad issues.
4. *Networking*: Use LinkedIn, Facebook, or Twitter to connect with other international education professionals by participating in group discussions. Find colleagues by searching on key words like study abroad, international or NAFSA.
5. *Alumni relations*: Encourage alumni to share their experiences with current and prospective students on Facebook. Use a LinkedIn group to connect alumni with current participants and recent graduates to discuss how to use their study abroad experience in their job search.
6. *Enhancing learning*: Set up a treasure hunt through Twitter or Facebook, which help familiarize program participants with their new surroundings. Give students an assignment where they share resources via Facebook or Twitter or create a video documentary cross posted on YouTube, blogs and Facebook.
7. *Internationalizing the campus*: Highlight or profile faculty, staff, and students from partner schools abroad and their contributions to campus using YouTube videos, podcasts or featuring them on Facebook with a link to an article on your website or blog. Reach out to campus community for suggestions on how they would like to internationalize the campus.
8. *Conducting classes/coursework*: Use Blackboard to begin classes online before students depart for abroad location or once they return home. Especially effective for programs that spend a short period of time in country or where students are not from the sponsoring (home) campus.
9. *Holding meetings with colleagues/students/parents scattered across the globe*: Skype can connect multiple callers in different locations. Staff from both the home campus and on-site program can interview a prospective employee without having to transport the applicant to either location.

10. *Sharing information*: Posting links on Twitter to useful resources or breaking news in a region where students and programs are located. Set up a Wiki for contributions on a best practices list or packing list for students going abroad.
11. *Building relationships*: Offer helpful advice, share links to useful resources, offer support, comment on photos/blog posts/etc., commiserate or share a funny anecdote. Have frequent interactions with stakeholders located across the globe over various social media channels.
12. *Improving customer service*: Encourage current program participants and alumni to share information with prospective students. Identify and deal with problems as they arise by monitoring participants and other stakeholders. Maintain open and honest communications, providing transparency to the process of studying abroad.
13. *Building a sustainable community*: Grow a network on Facebook, LinkedIn, and Twitter of all members responding to, sharing with, and supporting each other. Connect your online community to real world events like fundraising, alumni activities, internships and career fairs.

Tools

Start with the website. Consider this the foundation of your communications hub. It should be clear, concise, and correct. If you have target audiences whose first language is not English, provide relevant pages in their languages and provide a translator program for pages only published in English. You can provide access to your blog, Twitter, and Facebook updates by adding applications that scroll your latest posts.

Blogs

Most study abroad organizations using blogs have student bloggers who share photos, experiences, and personal insights while participating in the program. While this is effective for program promotion and advising, there is another use for blogging that is neglected. Very few schools have a blog targeting customer service or discussing current world events and issues that affect international education. In April 2007, the US State Department's Passport Services unit became severely backlogged in processing US passports when legislation was passed that required every US citizen to have a valid passport to fly between the United States, Mexico, and Canada. Many study abroad students, as well as the general public, were faced with the possibility of not getting their passport in time for their departure. The

State University of New York College at New Paltz's office blog, Study Abroad 101 notified students of this situation to encourage the summer students who had not applied for their passport to do so immediately. The comments and discussion that followed provided more information on processing time frames, as well as suggestions on how to expedite the process (Schouten, 2007).

During the Haiti earthquake disaster, The International Higher Education Consulting Blog shared links to news on schools with students in the disaster zone and health and safety planning resources to help international educators prepare for future emergencies (Comp, 2010).

Twitter

Twitter is great for program promotion, but if you only use it for that, those following you will quickly grow tired of the advertisements and unfollow you. Academic Programs International (API) uses their Twitter channel to share program-related information, field-related issues, deadline reminders, contest or scholarship announcements, breaking news, and study abroad–related trivia. They interact with their students, colleagues, and even their competition in an engaging, friendly manner.

If security is a concern, a Twitter profile can be kept private, which allows only approved followers to see tweets. For example, Academic Solutions, a program provider with programs in the United Kingdom, used Twitter to stay connected with students on excursions who went off in separate groups to explore their location. The program leader reminded students where they could meet the coach, as well as send out links relevant to the town they were visiting. Only the students could see the information, which they received on their cell phones.

Facebook

Facebook can be used in various ways. International educators use their profile to share career-related information like links to published articles, awards, and photos. By creating a fan page or group, they provide a space for students to share photos, travel expertise, and program experience. There is a tab to conduct discussions on how to apply, choose a program, or talk about course-related issues. The tabs within a page or profile can be customized, allowing the addition of applications to provide PDF documents and links to other social media applications.

LinkedIn

LinkedIn is a career networking tool that can be used to search or post job openings, find institutional or research partnerships and new employees. Groups can be created, discussions conducted, ideas shared, and events organized. Your profile can include your career history, as well as current blog posts, twitter feed, presentation calendar, PowerPoint slide-shares and other applications.

The Forum on Education Abroad (n.d) has an active discussion group which allows the group to update members on upcoming conferences, as well as allow members to post information on scholarships and programs that might be of interest to other members.

YouTube

Video production has become much easier with the variety of editing applications now available. Besides having videos of exciting study abroad locations with sound bytes and a music bed, pre-departure/re-entry orientations could be made available for students who are unable to attend in person. Videos can be instructional, promotional, inspirational, or simply share information. Interview alumni whose study abroad experience impacted their careers. Run video contests for students and alumni to create program advertisements or instructional "How to" videos that engenders brand buy-in and come from a participant's perspective.

SUNY Broome Community College created a pre-departure orientation video because many students participating in their Italy programs were unable to come to the Broome campus to attend orientation in-person (SUNY Broome Community College, 2008). Since it was on their YouTube account, students who were abroad could refer back to it while they were away, if necessary. They also produced videos walking students through choosing a program, the application process and financial aid for study abroad.

Learning Management Systems

Learning Management Systems (i.e., Blackboard) are ideal for study abroad programs, especially those that meet before the on-site portion of the program begins. Some study abroad programs accept students from other universities across the United States and abroad. Those students would not be able to attend classes on campus but could participate through web-based course management systems. A learning management system would also work for staff training. The office's history, relevant documentation, and links to training resources would be located in one place. Information shared would be consistent and always available.

Wikis

Wikis are web-based platforms that allow multiple collaborators to create, share, and edit documents. This is useful because contributors worldwide can login into a wiki document at any time and update it. This works for research projects, presentations, training manuals, etc. A study abroad office could set up a wiki of office procedures that is accessible to all employees. The wiki can be updated by anyone in the office, so if there is a change in office policy, it is reflected in the document and everyone is able to see it. A program fact sheet could be created by students for future students attending a specific program abroad. Each semester the sheet is updated or added to by current or returning students. Wikis make it much easier to collaborate on presentations, providing access to all presenters to edit one document, rather than e-mailing around a document and having one person collect and add all changes to a master document. Mike Stone from Study Abroad 101 uses Google docs to create PowerPoint presentations for sessions when he co-presents at NAFSA conferences (Schouten & Stone, 2008). Although the final product is always downloaded, there is some reassurance having an online backup if the downloaded file fails.

Skype

Skype offers free phone calls from anywhere with Internet access to anyone else using Skype. Not only is this a great option for students to call home at no cost, but it is also useful to study abroad professionals on a tight budget. International calling is expensive and necessary for study abroad administrators. Whether discussing a student problem, program issue, or communicating during a crisis, Skype is an effective communication tool. If staff is spread across the globe, office meetings can be held through Skype conference call. In the comment section of the NAFSA Technology Taskforce Survey, one administrator noted that they use Skype to have "virtual tables" at study abroad fairs. Skype also offers instant messaging and file sharing, which is helpful if you want everyone on the call to be discussing a specific document.

Academic Solutions, a program provider with clients around the world and offices in London and Barcelona, uses Skype to conduct staff and client meetings. The ability to communicate cheaply and easily also gave them the opportunity to hire an affordable and talented web designer located in Slovenia. Hiring someone of the same caliber in London or New York would've cost far more. The discussions on the development of the company's new website were conducted over Skype and GoogleTalk.

In spring 2010 Marist College conducted interviews for a new registrar assistant for their popular Scuola Lorenzo de Medici program on their campus in upstate New York, but their on-site program director located in Italy also participated in the interviews through Skype.

BEST PRACTICES

The following list of best practices developed from the author's professional experience using social media as the Marketing Director of SUNY New Paltz and Academic Solutions, as well as my discussions and interactions with international education colleagues over Twitter, Facebook, and LinkedIn:

Hire Staff with Social Media Skills and Experience

There is more to social media than just having an account and updating your status. You need to cultivate discussion and exchanges. Check out prospective employees' online presence and how they have interacted on various social media in the past.

Train Your Staff

Social media allows everyone to become an unofficial spokesperson for your office/institution. While you want your staff to be themselves, you also want their online discussions to reflect the organization's mission, goals, and brand identity with sensitivity to legal repercussions. When negative comments are posted, the response must be thought out. In some cases, the community will step up to defend an organization, but if the administrator of the profile or page needs to step in, the response should be non-defensive and transparent. Sometimes admitting a mistake might be called for, but not always. Arguing with someone over how they felt slighted or wronged will not help the situation. In some cases, no response might be the best response.

Monitor Your Brand/Relevant Names

It is not paranoia, people are most likely talking about your organization, programs, possibly even your staff. Use Google Alerts, social media alerts, and keyword searches to find out what is being said about your various entities. If you do not use social media, monitoring the conversations about your organization and related entities will most likely convince you that you need to become more involved. Some multi-platform search engines are:

- *Spy*: http://spy.appspot.com/
- *SamePoint*: http://www.samepoint.com/
- *SocialMention*: http://socialmention.com/
- *WhosTalkin*: http://whostalkin.com/

(Smarty, 2009)

Listen

This is different from monitoring. By actively listening you are aware of what is going on and can develop strategies to address issues that arise, both positive and negative. Positive conversations provide you with material that can be used for promotional efforts and blog posts. Negative discussions give warning if problems or issues are developing. Addressing a problem before it becomes a full-blown crisis is not just good customer service but effective public relations management.

Transparency/Authenticity

Avoid jargon, keep your communications open, honest, and clear. Although Heather Mansfield's article from University Business is discussing Twitter, her advice rings true for all social media: "Put authenticity before marketing. Have personality. Build community. Colleges and universities that are most successful at utilizing social networking websites like Twitter, Facebook, and MySpace know from trial, error, and experience that a 'marketing and recruitment approach' on social networking sites does not work. Simply put, it comes across as lame to the technologically hip users of social networking sites. Traditional marketing and development content is perfectly fine for your website, e-mail newsletters, and print materials, but Web 2.0 is much more about having personality, inspiring conversation, and building online community. Nowhere is this more true than on Twitter. Relax, experiment, let go a bit, find your voice, be authentic" (Mansfield, 2009).

Team Up with Others in Your Organization

If you are a college or university, it is more than likely your admissions office is using and monitoring social media for your institution. These responsibilities may be shared with web communications, public affairs or community relations, media relations, the legal department, and alumni affairs. They may already have plans and strategies that can be adapted by the study abroad office.

You can also team-up with other offices who are using social media to "cross-pollinate" your networks. Residence Life can publicize study abroad events and deadlines across their social media networks. Athletics can post a link to study abroad programs that would appeal to student athletes whose academic program is affected by training schedules. The Fine Arts Department can create a Facebook photo album of student photography from abroad. The study abroad office reciprocates by announcing housing deadline reminders for returning students, encourage students abroad to follow campus teams to stay in touch, or, making the Fine Arts fan page a favorite on the Study Abroad fan page.

Help Your Audience Find You

Publicize your channels on business cards, brochures, landing pages on home institution's website, on each channel, on landing pages, etc.

Participate

Just because you built it does not mean they will come and stay. If you are not contributing, why should your audience? Cultivate discussions and exchanges without dominating the conversation. Engage with your network, repost or retweet useful items from colleagues.

Time Management

One legitimate complaint against social media is the time that can be spent monitoring various channels, creating content and participating in discussions. Some organizations have one full-time staff member completely dedicated to social media content. In most study abroad offices, this will not be possible. Study abroad administrators have a few options. First, social media management should be scheduled into the daily/weekly calendar. Second, there are multiple application management tools like HootSuite and Tweetdeck, which allows an administrator to update and schedule posts across various channels like Facebook and Twitter from one control panel. SUNY New Paltz assigned Facebook fan page management to social media savvy (and trained) student workers who participated in discussions, posted photos, answered inquiries, monitored key word searches, and posted videos.

Measurement

In the business world they use the term return on investment (ROI), but in academe the term is assessment or evaluation or measurement. You could run a social media campaign that leads to a landing page where you can measure traffic that came directly from that link against the number of applicants you gain. Social media is not necessarily quantitative. Your numbers (followers or admits, etc.) increase after that campaign. Social media is not necessarily quantitative. In building a community, the success rate overall may be more qualitative. Measurement may also come through richer conversations and discourse through the channels, fewer complaints or fewer basic inquiry phone calls. Creating an effective measurement tool might be challenging, but it is possible (Fig. 1).

CONCLUSION

NAFSA recognizes their membership needs training in technology and social media. They have included articles in their International Educator magazine and encouraged conference sessions and online discussions about using technology in international education. In the article "Borderless Via Technology," Julie Little from EDUCAUSE says that "new tools – whether used for collaboration, co-creation or real-time interaction – have helped 'flatten the world'... Anybody can do a video, and anyone can get onto

Using Social Media in Study Abroad 143

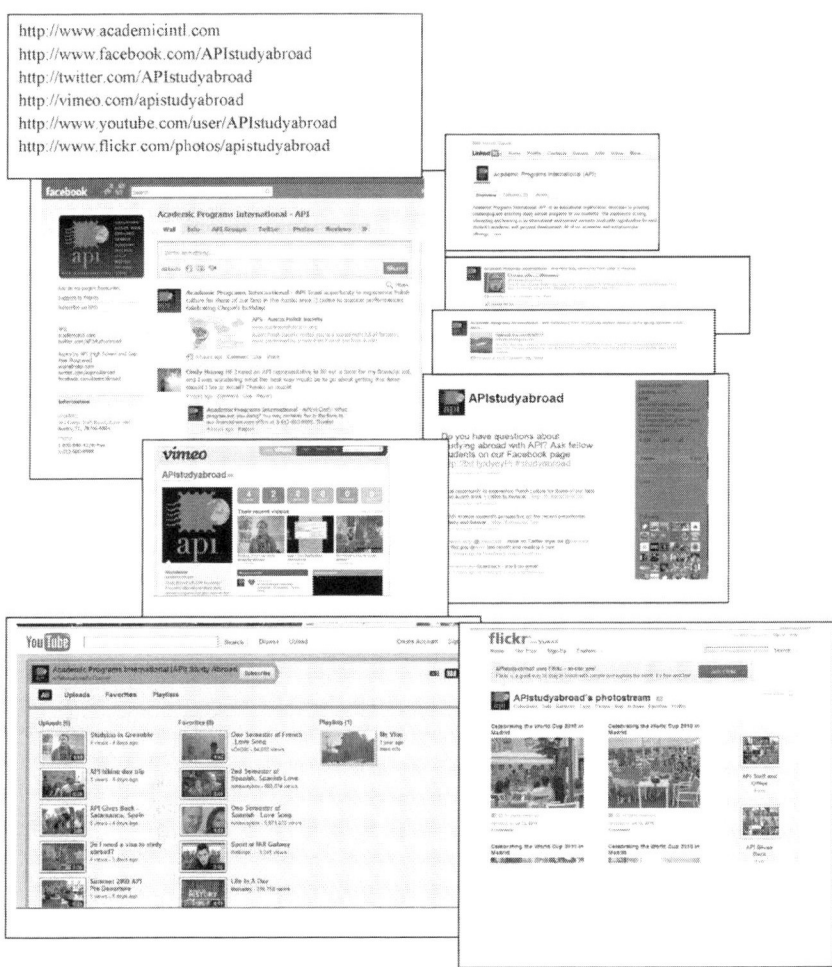

Fig. 1. Example of Cross-Channel Social Media Program. Academic Programs International (API) has an interconnected social media network which allows them to link back to their website, to Facebook discussions, to YouTube/Vimeo videos, and Flickr photos. Their students actively participate in this communications matrix. Not everyone will find this multisocial media strategy necessary, it will depend on their communication/marketing goals, target audience, staffing, and limitations set by administration.

Skype. A lot of these kinds of technologies that were previously very expensive and limited have put international experiences in everyone's hands" (West, 2010).

Social media helps international educators and study abroad service providers do their job more effectively and efficiently. It keeps them up-to-date with world events with immediate news reporting. It lowers advertising costs since most platforms are free. Using social media reduces time spent on general inquiries by connecting on-site staff and experienced alumni with prospective students. It increases an advisor's access to industry experts and resources. It strengthens relationships among partnered institutions abroad. It reduces travel costs because meetings can be held virtually rather than in-person. Social networking helps in fundraising efforts by cultivating the donor group, giving inclusiveness even if they are not a current member of the campus community.

A college campus is an interconnected, sustainable physical community that includes faculty, staff, administrators, campus departments, academic departments, students, parents, alumni, local businesses, and local residents. This model can be extended to a sustainable virtual community which in the study abroad field extends to include their counterparts on multiple campuses across the globe. The ability to connect the world, being able to share and unite across cultures and continents is not only the goal of study abroad, but the capability of social media when used effectively.

As technology continues to evolve, study abroad professionals will need to adapt, much like their students studying in foreign countries who must adapt and evolve in their newly adopted cultures and environments.

REFERENCES

Brogan, C. (2009, June 3.). Audience or community. Available at http://www.chrisbrogan.com/audience-or-community/. Retrieved on April 29, 2010, from ChrisBrogan.com

Cellan-Jones, R. (2008, May 12). Twitter and the China earthquake. Available at http://www.bbc.co.uk/blogs/technology/2008/05/twitter_and_the_china_earthqua.html. Retrieved on July 11, 2010, from BBC News dot.life blog.

Comp, D. (2010, January 14). International students and faculty in Haiti – Is your institution prepared for a crisis? Available at http://ihec-djc.blogspot.com/2010/01/international-students-and-faculty-in.html#comments. Retrieved on July 5, 2010, from International Higher Education Consulting Blog.

Forum on Education Abroad. (n.d). Forum on education abroad LinkedIn group. Available at http://www.linkedin.com/groupAnswers?viewQuestions=&gid=2310121&forumID=3&sik=1272553024311. Retrieved on April 29, 2010, from LinkedIn.com.

Mansfield, H. (2009, May). 10 Twitter tips for higher education. Available at http://www.universitybusiness.com/viewarticle.aspx?articleid=1285. Retrieved on August 29, 2010, from University Business.

Reinig, M., Schouten, P. & Bova, M. (2010, May 5). NAFSA Technology Taskforce: Uses of technology in education abroad. Available at http://www.nafsa.org/_/File/_/ea_tech_report.pdf. Retrieved from NAFSA.com

Schouten, P. (2007, April 19). Passport delay alert. Available at http://abroadblogs.newpaltz.edu/blog0607/2007/04/passport-delay-alert/#comments. Retrieved on July 5, 2010 from SUNY New Paltz Center for International Programs Study Abroad 101 blog.

Schouten, P., & Stone, M. (2008, November 9). Social media 101: Using social media to advise, connect & promote. In: P. Schouten & M. Stone (Presenters), *NAFSA Region X*. Brooklyn, New York: CNN website.

Simon, M. (2008, April 12). Student "Twitters" his way out of Egyptian jail. Available at http://www.cnn.com/2008/TECH/04/25/twitter.buck/. Retrieved on July 11, 2010 from CNN.com.

Smarty, A. (2009, March 19.). How to search multiple social media sites at a time. Available at http://www.makeuseof.com/tag/how-to-search-multiple-social-media-sites-at-atime/. Retrieved on April 29, 2010, fromMakeUseOf.com.

SUNY Broome Community College. (2008, July 29). SUNY Broome Community College on YouTube. Available at http://www.youtube.com/watch?v=zwcLUEAjhTo. Retrieved on April 29, 2010, from YouTube.com

West, C. (2010). Borderless via technology. *International Educator*, March/April, pp. 24–33.

USING SOCIAL NETWORKING SITES DURING THE CAREER MANAGEMENT PROCESS

Nancy Richmond, Beth Rochefort and Leslie Hitch

ABSTRACT

This chapter describes how higher education professionals and college students can use social networking sites and technology to manage their careers. Individuals can expect to change careers several times in a lifetime making the importance and role of social networks past and present central to the career management process. The way individuals communicate and interact through the use of social networking sites for the purpose of career development is discussed. The role of social networking sites in exploring career options, learning, making connections, searching for jobs, developing professionally, making decisions, and maintaining a professional image online is examined. A model is presented on using social networking sites to gather information and feedback during the career management process. Scenarios and examples are provided from higher educational professionals, hiring managers, college students, job seekers, and career changers. The chapter envisions the future of career management specific to higher education and addresses how higher education career advisors can respond to social networking sites and technology.

INTRODUCTION

The purpose of this chapter is to present and examine how social networking sites have reconstructed career management within the field of higher education. Beginning with Facebook then LinkedIn and Twitter, the use of social networking sites and electronic devices to build and maintain personal contacts has almost become de rigueur in daily life and increasingly as a way to establish and manage one's career. Once simply called "networking," physically meeting with friends and colleagues, has changed to a more multifaceted approach that interweaves "traditional" and "virtual" networking throughout the career development process. The role of social networking sites in exploring career options, searching for jobs, and maintaining a professional image online is examined. Examples are provided on how social networks sites such as Facebook, LinkedIn, and Twitter have changed the way individuals communicate, interact, and connect with one another online in relationship to careers. A model is presented on using social networking sites to gather information and feedback during the career management process. Scenarios from students, employers, and higher education professionals provide diverse perspectives on using social networking during the career management process.

SOCIAL NETWORKING PAST AND PRESENT

Individuals have been creating social networks and communicating with one another throughout history and therefore the idea behind social networking sites is not a new phenomenon. However, social networking sites are changing the landscape of how we relay information to our social connections as did the mail, telephone, fax machine, and email. In contrast to past communication tools, social networking sites allow individuals to communicate and to stay in touch with many social ties concurrently with little effort. In comparison, social networking sites allow users to connect with hundreds of friends, family, and professional relationships simultaneously from around the globe with a few keystrokes. When using the phone or email, it was easier to lose touch with social connections such as previous high school classmates, college friends, or previous co-workers. Today through using social networking sites one can more easily remain in contact with a larger social network throughout their lifetime, which is an asset during the career management process.

Social network theorist Granovetter (1973) researched the process of finding a job by studying several hundred workers and interviewed them about their employment history. He examined how people learn about available jobs and investigated the tie between the jobseeker and the person who supplied the information that led to a job. He found that 56 percent of those interviewed found their jobs through a personal connection. Additionally, Granovetter discovered that jobs were more likely to be found by one's weak ties instead of their strong ties. Typically our strong ties tend to move in the same circles that we do, the information they receive overlaps considerably with what we already know. These are often our immediate circle of friends. However weak ties, friends of friends, friends of acquaintances, know people that we do not know, and therefore are more important in finding out about new information as demonstrated in Fig. 1.

Granovetter's research suggests that weak ties or acquaintances are in fact more important than strong ties or close connections during the career management process. Individuals today can use this "weak ties" theory to their benefit through connecting and communicating with weak ties through the use of social networking sites. On the basis of Granvetter's research, it is plausible that using sites like Facebook, LinkedIn, and Twitter to interact with weak ties could help individuals gather information and discover opportunities more readily and quickly.

Now the range of possibilities in which we communicate with one another has changed. In the past if you wanted to know if a friend knew anyone who worked at a certain company you would give them a call on the phone or perhaps send them an email. Today finding out where others work and reaching individuals you would not normally interact with on a daily basis

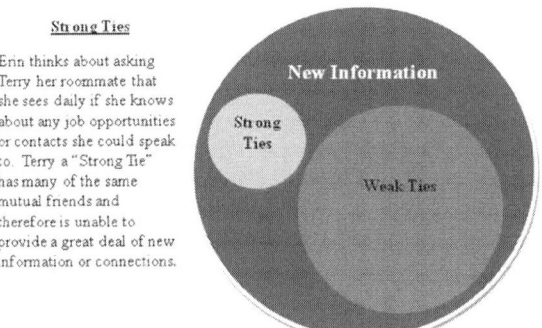

Fig. 1.   Understanding Weak and Strong Ties.

can be done in a relatively short period of time. Social networking sites have become a valuable tool as they have increased the flow and sharing of information with individuals who are outside of the immediate inner circle, which facilitates both learning and the creation of social connections. (Chi, Chan, Seow, & Tam, 2009) For example, Facebook, LinkedIn, and Twitter allow individuals to connect with people not normally interacted with on a daily basis. Although technology tools are forever changing, the importance of weak ties during the career management process will most likely remain.

CAREER MANAGEMENT

A career can be described as the sequence of roles or occupations a person holds in the course of a lifetime (Super, 1980; Tolbert, 1980). In recent times the role of an individual's career has shifted as employers can no longer guarantee job security and employees can no longer expect to stay in a position throughout their life. In fact, the average person can expect to change careers several times in their lifetime (Peterson & González, 2005). Owing to this constant change and refocusing of one's career, it has become increasingly important for individuals to learn how to manage career transitions. Career management can be defined as the ongoing process of gathering information, the self-assessment process, the creation of career goals, the creation and implementation of a career strategy, and the obtainment of ongoing feedback from our social networks (Greenhaus, Callanan & Godshalk, 2010). Another important factor in surviving changes in the workplace is the ability to develop career resiliency. Career resilience characterizes a person who is self-aware, dedicated to continuous learning, future-focused, connected, and flexible (Collard, Epperheimer, & Saign, 1996). Career management and resilience are important as they can significantly change the quality of one's life, one's sense of purpose, immediate and potential income, and a person's connection to society.

SOCIAL NETWORKS IN AN ELECTRONIC WORLD

A "social network" can be defined as "a set of nodes" (e.g., persons, organizations) linked by a set of social relationships (e.g., friendship, over lapping memberships) of a specified type (Laumann, Galaskiewicz, & Marsden, 1978). An individual may also use a social network to explore career options, to help create career goals, to research an effective strategy, and to gain feedback from others. Developing and maintaining a strong network is a lifelong process of central importance to the career management process. Yet, for many individuals creating and maintaining social networks can often seem frightening and maybe viewed as a chore that will only be taken on if absolutely necessary. A common error that individuals make is only thinking about social networks when they have an immediate need such as finding a job. Fortunately, creating and maintaining a social network has become easier with the use of social networking sites.

boyd & Ellison (2007) define "social networking sites" as web-based services that allow individuals to (1) construct a public or semi-public profile within a bounded system, (2) articulate a list of other users with whom they share a connection, and (3) view and traverse their list of connections and those made by others within the system. In addition, individuals use these social networking sites for information sharing, continued learning, research, collaboration, support, and discovering opportunities. For example, in the past you would go to a networking event and collect business cards to put in your rolodex for later, making social networking more difficult. Today through the use of electronic tools social networking can be as simple as meeting an interesting contact at a conference and sending them a LinkedIn invitation while still at the event from a smart phone. This example shows that creating and maintaining connections has in many ways become easier through use of social networking sites such as Facebook, LinkedIn, and Twitter. Table 1 outlines some of the advantages and disadvantages of using these social networking sites. In addition, information is provided on factors to consider when creating a profile on one of the below social networking sites.

Facebook

Currently, Facebook is the largest and most widely used social networking site in the world with over 400 million users (Facebook, 2010). Initially used only by college students, Facebook now allows anyone to create a profile and age groups across the board are now using this social networking site. Facebook is often viewed as a social networking site for one's personal network due to the ability to share photos, to create groups, send event invitations, to comment on friend's wall, and share personal status updates. Facebook complements the network of relationships present in the offline world by providing a platform for active communication between friends and more passive aggregated streams of social news (Burke, Marlow, & Lento, 2010). Facebook

Table 1. Using Social Networking Sites for Career Management.

	Facebook	LinkedIn	Twitter
Getting started: Creating a profile	Carefully consider what personal information is posted. Make sure photos and information will not undermine your ability to create a professional online image	Fully fill out profile information including past work experience and education. Post a professional photo so that you can be recognized at the next networking event	Create a professional twitter background, use twitter bio to self-promote and post a professional photo
Advantages	More people are using Facebook than any other social networking site, allowing users to further extend their social networks	Designed specifically for professional networking. More control over information posted	Open access allows a user to communicate with hundreds of followers at a time for either personal or professional use
Disadvantages	Designed for communicating with personal connections and less control over information posted	Not all contacts maybe using LinkedIn and not as many users as Facebook	Not as many users as Facebook

is an interesting platform to discuss in relationship to career management, because of the transition periods in user's lives and the difficulty of navigating into a more professional online image (Peluchette & Karl, 2009).

Individuals are faced with questions like, "Do I accept my co-worker as a friend on Facebook?" "What if a Facebook friend becomes a hiring manager at a company I want to work for?" "What if you are interviewing for a job and your current manager hears about this from a Facebook update?" These are real situations that are taking place every day to students and working professionals. Owing to the rapid changes in technology the answer to these questions are currently in flux, and researched guidelines have not yet been established. Instead the answer to these questions is often left up to the individual and the solution maybe different depending on an individual's personal preferences, career goals, and values. However it can be said that any information posted online should undergo careful consideration in relation to an individual's present or future career goals. Also, Facebook users need to be aware of privacy setting options available to them to help minimize the risk of personal information being easily accessed (Collins, 2010).

Additionally, there are more serious questions regarding Facebook: some employers could use personal information to discriminate against current or potential employees based on Facebook status updates related to one's religious views, political ideas, relationship status, age, gender, or the color of one's skin. These concerns are often outweighed by the fact that individuals may find that they have an extended Facebook social network that could be valuable in both sharing information and finding out about job opportunities in the future. In addition, some employers in recent years have been using Facebook to reach out to individuals who might be interested in working for their companies (Hagel & Brown, 2008).

LinkedIn

LinkedIn is a social networking site that has over 65 million registered users (Linkedin, 2010). LinkedIn was specifically designed for creating and maintaining a professional network. Individuals can use the site to connect with professionals in their fields, co-workers, and new social connections. LinkedIn has changed the way in which we can stay in contact with our professional social network. In the past an individual may have handed over a business card to stay in touch, however that individual most likely will change jobs in the future and the information on the business card is soon out of date resulting in a lost connection. However, today social networking sites like LinkedIn make it easier to stay in touch with professional connections as the information on where an individual works is constantly being updated.

Individuals can use LinkedIn to conduct research on both individuals and companies. LinkedIn can be used to find connections at a company of interest, to conduct research on hiring committee members, to search for job openings, to create professional groups and to provide examples of previous presentations. Companies and hiring managers can use LinkedIn to post jobs, to read recommendations, and to search for more information about candidates who are applying for jobs.

Twitter

Twitter has over 100 million users and is a social networking site used for microblogging (Twitter, 2010). Twitter users send short posts known as tweets that are no longer than a 140 characters. Tweets can be displayed on the Twitter users profile page and delivered to the Twitter user's subscribers who are known as followers. Although privacy restrictions are available most Twitter users post information that is open for all to read. Owing to the open access of Twitter, it is important to carefully consider what information you are posting. Twitter's open access allows users to communicate with high profile and influential professionals that in the past may have been harder interact with online. Furthermore, Twitter allows individuals who have interests in common to share information online (Dunlap & Lowenthal, 2009). In addition, through the use of Twitter an individual can post interesting professional information that can help them become better known in their field of interest.

MODEL DEVELOPMENT

As mentioned before, during the career management process an individual gathers information, explores career options, develops career goals, implements a career strategy, and obtains ongoing feedback from social networks (Greenhaus et al., 2010). In addition, an individual who is career resilient is dedicated to continuous learning and is able to make connections (Collard et al., 1996).

Fig. 2 demonstrates how an individual could both gather information and feedback through social networking sites during the career management process. Note that Fig. 2 does not indicate where an individual should start in the career management process since the location to start could be different depending on an individual's specific needs. The process outlined in Fig. 2 was developed from several related theories and models (Bandura, 1986; Greenhaus et al., 2010; Graham & Ali, 2000; Lent, Brown, & Hackett, 2000). The following sections presents different aspects of the model and in some instances scenarios will further explain how social networking sites can be used during the career management process.

Taking Responsibility and Action

An important aspect to using social networking sites for professional growth is becoming a user through taking responsibility and action. An individual will first need to understand the added value of using social networking sites for the purpose of creating a professional brand online. According to

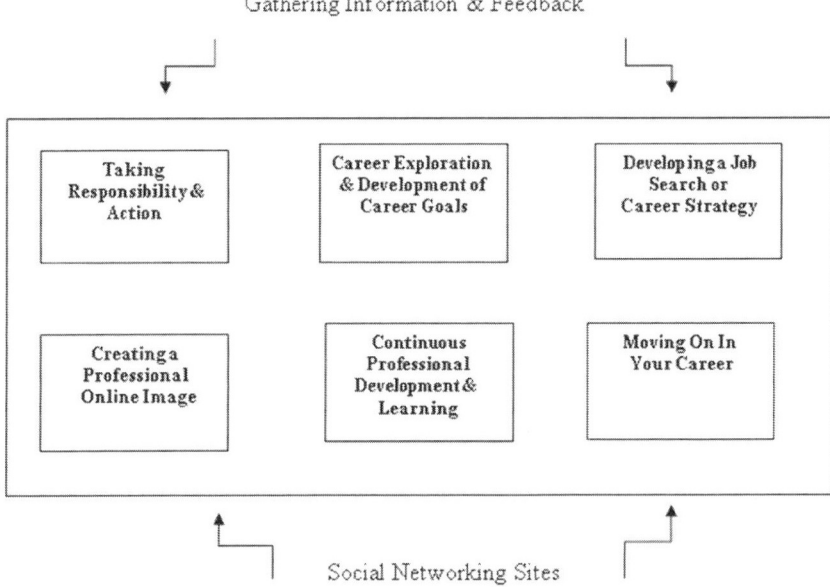

Fig. 2. Using Social Networking Sites to Gather Information and Feedback during the Career Management Process.

Bandura's Social Cognitive Theory (1977), self-efficacy is mediated by a person's beliefs or expectations about their capacity to accomplish certain tasks successfully or demonstrate certain behaviors. One could conclude from Hackett and Betz (1981) that using social media during the career management process might be determined by whether or not a certain behavior will be attempted, the amount of effort the individual will contribute to the behavior, and how long the behavior will be sustained when obstacles are encountered. When individuals have low self-efficacy expectations regarding their behavior, they limit the extent to which they participate in an endeavor and are more apt to give up at the first sign of difficulty. Therefore, individuals helping with the career management process may want to consider using encouragement and perhaps additional training to increase confidence and self-efficacy.

Therefore, another factor to consider is how comfortable an individual feels using technology as they may need additional information and feedback from others. In order for higher education professionals to help college students with using social networking sites technical training and professional development might be needed. Taking responsibility and action of using social networking sites during the career management process may be more plausible if potential obstacles can be overcome or reduced. Barriers could be reduced by sharing ideas, feedback and information with one's social network through the use of social networking sites. In addition, both college students and higher education professionals will need to be educated in understanding how social networking sites can help during the career management process.

Career Exploration and Creating Career Goals

As noted in Fig. 2 social networking sites can be used during the career exploration process and in helping individuals become more aware of their self and needs through gathering information and feedback from others. For example, social networking sites give individuals the opportunity to further explore their interests and to learn more about various career options available. Numerous career development theories have shown the importance of understanding one's interests during the self-assessment process (Parsons, 1909; Holland, 1997; Super, 1976).

Knowledge about one's interests is crucial in the development of career goals (Holland, 1997). For many college students, developing career goals can be both confusing and stressful. However one re-occurring theme in retention literature is that the development of career goals can strongly influence a student's decision to remain in school (Tinto's, 1993). The presence of long-term goals positively predicts academic performance (Ting, 1997; Chiu, 1990). Previous research shows that career goals motivate students to continue on despite daily challenges (Ting, 1997). Individuals can use social networking sites to both gather information and receive feedback from their social networks to help them both understand career options and to help them find ways to reach their career goals.

The following five scenarios are based on cases from higher educational professionals, hiring managers, recruiters, college students, job seekers, and career changers. Note the details and names have been modified to protect the identity of the individuals involved.

Scenario
Sammy is a career changer thinking about entering the field of higher education. However she is unsure about the difference between roles within the field and what kind of education she would need to enter this new career.

Sammy feels a bit overwhelmed with the information available online and would like to talk to individuals who are actually working in the positions she is considering. Sammy recently created a "LinkedIn" account and uses this social networking sites tool to search for potential contacts at a college that is near the city in which she lives. Sammy discovers that she has a LinkedIn connection who works at the college and four additional LinkedIn connections who know someone working at the college. Sammy reaches out to her LinkedIn connections to see if she can connect with anyone in person for an informational interview to learn more about the culture of the college and to find out more about different career options within the field of higher education. After using social networking sites to make in-person connections, Sammy feels more confident in her interest in working in higher education and has been able to narrow down her career goals to working in the area of resident life.

Developing Job Search or Career Strategy

Fig. 2 depicts how individuals can use social networking sites for gathering information and feedback to develop either a job search or career strategy. Social networking sites can be used to find out about job opportunities. In addition, an individual can use these tools to let others know about their skills, interests, and career goals helping them in the development of a strategy for their job search or career in the future. Furthermore individuals can evaluate whether their career or job search strategy is working from gathering feedback and information from the extended social network.

Scenario
Linda Lou is looking for a full-time job and tells her academic advisor that she spends many hours each week searching job postings online and applying to jobs in marketing, but she is getting frustrated because she has not been able to get an interview. When her academic advisor asks her if she has been using her social network to help her during the job search process she says she doesn't like to ask for favors and doesn't really know anyone who could be of use. After some discussion, the academic advisor discovers that Linda Lou has a Facebook account with over 230 friends, and it is determined that the information posted online would be seen as appropriate by employers. The academic advisor suggests that she writes in her update status on Facebook, "Does anyone know anyone working in marketing that might be a good person for me talk to – looking to find out more about this type of career?" Linda skeptical about this new job search strategy, but decides to give it a try since

nothing else is working. After posting this message on her Facebook page, Linda receives a few messages back from her Facebook friends giving her suggestions on people they know working in the area of marketing. Linda Lou reaches out to these connections and meets up with a woman working in marketing to learn more about what she does for work and discovers that they might have an upcoming job opening. A few weeks later Linda receives a phone call about scheduling an interview for the new position.

Creating a Professional Online Image

Fig. 2 depicts the importance of both gathering information and feedback from others to ensure you are creating a professional online image. In order for an individual to market their skills and interests effectively the image they portray online is an important part of the career management process. An individual may want to think carefully about what kind of brand or image they would like others to have of them based on the professional image they are trying to portray. For example, an individual may want to consider being consistent with the photos used on profile pages so that they can be easily recognized and not confused with another individual with the same name. In addition, if they decide to use a social networking site the profile information should be filled out completely with information that helps promote both their skills, interests and career goals.

Scenario
A hiring manager has a pile of resumes on her desk for a recent job opening. The hiring manager would like to bring in candidates from Livermore University and wants to find out more about the candidates from this particular institution. First the hiring manager goes onto Facebook to learn more about the potential candidates who submitted their resumes, however due to their strict privacy settings she is unable to view their information. However, the hiring manager has an intern working in the office that attends Livermore University and she asks the intern if they could login into their account for the recruiting manager. The Livermore University intern gives access to the hiring manager through their login information.

Logged in as a Livermore University student, the hiring manager begins searching for individuals that applied for the position and finds some disturbing information on "John Smith" who is a Facebook friend to the intern. John has a friend who has posted information on his page that says, "Great party last night man, you were totally wasted." In addition, another friend has posted a photo of John playing a beer drinking game in his underwear. The hiring manager decides that John will not be a fit for the organization and moves onto another candidate.

Sue Brown on Facebook has information posted on her recent trip to Italy, in her interest section she talks greatly about her passion for sports and in many of her photos she is wearing athletic gear with the names of her favorite sports teams. The hiring manager actually is looking for a candidate to help a sports consulting firm, which will require a great deal of international travel. The hiring manager decides to send Sue an email asking her to come into an interview for next week.

The above scenario depicts how online information can negatively and positively help an individual reach their career goals. The take away message from John Smith's situation is that online information is not private and one never knows who could look at it, report it, or distribute it to an employer or others. Furthermore, when using Facebook, it is important to monitor what information others are posting about you online. In contrast, the example of Sue Brown shows that you can portray a positive image online while still being a real person and sharing appropriate personal information that in the end could show an employer about your true interests perhaps leading to a job opportunity. Both cases demonstrate the importance of considering what kind of information you should post online about yourself and to think carefully about what kind of image you are trying to portray to others.

Continuous Professional Development and Learning

There are many ways an individual can use social networking sites to continue to grow professionally and to learn about new trends in one's field. As shown in Fig. 2 and the scenario below social networking site users can continue to gather information and feedback throughout their career to aid in continued learning and professional development.

Scenario
When you Googled the name Nancy Richmond a year ago you would find that there were many individuals with this name and none of the information was related to the Nancy Richmond writing this chapter. You may have been able to find one of the authors on the fourth page of the search results. That is when I realized that I needed to do a better job at creating a professional brand online. I previously had a LinkedIn profile but I wasn't actively engaged in creating connections and sharing information online. That said, I thought it

might be a good idea to start reaching out to my contacts online and creating a professional group called the "Career Counselor Technology Forum." To further reach out to members and encourage use of the new LinkedIn group I organized free webinars and online panel discussions for members to learn more about topics related to technology and career counseling. In a year this new professional online group had over 320 members, who are actively engaging in online discussions by asking questions, sharing information, discussing articles online and posting interesting videos. Creating the "Career Counselor Technology Forum" has enabled me to develop new connections, discover how others were using technology across the nation in my field, and in the process was able to improve my professional brand online.

Personally I have decided to use Facebook strictly for my personal connections which in my case would be classified as my high school friends, college friends, family, and trusted personal connections. Everything that a Facebook friend posts on my page or that I post will be carefully critiqued and analyzed for appropriateness. When viewing information on my Facebook page I consider if I would feel comfortable having a reader of this chapter, a college student, co-worker, or future manager view the posted information. I greatly enjoy seeing Facebook updates about my friends new baby, trips, or personal life experiences which allows me to feel more in touch with my personal connections that could be an asset to managing my career in the future. Through using Facebook I have managed to create a stronger and larger social network.

In addition, to using LinkedIn and Facebook I created a Twitter account @NancyRichmond where I created a tag line "Creating Meaning in Work and Life one Tweet at a Time." Using Twitter I posted inspirational quotes, tips related to job acquisition, advice on changing careers or other information related to my fields of interests. Through this new online experience I was able to learn a great deal from others, discover new pulsing trends in technology, communicate daily with interesting professionals online from around the world, and gained over 400 Twitter followers in less than a year. Though there is more that could be done in the future to continue to build my professional brand online I was happy to see that when writing this book chapter I found that my Twitter account @NancyRichmond is currently the first item that now appears if you Google my name.

Moving on in Your Career

As mentioned previously individuals will most likely change careers many times in their lifetime. Social networking sites can help an individual decide if it is time to move on and help provide support during this time of career transition through the providing of ongoing feedback and information as shown in Fig. 2. In addition, moving on in your career may not mean changing careers but instead how you are perceived in your current role by co-workers or professionals in your field. Once the decision has been made to move on in your career one must evaluate how they can best manage their career through the use of social networking sites.

Scenario
Wally Le works in higher education and is thinking about moving into a new career and is considering applying for a research position at an elite university. However, Wally is concerned because when he recently Googled his name "Wally Le" and found some unflattering inaccurate information online posted by a previous student who failed one of the courses he previously taught. Wally is concerned that a search committee or hiring manager could stumble upon this uncomplimentary online information, which could put his career at risk. Wally meets with a career counselor and who suggests several different ways to help Wally bury this unflattering information online such as creating a LinkedIn account, using Twitter, creating a blog or buying a web domain with one's name in it. Wally decides to start using LinkedIn and Twitter to communicate with his connections about research and to help create a professional brand online. In the process Wally finds that he is learning more about his field, creating a stronger social network and overtime is able to bury this unwanted information in a Google search.

Considering the above some individuals may take the approach that they will avoid posting any information online, "If I ignore social networking sites it will go away and then I am not at risk." However, not participating in social networking sites and becoming a non-user may not be the best answer. Not using social networking sites means being unaware of what other individuals may be posting about you online. In essence, by not participating in social networking sites one is likely to lose access to a large percentage of the professional world that is participating in using social networking sites. In addition, by not using social networking sites an individual has the potential to eliminate possibilities for professional advancement, informal learning, and extending their social network. Perhaps the key to create a professional image instead is to change security settings, think before posting, monitor closely one's online image, and find ways that help others find one's professional online information easily.

FUTURE: HIGHER EDUCATION, SOCIAL NETWORKING SITES, AND CAREER MANAGEMENT

Social networking sites have become a valuable way to communicate in our society. In addition, finding ways to develop a professional image has become an important challenge that both students and working professionals will face in the future. Developing innovative solutions in using social networking sites during the career management process is an increasingly important topic for higher education professionals to address.

Higher education professionals will play an important role in helping college students understand the importance of creating a professional image online and in being aware of how information could be perceived by others (Peluchette & Karl, 2009). In addition, higher education professionals have the opportunity to help model best practices of using social networking sites so that students have a better understanding of what is seen as appropriate information to post online. During the process of using social networking sites, individuals will have the opportunity to begin creating their own professional brand online. Perhaps start small by creating and starting to use one social networking site at a time to find out what works best for your particular needs and career goals.

Today there is a new and great opportunity where both college students and higher education professionals can use these electronic tools to share information and learn from one another. It will be up to higher education professionals to find creative ways to integrate social networking sites into the college experience and during the career development process to help college students create a larger and more dynamic social network for their future careers. In addition, institutions can help by researching ways to better understand how social networking sites can be used to help students manage their careers more effectively in the future.

CONCLUSION

Today part of the career management process includes creating a professional image online. It is important to remember that employers are increasingly using the Internet to search for information, both positive and not so positive, about potential candidates and employees. Social networking sites are creating an interesting dynamic where one's personal and professional life often are becoming blurred. While the sites themselves

(Facebook, Twitter, etc.) may morph to a more current application, society's reliance on technology for social connections, to share information and to stay connected will remain a critical component to the career management process – to network with others for social and professional reasons.

REFERENCES

Bandura, A. (1977). *Social learning theory. Prentice Hall series in social learning theory*. Englewood Cliffs, NJ: Prentice Hall.
Bandura, A. (1986). *Social foundations of thought and action: A social cognitive theory*. Englewood Cliffs, NJ: Prentice Hall.
boyd, D. M., & Ellison, N. B. (2007). Social network sites: Definition, history, and scholarship. *Journal of Computer-Mediated Communication, 13*(1), 210–230.
Burke, M., Marlow, C., & Lento, T. (2010). *Social network activity and social well-being*. ACM CHI 2010: Conference on Human Factors in Computing Systems, 1909–1912. New York: ACM.
Chi, L., Chan, W. K., Seow, G., & Tam, K. (2009). Transplanting social capital to the online world: Insights from two experimental studies. *Journal of Organizational Computing and Electronic Commerce, 19*(3), 214–236.
Chiu, L. (1990). The relationship of career goals and self-esteem among adolescents. *Adolescence, 25*(99), 593–597.
Collard, B. A., Epperheimer, J. W., & Saign, D. (1996). *Career resilience in a changing workplace*. Columbus, OH: ERIC Clearinghouse on Adult, Career, and Vocational Education, Center on Education and Training for Employment, College of Education, the Ohio State University.
Collins, J. (2010). Fortify your Facebook privacy settings. *Journal of Accountancy, 209*(6), 42–45.
Facebook. (2010). Available at http://www.facebook.com/press/info.php?statistics. Retrieved on May 1, 2010.
Graham, B., & Ali, L. (2000). *Moving on in your career: A guide for academics and postgraduates*. London: RoutledgeFalmer.
Granovetter, M. S. (1973). The strength of weak ties. *American Journal of Sociology, 78*(6), 1360–1380.
Greenhaus, J. H., Callanan, G. A., & Godshalk, V. M. (2010). *Career management*. Thousand Oaks: Sage Publications.
Hackett, G., & Betz, N. E. (1981). A self-efficacy approach to the career development of women. *Journal of Vocational Behavior, 18*(3), 326–339.
Hagel, J., & Brown, J. S. (2008). Life on the edge: Learning from Facebook. *Business Week* (Online). Available at http://www.businessweek.com/innovate/content/apr2008/id2008042_809134.htm. Retrieved on May 2010.
Holland, J. L. (1997). *Making vocational choices: A theory of vocational personalities and work environments*. Odessa, FL: Psychological Assessment Resources.
Laumann, E. O., Galaskiewicz, J., & Marsden, P. V. (1978). Community structure as interorganizational linkages. *Annual Review of Sociology, 4*, 455–484.

Lent, R. W., Brown,, S. D., & Hackett,, G. (2000). Contextual supports and barriers to career choice: A social cognitive analysis. *Journal of Counseling Psychology*, *47*, 36–49.

Linkedin. (2010). Available at http://press.linkedin.com/about

Dunlap, J., & Lowenthal, R. (2009). Tweeting the night away: Using Twitter to enhance social presence. *Journal of Information Systems Education*, *20*(2), 129–135.

Parsons, F. (1909). *Choosing a vocation*. Boston: Houghton Mifflin.

Peluchette, J., & Karl, K. (2009). Examining students' intended image on Facebook: "What were they thinking?!". *Journal of Education for Business*, *85*(1), 30–37.

Peterson, N., & González, R. C. (2005). *The role of work in people's lives: Applied career counseling and vocational psychology*. Belmont, CA: Thomson/Brooks/Cole.

Super, D. (1976). *Career education and the meaning of work. Monographs on Career Education*. Washington, DC: The Office of Career Education, U.S. Office of Education.

Super, D. E. (1980). A life-span, life-space approach to career development. *Journal of Vocational Behavior*, *16*(3), 282–296.

Ting, S. (1997). Estimating academic success in the 1st year of college for specially admitted white students: A model combining cognitive and psychosocial predictors. *Journal of College Student Development*, *38*(4), 401–409.

Tinto, V. (1993). *Leaving college: Rethinking the causes and cures of student attrition*. Chicago: University of Chicago Press.

Tolbert, E. L. (1980). *Counseling for career development*. Boston: Houghton Mifflin.

Twitter. (2010). Twitter snags over 100 million users, eyes money-making. Available at http://economictimes.indiatimes.com/infotech/internet/Twitter-snags-over-100-million-users-eyes-money-making/articleshow/5808927.cms. Retrieved on May 1, 2010.

PART III
SOCIAL MEDIA AND PUBLIC RELATIONS

AMPLIFICATION AND ANALYSIS OF ACADEMIC EVENTS THROUGH SOCIAL MEDIA: A CASE STUDY OF THE 2009 BEYOND THE REPOSITORY FRINGE EVENT

Nicola Osborne

ABSTRACT

Social media tools are in increasing use across higher education and Twitter hashtags, live blogs, Facebook events, and Flickr groups are becoming a regular feature of academic conferences and event. In this chapter the author reflects on the experience of planning, moderating, and analyzing social media amplification of the 2009 Beyond the Repository Fringe event. Based upon this experience several important issues regarding social media usage are considered and a series of practical guidelines for planning amplification of higher education events are proposed.

INTRODUCTION AND BACKGROUND

In this chapter I will be considering the possibilities, as well as the practical issues, of using social media to amplify higher education events. These topics are framed by the experience of arranging and moderating amplification for the 2009 "Beyond the Repository Fringe," an informal annual "unconference" that focuses on innovations and opportunities in repository technology, policy and practice, provides a discussion and networking space for practitioners, and allows practical exchange of experience and ideas. The event takes the form of a physical event with a venue and structure designed by the organizing committee and a program of talks volunteered by Repository Fringe attendees. Participants are drawn from a diverse array of Higher Education institutions, libraries, and technology companies based in the United Kingdom and software engineers, academics and researchers, digital curators and senior library professionals.

I will be analyzing and reflecting on the Beyond the Repository Fringe experience touching on the use of various tools, including Flickr groups and live blogging, and considering the complexities of identity and moderation in social media amplification. In particular I will look at the role that Twitter can play in event amplification and in subsequent reflection on the success of an event. In addition I offer, at the end of this chapter, practical advice and guidance intended to assist event organizers in planning, running, and measuring the success of amplifying academic events.

The experience described in this chapter should be of particular interest to those who plan academic events. Repository Fringe is an unconference but the experiences and techniques could also be applied to traditional conferences, workshops, some training contexts and many medium to large-scale meetings and events. The author has also seen similar techniques deployed in successful pedagogical contexts though here negotiations of identity can be more complex. As the event described is open and public facing these techniques are not as suitable for contexts in which sensitive or private information is discussed.

WHAT IS "AMPLIFICATION?"

In the course of this chapter I will be looking at the process of "amplifying" an event and it thus seems useful to define what I mean by this. The Oxford English Dictionary (OED Online, 1989) defines amplification as *the action of amplifying, extending or enlarging*. This notion of extending and enlarging an event beyond its temporal or physical bounds is key in understanding the productive possibilities of using social media at events. Although technical definitions of amplification have some relevance here, since people and intellectual content are being amplified by social media technologies, the benefits of "amplifying" what is said, presented, experienced, or discussed can be best understood through the specific rhetorical sense of amplification (OED Online, 1989):

> 4. Rhet. The extension of simple statement by all such devices as tend to increase its rhetorical effect, or to add importance to the things stated; making the most of a thought or circumstance.

Although the term "amplification" is established as a colloquial term around social media for broadcast or extensions of events or experiences (e.g., Kelly, 2010a; Haydon, 2010 or in the naming of the not-for-profit events amplification organization "Amplified," 2010) I would like to propose a specific definition for the social media amplification of events as:

> The extension of a physical event (or a series of events) through the use of social media tools for expanding access to (aspects of) the event beyond physical and temporal bounds. Such amplification takes place in the context of intent to make the most of the intellectual content, discussion, networking and discovery initiated by the event through the process of sharing with co-attendees, colleagues, friends and wider informed publics.

Experiments around event amplification (sometimes referred to by different but connected terms) have been taking place in many interesting and innovative ways for at least the past two years. There is, however, very little literature on this topic, though early work on emergent communications technologies for conferences (such as Kelly, Tonkin, & Shabajee, 2005) and recent work on transliterate approaches (McGill, 2010) are useful and notable exceptions. The rise of transmedia approaches to entertainment also provide many inspiring examples which may be applied to event amplification and hybrid virtual/physical events (Cheshire & Burton, 2010).

#RF09: A CASE STUDY OF AMPLIFYING AN ACADEMIC UNCONFERENCE

In July 2009 the "Beyond the Repository Fringe" unconference took place in Edinburgh organized by EDINA, the Digital Curation Centre (DCC), and the University of Edinburgh School of Informatics. This was the second "Repository Fringe," with both having run on an informal "unconference" format. The term "unconference" refers to various nontraditional event formats, most often associated with a physical event with a fixed location and date but with a structure and/or program defined by volunteer speakers and attendees. In the case of the Repository Fringe the format is an informal, participant-driven facilitated physical event, with no fee for participation or attendance, which is intended to draw in a wide selection of participants and encourage active and enthusiastic participation. In order to provide structure, the organizers provide a draft timetable and keynote speakers are selected and confirmed before the event is publicized. The majority of speakers and workshop facilitators identify themselves by responding to a call for participation circulated through various repository email lists and websites. Potential speakers are encouraged to add proposals for talks and workshops directly to the Repository Fringe wiki, http://wiki.repositoryfringe.org/. The format for the event changes somewhat from year to year but the core idea of an open, accessible, inexpensive event that encourages active dialogue between a self-selected audience from the UK repository community remains core to the event.

The Repository Fringe events have both received healthy levels of interest with around 80 participants attending the first event in 2008 and 92 participants registered for the 2009 Beyond the Repository Fringe event (via EventBrite, an online event booking system). The maximum capacity of 100 free places on the event was made possible by funding from the JISC Repositories and Preservation Programme (http://www.jisc.ac.uk/whatwedo/programmes/reppres.aspx), which supports innovation around digital repositories and preservation for education and research. Since the Repository Fringe events take place in Edinburgh the organizers are aware that there are further potential participants who, even when not paying a conference fee, may not be able to secure time or funding to travel and stay in the city for several nights. Some participants will, of course, be able to disseminate experiences and information to colleagues but there remains a sense of a wider audience interested in the events but unable to attend in person. Many of the potential attendees are, however, adept and enthusiastic about the use of new technology and the event thus provided an excellent opportunity for experimenting with social media amplification in order to reach out and extend the event beyond its physical boundaries.

Following successful use of an event wiki and a Flickr account for the previous Repository Fringe event, the core organizing team had already identified video streaming and live blogging as useful amplification tools for the 2009 event. During discussions over the role of live blogging in the event, we identified a wider variety of additional amplification tools that could be trialed at the Repository Fringe 2009.

ESTABLISHING GOALS FOR SOCIAL MEDIA AMPLIFICATION AT REPOSITORY FRINGE

The participative nature of the unconference model used by Repository Fringe is such that the organizers were confident of some level of participation around the event. In addition, social media mentions of the first Repository Fringe (in 2008) were known of but had not been related back to official web presences. The goals for social media amplification were therefore to:

1. Provide access to the presentations of Repository Fringe 2009 to those unable to attend through video streaming and live blogging.
2. Enable rich networking opportunities for attendees (physical and virtual).
3. Collect attendee images of the event in lieu of access to professional event photographers.
4. Provide an accessible backchannel for attendees to comment on the event.
5. Ensure any follow up social mentions were available to organizers for use in assessing the success of the event and planning for future events.
6. Gain experience in using multiple social media tools for event amplification with a view to feeding this experience into future events and project work.

SELECTING SOCIAL MEDIA AMPLIFICATION CHANNELS

In discussing possible social media spaces for use in amplifying Repository Fringe, the organizing team drew on their own experience as representatives of the repository community. The repository community is demographically complex – individuals tending to use tools according to roles, interests, or technical experience rather than age, location, or similarly easy to identify dimensions. With this in mind we considered the spaces we knew were already in use by our audience: popular blogs, microblogging activity, wikis, photo sharing sites, etc. Although we could have deducted that most attendees would (demographically speaking) be on Facebook we excluded some such sites as unlikely spaces for productive or public discussion.

The *DISC UK DataShare Blog* (http://jisc-datashare.blogspot.com/) was identified as the best location for live-blogging the event as this project was hosting a meeting in a parallel theme within the Repository Fringe and therefore had a strong and specific association with the event and many attendees. *Twitter* was also felt to be an important amplification channel as the Repository Fringe followed several months of events and reports in the UK Higher Education community that had benefited from ongoing discussions on assigned hashtags (e.g. JISC, 2009). Visible Tweets (http://visibletweets.com/) was also identified as a tool that would enable a simple hashtag-based visualization of Tweets for a "Twitter Wall" (a projection of incoming Tweets around the event) although this functionality was little used during the day.

The organizers were aware that Twitter usage could not be assumed of all participants, we were also aware that the number of social channels in use might cause some confusion unless they could be coherently combined. *CoverItLive* (http://www.coveritlive.com/) was therefore identified as a suitable tool, enabling the combining of event streams including tweets, comments, pre-populated event information, and images in an embeddable interface and combined RSS stream. The CoverItLive stream could also be retained after the event for replay (via the website) or archiving. The existing Repository Fringe *Flickr* account would be used to share images of the event and a Flickr group (http://www.flickr.com/groups/repofringe09/) was also set up to enable easy pooling of both organizer and attendee images of the event.

All social media channels were listed (and linked to) on the Repository Fringe wiki so that any interested participants or online viewers would be able to find and access the blog, images, and hashtag easily. The CoverItLive event was also embedded on the front page of the Repository Fringe web presence, http://www.repositoryfringe.org/, and on an additional live coverage page hosting streaming video of the event. Over the course of the event a further page (http://wiki.repositoryfringe.org/index.php/Coverage_of_the_event_online) was created to track both official online coverage of the event and postings by attendees, interested colleagues and viewers on their own blogs and websites. This page has subsequently been updated to reflect the online impact of the event, connecting to all known mentions and postings about Beyond the Repository Fringe.

SET UP AND MANAGEMENT OF AMPLIFICATION TOOLS DURING THE EVENT

Wherever possible the selected social tools were branded with the Repository Fringe 2009 logo – an image of the annual Edinburgh Festival

Fringe, the inspiration for the event ethos and name due to its reputation as the energetic, creative, irreverent, and informal antidote to more official events. Before the event the logo was also uploaded to the Flickr group so that it could be used by organizers and both official and independent bloggers. The "event" in CoverItLive began several days before the in-person event started allowing early comments to the Twitter Stream to be collated and published. Before this launch the template was populated with short information texts about each scheduled item in the program (which included keynotes, Pecha Kucha (http://en.wikipedia.org/wiki/Pecha_Kucha) sessions, "Show & Tell" sessions, workshops, round table discussions, and a developer competition) ready to be instantly published to the CoverItLive stream at appropriate times during the event. And indeed these prepared announcements made up most of the 40 alerts and notes posted by the organizers to the CoverItLive stream during the 2-day event.

A Twitter "hashtag" (a single tag for related comments which is preceded by the # sign to enable easy filtering of tweets) was identified as important for effective amplification but selecting the *right* hashtag proved challenging. There is no official way to register a hashtag despite the existence of websites like http://hashtag.org/, which was set up as an attempt to register all hashtags as they appeared on Twitter but has now become a community site, built on the Ning platform, around hashtag usage. The unofficial way to check a potential hashtag is to run a search on Twitter (or a third party Twitter application such as Tweetdeck (http://www.tweetdeck.com), Brizzly (http://brizzly.com/), or Soda.sh (http://soda.sh/)) for existing mentions of the chosen word. Initially "#RepoFringe" seemed like a good choice as it was not in use already and is the commonly used abbreviated form of the event name (also in use on the official Flickr account). However it was felt that #RepoFringe might, at 11 characters, be too long for the 140 character limit Twitter imposes. #RF09 was selected as a more suitable and more concise alternative and initial search found only a small amount of activity associated with the tag. By the time of the event it became clear that the hashtag was also in use for a motorsports event, a World of Warcraft contest and the Roskilde Festival, a Danish music festival. Since #RF09 had already been publicized the hashtag was used despite these clashes and, over the course of the event, most tweets to #RF09 were directly related to Beyond the Repository Fringe. Visual inspection allowed the removal of a small handful of tweets intended for these other events from any further analysis.

Although there are continuing discussions and experiments around the use of additional Twitter hashtags to identify specific sessions or themes at events such as Beyond the Repository Fringe we did not choose to identify any additional hashtags for specific workshops or parallel discussions. Even for this relatively small event this decision led to some confusion in marrying up tweets to different simultaneous sessions and is a technique that will be considered again in planning the 2010 Repository Fringe event.

In addition to the online set up process a physical inspection of the Beyond the Repository Fringe venue took place in order to assess the availability of electrical sockets, wireless internet and presentation facilities. For amplified events, access to power and internet connections is particularly important both to support official live blogging and to support attendees wanting to contribute to amplification channels.

METRICS

Credible social media metrics are still emerging (e.g., Owyang, 2010). Many existing measures relate to commercial objectives (such as lead generation and impact on sales) which can be difficult to relate back to the goals and practice of academic organizations. Identifying useful impact measures that reflect the (generally) not-for-profit nature and academic tone of Higher Education events can therefore be challenging. However, as in a commercial setting, identifying the desired outcome is important to designing appropriate metrics. In the case of Beyond the Repository Fringe the main goal was to generate discussion and feedback around repositories so assessing the level of participation, the extended online discussion and the key issues highlighted by commentators was important for us. Because we were also trialing a variety of social media amplification tools we were also looking for useful reactions and reflections on these tools.

ACHIEVEMENT OF GOALS

1. Provide access to the presentations of Repository Fringe 2009 to those unable to attend through video streaming and live blogging.

    The video streaming provided at the event was useful for remote participants but a number of technical issues prevented remote participants from seeing all of the sessions available. The live blogging was, however, a significant success. In addition to being used by both the closing keynote speaker and remote participants the blog posts were also

subsequently used as a core record of the event by a number of attendees who blogged their experiences. The live blog thus allowed these bloggers the space to reflect and discuss the Repository Fringe rather than describe the presentations seen. Additionally, the live blog has provided a long lasting record of the event that is easier to access and understand than the more dense Twitter or CoverItLive records of the event.
2. Enable rich networking opportunities for attendees whether attending in person or virtually.

Twitter worked well as a networking tool for attendees whether or not they were on campus. It retrospect the addition of a delegate list including twitter identities (and linking them back to real names) might have been useful. We also received feedback via Twitter, and paper feedback forms, that some attendees would have liked for some social activity to be arranged for the night preceding the Repository Fringe. This has been noted for the 2010 event and the new website includes an area to post any updates or notes about entertainment and social activities, additionally several light early evening Repository Fringe social activities are build into the 2010 program.
3. Collect attendee images of the event in lieu of access to professional event photographers.

The use of a Flickr group built on the 2008 Repository Fringe's use of Flickr. The group attracted only a small number of participants but enabled the collection and use of a large number of very high-quality images. The number of contributors did seem to reflect the number of photographs taken at the event but there is scope to develop this further, and to perhaps integrate images from mobile phones, in the future.
4. Provide an accessible backchannel for attendees to comment on the event.

Twitter worked well as a busy and engaging backchannel for Repository Fringe with both those attending in person and those participating remotely finding great value in the use of an event hashtag for networking and discussion. It had been initially hoped that the backchannel could be highlighted through displaying visualizations of recent Tweets on LCD and/or projector screens which are in place around the venue though this was, in the event, not possible. One of the challenges of an individual engaging in the Twitter stream and the live blogging of an event is the competition for attention between these two channels. A solution to this, where feasible, would be to split the task between two individuals with one committed to updating blog postings, the other to monitoring and updating Twitter comments.

CoverItLive did not prove to be a successful backchannel for those without Twitter accounts – one of the reasons it was initially used – as the tool was not as familiar to the Repository Fringe attendees and most of those who wished to make real-time comments elected to do so through their Twitter accounts. CoverItLive did, however, provide an attractive and simple way to archive and replay the Tweets from the #rf09 hashtag.
5. Ensure any follow up social mentions were available to organizers for use in assessing the success of the event and planning for future events.

The use of TwapperKeeper, CoverItLive, and the JISC DataShare Blog all successfully allowed the organizers access to comments and feedback made during the Repository Fringe event. Follow up blog postings, tracked through Google and social search tools, also provided invaluable feedback to compliment comments gathered via paper feedback forms at the end of the on-campus event.
6. Gain experience in using multiple social media tools for event amplification with a view to feeding this experience into future events and project work.

Repository Fringe was an extremely useful event for trialing a rich mixture of social media amplification tools and techniques. Although the audience for this event includes an unusual level of engagement with technology the experiences have already fed into further thinking around event amplification and recent events such as the first Open Knowledge Scotland meeting (http://wiki.okfn.org/OpenKnowledge ScotlandEventPage/) in May 2010.

PARTICIPATION LEVELS

One of the most simple measures is the extent to which each channel is used – both in terms of the level of participation and the volume of content (e.g., number of comments) produced. In the case of Beyond the Repository Fringe some channels were clearly more successful than others. Around 40 people watched the CoverItLive aggregated feed during the event but no comments were submitted via the tool despite this functionality providing a way for those without Twitter accounts to take part in the live stream. The stream was embedded on a special live feed page of the Repository Fringe website with little interactive content so it may be that viewers did not realize that they had the ability to actively comment or it may be that all of those who wished to participate, contributed directly via Twitter (which fed into the CoverItLive stream). The CoverItLive event did, however, have impact beyond the event with 80 people viewing the replay since Beyond the Repository Fringe took place.

The Flickr group (http://www.flickr.com/groups/repofringe09/) was a more mixed experience. Only one participant joined the group but he shared a large number of high-quality images and, like the organizing team, posted images under a Creative Commons Licence allowing reuse. The Flickr group enabled sharing, whilst ensuring that photographers, including individual organizers, retain credit (and ownership) over their images. The group also allowed individual organizers to use existing storage space and settings associated with personal "Pro" accounts (which, unlike free accounts, allow unlimited upload and sharing of high resolution images) when contributing images to the official coverage. The use of personal Flickr accounts, potentially introduces substantial blurring of personal and professional identities and whilst this blurring is commonplace there are privacy and organizational policy complexities associated with such ambiguity. I will reflect on this recent form of tangled identities and roles in professional and quasi-professional contexts later in this chapter as I consider broad considerations for the use of social media amplification.

The live blog of Beyond the Repository Fringe, though one of the less innovative social media channels, demonstrated some of the most tangible benefits. Producing detailed timely blog postings was extremely labor intensive but they allowed remote participants to follow the event in some depth. The closing keynote speaker, Clifford Lynch, was one such participant as he was traveling from an event in the United States on the first day of the Repository Fringe and was only able to attend a few sessions before his own keynote brought the event to a close. In his presentation he indicated that he was able to follow the event via the live blogging and went on to make specific reference to earlier speakers and the content of presentations which the blog coverage had allowed him to experience from afar. The blog has also had currency since the event as it has provided a core record for attendees and other repository bloggers to link back to. At least nine blog postings about Beyond the Repository Fringe have appeared since the event and most link back to the live blog coverage as well as the website for the event.

TWITTER

Twitter was by far the most active channel at Beyond the Repository Fringe with over 300 tweets posted to the #rf09 hashtag over the course of the

2-day event by a total of 45 Twitter accounts. Additional tweets appeared over the following days offering feedback or linking to blog postings and follow up content. It thus warrants further attention since comments provide a rich archive of feedback on the event as well as revealing social connections between participants.

TWITTER ANALYSIS

For Twitter usernames that contributed at least one tweet to the #rf09 hashtag a new entry including name, username, and an anonymous form of attribution (Tweeter1, Tweeter2, etc.) was created in a spreadsheet. The username was looked up using the Twittergrader tool (Shah, 2009) which queries Twitter profiles (via the API – the Application Programming Interface) for information including the number of people who subscribe to a user's updates, the number of updates they have posted, etc. This provided a snapshot of the Twitter activity, popularity and personal networks of each Beyond the Repository Fringe Twitter commentator.

The usernames were checked against each other in order to analyze how many participants "follow" each other and are connected on Twitter. This check was performed using two methods: the DoesFollow tool (Clinkscales, 2010) and a direct call on the Twitter API which can be made with the following command (where NAME1 and NAME2 are both Twitter usernames):
http://twitter.com/friendships/exists.xml?user_a=NAME1&user_b=NAME2 (via Morrison, 2009).

As this analysis of connection has taken place some months after the event it is impossible to gauge how many of the participants began following each other during or after Repository Fringe 2009. However, many of the connections found through this analysis do support patterns of users quoting or "retweeting" (forwarding) each other repeatedly during the event which suggests that connections may have already been established in July 2009.

Of 42 active (nonautomated) Twitter commentators only 2 individuals lack connections to any other participant. Around half of those who tweeted have 10 mutual connections (where they both follow and are followed by other participants) within the participant group – so they are connected to a quarter of those posting tweets to the event hashtag. The most popular Repository Fringe Twitter participant is connected to more than half of the other participants. A visualization (Fig. 1) compares total popularity of Twitter participants with mutual and unrequited/fan relationships within

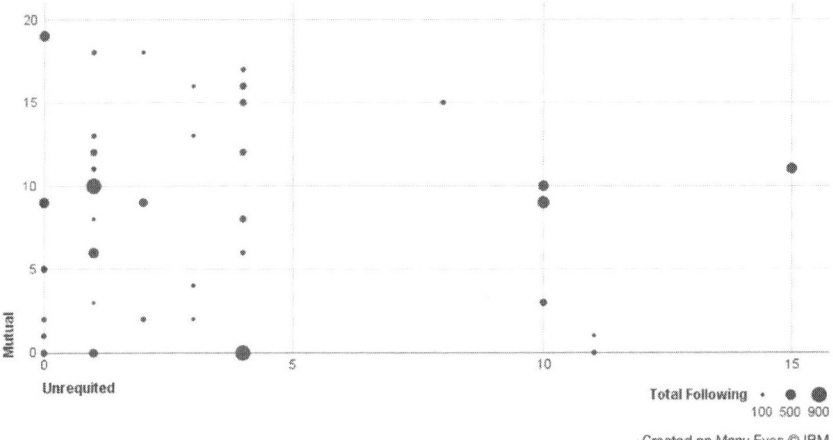

Fig. 1. Visualization, Created using the ManyEyes Visualization Tools (http://manyeyes.alphaworks.ibm.com/manyeyes/), Comparing the Number of Mutual and One Directional "Unrequited" Connections (Followers Who are Not Followed Back) between Beyond the Repository Fringe Twitter Participants. Each Dot Indicates a Different Twitter Username with the Size of the Dot Scaled According to the Total Number of Followers that Participant Has.

the #RF09 group. As might be expected those with high follower (500+) counts have more "fans" than mutual connections.

The UK repository community is relatively small and well-connected but the dense Twitter connections between Repository Fringe Twitter commentators gives insight into the enthusiastic uptake of this channel. Participation in the #RF09 hashtag may well have been boosted by pre-existing social relationships and comfort with the site. These relationships could be explored further through techniques including digital ethnography (e.g., Bardzell & Odom, 2008; Gatson & Zweerink, 2004; Hine, 2000). This can be an extremely useful method for understanding the relationships and impact of an event but for a group as large and densely connected as the #RF09 Twitter group this would be a very substantial undertaking.

TWITTER COMMENTS

Twitter offers a rich time-stamped archive of feedback on the content and organization of the event since many of those participating in the Twitter stream were attending Beyond the Repository Fringe in person and reporting on their experiences of presentations, workshops, etc. The Twitter participation rate was particularly high with a third of all event attendees (based on Twitter profiles, event registrations, and tweet content) posting at least one tweet. This may not be representative of Twitter usage across the sector but is in keeping with the Repository Fringe's focus on new technology and active participation. A more interesting distortion can be seen when looking at the number of tweets per username with over 100 of the tweets posted by a single user who commented regularly throughout the 2 days and subsequently posted a number of reports on the event to his personal blog. The advantage of this level of real-time commentary to provide information that could never be collected via traditional feedback forms (which were also used for Repository Fringe 2009) can be seen in the following comments posted only an hour apart by this same prolific in-person attendee (Tweeter8):

> Pre #rf09 thoughts. An event of shock and awe but thin on practicality. Hoping I'm wrong.

> This session has set a very high point for the conf. I could probably go home now and the trip would have been worth it.

Even if this participant gave detailed and honest responses on their feedback form (presuming they completed one – only 23 attendees returned feedback forms) it would be hard to capture such a clear snapshot of expectations and to so easily identify the talk which triggered such a swift change of heart. In this case, I can immediately compare the timestamp of the tweet to the presentation schedule and see that it was the opening keynote, "A sneak preview at the A-list stars of future repositories: blockbuster technical developments and the cultural drivers behind them" by Ben O'Steen and Sally Rumsey of Oxford University which entirely shifted this participant's expectations. For assessing the success (or failure) of topics, presenters, and format the tweets are a very powerful analysis tool. However, the sequence of comments by Tweeter8 also indicates how challenging it can be to moderate comments in real time. For a moderator, it is tempting to reduce the risk of negative comments by intervening with reassurances. However, this could have stifled honest discussion particularly as the critical tweet was posted early in the event as activity on the Twitter stream was just gaining momentum. It was, of course, pleasing to see the risk pay off when the positive contradictory comment from the same tweeter appeared just an hour later.

The time stamping of tweets also offers more sophisticated potential for amplified events. In the case of Beyond the Repository Fringe we provided a webpage that showed the embedded video stream alongside the CoverItLive stream (including all Twitter comments) and made both artifacts available for viewing after the event. However more direct integration of Tweets with video feeds has been explored in a variety of experiments – using pre-recorded rather than live video streams – notably in the work of Tony Hirst (Hirst, 2010) and Martin Hawksey Hawksey (2010). The value of linking commentary with presentation footage lies partly in the wealth of referrals to further reading, relevant URLs, and additional information that is supplied in Twitter comments. For instance at Beyond the Repository Fringe several tweets referred to resources that were under discussion at the event:

> Hugh Glaser now demonstrating RKBExplorer (http://www.rkbexplorer.com/ at #rf09 (Tweeter26).

The ability to match public Twitter comments to each item on the program can be extremely helpful for organizers no matter what the tone of the Tweets but for speakers this feature means immediately seeing and taking on board comments no matter how critical or fair they may be. This potential for upset or conflict is particularly worth noting if public tweets are being shown alongside individual presentations since Twitter hashtags can become a very disruptive and unmanageable form of heckling. One possible solution is to display comments via a tool which allows the editing of tweets pre- or post publication. One of the drivers for using CoverItLive for Repository Fringe was the fact that it allowed editing and/or removal of comments at any point though for this event the functionality was used to remove a single tweet, on the basis that it related to another event using the #rf09 hashtag.

Viewing the Wordle (Fig. 2), it is immediately apparent that "data," "repository," "repositories," and "deposit" stand out as the most tweeted words. Terms including "Need," "like," "now," "good," and "interesting" also feature very strongly reflecting the tone of talks for this event, many of which were position papers and presentations on innovative projects and initiatives. More interestingly "Pecha" and "Kucha" are also mentioned very frequently. The terms refers to the short "Pecha Kucha" presentation format, in which presenters show and explain 20 slides for 20 s each. As this is challenging and relatively novel, it was of particular interest to those attending the event in person:

> @tweeter13 Well done on your pecha kucha! (Tweeter12)

Fig. 2. A Wordle (Created with the Visualization Tools at http://www.wordle.net/), Showing the Distribution of Words in the #rf09 Tweets (Words are Sized According to the Frequency with which They Appear in Twitter Comments).

pecha kucher session is really funny! Trying to grasp all concepts in 20 secs is also a challenge ... (Tweeter24)

Glad I didn't volunteer to do one of these sessions with my tendency to waffle (Tweeter8)

The Wordle, though a rather blunt tool, also highlights trends including positive interest in our keynote speaker Clifford Lynch (indicated by the popularity of "cliff" and "lynch") as well as some irritated tweets that questioned the time keeping on one Pecha Kucha talk.

SOCIAL TOOLS: THE GOOD, THE BAD, THE UNPROVEN

Images, Consent, and Timeliness

Photographs and video can be extremely powerful tools for amplifying academic events but, particularly for events taking place over several days, the timeliness of posting and sharing links and materials is crucial. Participants only engage fully in the conference whilst it is taking place so capturing their interest and participation then is key. In order to speed up the process of taking and sharing images, it is important to secure agreement from attendees for their images to be used at or before the point of registration on the day. This can raise some challenges since the easiest systems for doing this – requiring use of an attendee's image as part of the agreement to take part in the event, with the option to request that specific images are taken down – can be perceived as invasive to participant privacy. The Repository Fringe followed practice at many unconference events in explicitly encouraging participants to document the event and thus, implicitly, requiring attendees to personally opt out of images or avoid being photographed. However to remove any doubt about the use of images it is likely that a short note specifying this situation will be included in the information for the 2010 event. For smaller or more politically sensitive events (such as focus groups) it may be much more appropriate to provide more explicit consent forms on an opt-in basis.

Video can be a particularly sensitive area as it makes permanent both formal and informal comments made at an event so it is important to gain agreement from speakers to capture and use their performance. This allows content to be uploaded and/or streamed as quickly and efficiently as possible. Written consent that waives speaker performance rights will also help secure rights for future re-use and archiving. In some cases the balance between privacy and public access is met by recording formal presentations but not informal, panel, or networking elements. This is a practical solution that will reassure speakers but compromises the experience of participation for remote attendees.

IDENTITY ISSUES

The digital identity (or digital identities) of participants is often a secondary thought in the promotion of social tools at events – invitations to tweet, blog, etc. do not require any particular context to be set so participants may choose to publicly post under professional, personal, or blended personas. For the participants this may not be an issue but for the event organizer to be able to analyze, quote, or publicize comments the issue becomes more complex. Social media communications (particularly Twitter and in-person discussions captured on video) are believed to be inherently ephemeral so presenting these comments in the context of permanence enables a different type and degree of scrutiny and accountability (Chun, 2008). This can have real consequences for those quoted and therefore attempts to quote, publish, or disseminate comments in permanent (particularly print or broadcast) formats risks breaching the trust of participants and, ultimately, reducing participation to banal statements of fact. The decision to share and blend social identities is deceptively complex (e.g., Lundblad & Masiello, 2010) and is an issue under increasing scrutiny in social and cultural (e.g., danah boyd, 2008), pedagogical (e.g., Hemmi, Bayne, & Land, 2009) and professional (e.g., Williams, 2009) contexts. However as the impact of social tools increases, so do moves to store, analyze, and archive comments made in these spaces, for instance the Library of Congress has recently announced plans to archive all Tweets (Library of Congress, 2010), whilst JISC, the major funding body for the United Kingdom further and higher education technological innovation, is supporting development to the TwapperKeeper (http://www.twapperkeeper.com/) service (Kelly, 2010b).

MODERATION

One of the inherent risks of integrating real time social communications into an event is the possibility of erroneous, offensive, or irrelevant content being published under the auspices of your organization. There have been several notable cases of respected media brands incorporating live comment streams into their publications or broadcast streams only to have posters add offensive, silly, or libellous comments (e.g., Jones, 2009). Indeed, personal liability for social media comments have resulted in significant consequences for some with teachers, political candidates (Siddique & Carrell, 2010), and journalists (Heinz, 2010) all finding contracts terminated for social media comments either explicitly or implicitly tied to their professional identity. Meanwhile academics are engaged in complex cases stemming from social media and user generated comments (e.g., Service, 2010) whilst celebrity feuding, offensiveness or upset (Cofield, 2010; Siegler, 2010) are common across various social media sites. Some see a level of offence and noise as an inevitable and perhaps acceptable feature of social networking usage (e.g., Buchanan, 2010) but many organizations have or are developing guidelines specifically with the unintended consequences of casual spaces in mind (e.g., IBM, 2010). However monitoring and light moderation should, in most cases, be suitable for most academic amplification contexts.

ASSESSING SOCIAL TOOLS

Kerawalla, Minocha, Kirkup, and Console (2009) suggest a useful framework for the use of blogging which, although intended for distance and e-learning contexts, may be useful in considering the comfort and likely behaviors of an academic audience's engagement with social media amplification tools. They propose a model for designing courses that address prior participant experience of social media tools (see also Clark, Logan, Luckin, Mee, & Oliver, 2009) and their comfort with technology and the comparison of organizer and participant expectations. Although this framework is not explicitly designed for use with academic events I believe it offers a constructive starting point to planning a blend of social amplification tools.

There is, however, no substitute for experimentation with social media tools but this can be done in a variety of ways. Attending virtual events as a participant will immediately help highlight both positive and negative qualities of various amplification tools and these experiences can then be built on for future events. It can often be quite strange and disembodying to experience an event as a remote participant as a break in the video stream, an unexplained comment and events as insignificant as a coffee break can appear confusing to a participant who has just logged in to view the coverage of a conference. Attending physical events and participating in the Twitter and blogging back channels can also be a valuable experience for judging the balance, integration, and filtering implications of these tools. I have personally found that trialing more unusual and unproven social media tools for local or personal social events can also give useful initial indications of future usefulness.

PRACTICAL CHECKLIST FOR PLANNING AN AMPLIFIED EVENT

Based on the experiences of Beyond the Repository Fringe 2009, the planning process (currently taking place) for the 2010 event, and reflecting on substantial experience of participating in the social media amplification of academic events I have attempted to distil the social media planning process into the following practical guidelines:

1. Begin your amplification planning by carefully considering the needs and expectations of the event audience as well as the desired goals for your event. Ensure you use tools and communication methods that will be familiar and of interest to your audience. If many speakers and attendees regularly update blogs then this may be a suitable method of communication whereas if few organizers or expected participants

use Twitter then it is unlikely to be useful. Judging the mixture of channels to use will require speaking to peers, fellow organizers, colleagues and, when possible, attendees or speakers to assess their interest and usage of social media tools and their expectations for the event.
2. *Prepare your participants.* Events arranged online will benefit from printable elements of traditional delegate packs – local transport, restaurant, and entertainment information for instance – will still be worth distributing online. Even if social events are not part of the official program facilities for participants to arrange meet ups may also be expected.
3. *Prepare the physical event space.* You need to support and enable bloggers or event attendees to participate and making sure that there is access to power and internet connections will make a substantial difference to participation levels.
4. *Prepare the virtual event space.* Ensure that the online presence for your event is clear and consistent. Links to all amplification channels should be easily found and checked throughout the event, particularly if you are using streaming video or audio. If you can share presentation materials ahead of the event this will help ensure that those participating solely online have good access to the core content of the event as it is presented or discussed. If your event is likely to feature many acronyms or niche references consider creating an online glossary of terms that will help clarify terms for remote participants in particular.
5. *Ensure there are clear roles for updating and monitoring amplification channels throughout the event.* Curating engaging social media amplification is labor intensive but will be more manageable if responsibility for each element of the amplification is clearly planned. If there are multiple parallel themes, ensure one person will record and amplify each theme. Ensure there is a mechanism for registering and responding to technical problems or urgent queries. A short list of contact details held by all organizers may help with this.
6. *Request consent from participants.* This will help ensure that materials can be shared in a timely and relevant fashion. Permission may need to be sought for capturing still images, streaming and/or recording video or audio material, and for sharing presentation materials or public comments (particularly if publication of any type is planned). Issuing a waiver as part of the registration process and on the website will be a practical compromise at some events (especially larger events) for alerting

participants that their image, contributions, comments, or presentations may be made available or publicized by the event organizers.
7. *Moderate social media channels lightly.* Although comments in these spaces are public and comments may occasionally prove inaccurate or inappropriate it is important for organizers to inhabit and engage in social media as honest and human voices rather than over formal or censorious presences.
8. *Monitor social media coverage regularly.* This should begin before the event takes place so that any erroneous links can be corrected and all mentions can be recorded as they appear so that supporting evidence of the event's impact is readily available to organizers, funders, etc. Tools such as Google alerts (http://www.google.com/alerts), Tweetbeep (http://tweetbeep.com/), Collecta (http://collecta.com/), and RSS readers such as Feed Demon (http://www.feeddemon.com/) can all be useful in monitoring social media mentions.
9. *Consider feedback from social media channels alongside traditional feedback methods.* Blogs, Twitter, comments, and any other social channel your participants may use will all provide valuable feedback on an event but they should not entirely replace traditional feedback forms as some attendees will not be participating online and others will be keen to make anonymous comments on paper rather than traceable comments online.
10. *Reflect and learn from social media experiences throughout the event.* It can be hard to assess which social media channels will be most appropriate to an event ahead of time and it is therefore important to assess how the blend of tools is working throughout the event. If a particular tool or channel is immediately problematic or unused you can then discontinue use early in the event in order to focus energy elsewhere. If comments from one channel are particularly helpful, that can be promoted or highlighted to participants in the physical event space.

What has become clear through the experience of managing the Repository Fringe amplification, and the experience on leading or advising on the amplification of subsequent events, is the centrality of understanding your target audience. Social media tools should be deployed in concert with relevant traditional communications in ways that genuinely speak to and connect with your potential or identified attendees. It is therefore crucial to adapt and target any social media amplification work on the needs and expectations of the audience, with an appreciation of the skills and experience of the event organizers themselves. When used successfully social media amplification can not only increase the impact of an event online but can also enrich the experience of the whole event.

REFERENCES

Amplified (2010). Amplified. Available at http://www.amplified10.com/. Retrieved on July 5, 2010.
Bardzell, S., & Odom, W. (2008). The experience of embodied space in virtual worlds: An ethnography of a second life community. *Space and Culture, 11*(3), 239–259. doi:10.1177/ 1206331208319148.
Buchanan, R. (2010). If you want young people in politics, tweeting comes too: Do we veto everyone who shown themselves up online? In TimesOnline Comment section, 12th April. Available at http://www.timesonline.co.uk/tol/comment/columnists/guest_contributors/article7094779.ece. Retrieved on April 20, 2010.
Cheshire, T., & Burton, C. (2010). Entertainment reimagined. In: Wired (UK edition), 08-10, pp. 88–97.
Chun, W. H. K (2008). The enduring ephemeral, or the future is a memory. *Critical Inquiry, 35*(1), 148–171. doi:10.1086/595632.
Clark, W., Logan, K., Luckin, R., Mee, A., & Oliver, M. (2009). Beyond Web 2.0: Mapping the technology landscapes of young learners. *Journal of Computer Assisted Learning, 25*, 56–69. doi:10.1111/j.1365-2729.2008.00305.x.
Clinkscales, D. (2010). Doesfollow.com. Available at http://doesfollow.com/. Retrieved on March 10, 2010.
Cofield, S. (2010). Another Twitter gaff: Berto the culprit today. In Yahoo! Boxing Expert Blog, April 19. Available at http://sports.yahoo.com/box/blog/box_experts/post/Another-Twitter-gaff-Berto-the-culprit-today?urn=box,235238. Retrieved on April 10, 2010.
danah boyd. (2008). *Taken out of context: American teen sociality in networked publics.* PhD Dissertation. University of California-Berkeley, School of Information. Available at http://www.danah.org/papers/TakenOutOfContext.pdf. Retrieved on April 10, 2010.
Gatson, S., & Zweerink, A. (2004). Ethnography online: 'Natives' practising and inscribing community. *Qualitative Research, 4*(2), 179–200. doi:10.1177/1468794104044431.
Hawksey, M. (2010). JISC 2010 conference keynotes with Twitter subtitles. In MASHe: The Higher Education blog from the JISC RSC Scotland North & East, April 19. Available at http://www.rsc-ne-scotland.org.uk/mashe/2010/04/jisc10-conference-keynotes-with-twitter-subtitles/. Retrieved on April 25, 2010.
Haydon, J. (2010). Amplify your nonprofit event with facebook's new live stream plugin. In John Haydon: Discussing social media marketing for non-profits, 30 April. Available at http://johnhaydon.com/2010/04/amplify-nonprofit-event-facebooks-live-stream-plugin/. Retrieved on July 6, 2010.
Heinz, F. (2010). Radio host suspended for "Dirty Mexicans" Tweet. In NBC Dallas-Fort Worth website, 26 April. Available at http://www.nbcdfw.com/news/sports/Radio-Host-Suspended-Following-Off-Color-Tweet-92120704.html. Retrieved on April 27, 2010.

Hemmi, A., Bayne, S., & Land, R. (2009). The appropriation and repurposing of social technologies in higher education. *Journal of Computer Assisted Learning*, 25, 19–30. doi:10.1111/j.1365-2729.2008.00306.x.

Hine, C. (2000). *Virtual ethnography*. London: Sage.

Hirst, T. (2010). OUseful.info, the blog... Available at http://blog.ouseful.info/. Retrieved on April 25, 2010.

IBM. (2010). IBM social computing guidelines: Blogs, wikis, social networks, virtual worlds and social media. Available at http://www.ibm.com/blogs/zz/en/guidelines.html. Retrieved on April 25, 2010.

JISC. (2009). Higher education in a Web 2.0 world: Report of an independent committee of inquiry into the impact on higher education of students' widespread use of Web 2.0 technologies. Available at http://www.jisc.ac.uk/publications/generalpublications/2009/heweb2.aspx. Retrieved on April 20, 2010.

Jones, S. (2009). Twitter fail at the Telegraph – #Telegraphfail? In Financial Times Alphaville Blog, April 20. Available at http://ftalphaville.ft.com/blog/2009/04/20/54882/twitter-fail-on-twitter-fall-at-the-telegraph/. Retrieved on April 20, 2010.

Kelly, B. (2010a). Amplified events: Plans for #IWMW10. In UK Web Focus, July 5, 2010. Available at http://ukwebfocus.wordpress.com/2010/07/05/amplified-events-plans-for-iwmw10/. Retrieved on July 6, 2010.

Kelly, B. (2010b). JISC-funded developments to Twapper Keeper. In TwapperKeeper Blog, April 16, 2010. Available at http://twapperkeeper.wordpress.com/2010/04/16/jisc-funded-developments-to-twapper-keeper/. Retrieved on April 20, 2010.

Kelly, B., Tonkin, E. and Shabajee, P. (2005). Using networked technologies to support conferences. *In: EUNIS 2005 Conference Proceedings*, n.p. Manchester: University of Manchester. Available at http://opus.bath.ac.uk/439/. Retrieved on July 5, 2010.

Kerawalla, L., Minocha, S., Kirkup, G., & Console, G. (2009). An empirically grounded framework to guide blogging in higher education. *Journal of Computer Assisted Learning*, 25, 31–42. doi:10.1111/j.1365-2729.2008.00286.x.

Library of Congress. (2010). How Tweet it is!: Library acquires entire Twitter Archive. In Library of Congress Blog, April 14. Available at http://blogs.loc.gov/loc/2010/04/how-tweet-it-is-library-acquires-entire-twitter-archive/. Retrieved on April 14, 2010.

Lundblad, N., & Masiello, B. (2010). Opt-in Dystopias. *Scripted*, 7(1), 155–165. doi:10.2966/scrip.070110.155.

McGill, K. (2010). Remote Audiences [abstract and summary]. In Sue Thomas (chair), *Action*. Transliteracy Conference 9 February, Digital Media Centre, Leicester, UK.

Morrison, M. (2009). A first stab at a perl script to create Twitter friend/follow matrices. In Mediaczar: a blog by Mat Morrison, 14 July. Available at http://mediaczar.com/blog/2009/07/a-first-stab-at-a-perl-script-to-create-twitter-friendfollow-matrices/.

OED Online (1989). *Amplification. In the Oxford English Dictionary* (2nd ed.). Oxford: Oxford University Press. Available at http://dictionary.oed.com/cgi/entry/50007582. Retrieved on July 6, 2010.

Owyang, J. (2010). List of social media measurement KPIs. Available at http://www.flickr.com/photos/jeremiah_owyang/4251106041/. Retrieved on April 20, 2010.

Service, R. (2010). The shame of Orlando Figgs. In guardian.co.uk Comment is Free, April 23. Available at http://www.guardian.co.uk/commentisfree/libertycentral/2010/apr/23/figes-shameful-admission

Shah, D. (2009). Twittergrader. Available at http://www.twittergrader.com/. Retrieved on April 10, 2010.
Siddique, H., & Carrell, S. (2010). Election 2010: Labour sacks candidate Stuart MacLennan in Twitter row. In guardian.co.uk, April 9. Available at http://www.guardian.co.uk/politics/2010/apr/09/stuart-maclennan-sacked-twitter-general-election. Retrieved on April 10, 2010.
Siegler, M. G. (2010). John Mayer predicts deadpool for Twitter. In TechCrunch, April 27. Available at http://techcrunch.com/2010/04/27/john-mayer-twitter/. Retrieved on April 20, 2010.
Williams, N. (2009). Template Twitter strategy for government departments. In Cabinet Office Digital Engagement Blog, 21 July 2009. Available at http://blogs.cabinetoffice.gov.uk/digitalengagement/post/2009/07/21/Template-Twitter-strategy-for-Government-Departments.aspx. Retrieved on April 10, 2010.

CONNECTING FANS AND SPORTS MORE INTENSIVELY THROUGH SOCIAL MEDIA

Karen Weaver

ABSTRACT

Many of the largest athletics programs in the United States today are dependent upon revenue streams to sustain their teams. While still in the earliest stages, athletic professionals are finding ways to deepen the engagement with potential and current fans and donors with their department's mission and values. Social media is being used to put fans in the seats as well as create new paid content. No longer limited to the column inches in a newspaper or 30 seconds of highlights on the local news, athletics programs are breaking new grounds in the world of social media.

Another area of campus that has seen a social media explosion is intercollegiate athletics. This chapter will bring the reader through the various techniques that collegiate athletics directors and their staffs have used "social networking" for decades to promote their teams. Today, using the latest internet technologies, they continue to embrace ways to further engage their already passionate fan base. Today's athletics departments are using social media in ways that academia is just beginning to embrace. Why was athletics such an early adopter of social networking? Because it has always sought out new revenues to pay for department expenditures, including facilities, personnel, and equipment.

Intercollegiate athletics has long been a haven for embracing technological advances in the chase for dollars and victories. Dating back to 1912 when the first college football game was aired on the radio, athletics directors have sought ways to spread the gospel about their teams (Watterson, 2000). Competitive advantages were sought through building bigger stadiums, selling more tickets, hiring and paying top coaches, and providing athletic scholarships to student athletes. When University presidents asked athletics directors to raise the money for their budgets – they did so through ticket sales, media broadcasts, sponsorships, and promotions with local businesses (Smith, 2001).

Athletics departments built early social networks through promoting and enhancing their teams to the local media and fans. Football teams in the 1930s and 1940s hired newspapermen to write about their teams and players. Colorful radio personalities were hired to describe the live events, describing the on the field action as if they were warring Greek city-states (Watterson, 2000). The stories of the game were repeated all week in preparation for the next week's battle. The University of Notre Dame spread their message one step further as they became "America's team" in the 1940s when Ronald Reagan famously played George Gipp (All-American halfback who died at age 25 in the movie *Knute Rockne, All American*; University of Notre Dame Football Archives). The Catholic Church saw football and film as ways to further promote the mission of this religious institution across the United States (Smith, 2001).

Colleges embraced television and radio as mediums in which to connect with fans and promote their teams. As television moved into the golden era of the 1950s and 1960s, network producers looked for more content to fill the airwaves of three or four national broadcasting companies (Smith, 2001). Saturday afternoon football soon became "must see TV" for thousands of fans who became enamored with the ability to watch a live game from hundreds of miles away in their living rooms. Television networks paid schools thousands of dollars for the right to broadcast those games, and created "shoulder" programming both before and after the games. Shoulder programming allowed local broadcasters to make even more money off of the separate shows, and to create highlight packages of video clips that could be shown during the week.

The demand for more information about teams led to the creation of media specialists who were housed within athletics departments and charged with compiling game-by-game statistics, weekly press releases and generally hobnobbing with the local media, all in the hopes of creating favorable publicity for their colleges. Newspapers in the 1940s enhanced this development through the creation of "Sports" pages dedicated to local, regional, and national sports news.

To gather all of the historical data in one place, athletic departments created "media guides" for the purpose of informing the media of all data related to the team. Coaches quickly realized the value of media guides for prospective recruits, describing in words and photos the athletic prowess of the program. Media guides soon became the vehicle to dazzle recruits and fans with the history and traditions of the team. Media guides can be thought of as an early version of a website.

COMPETING INTERESTS

Its easy to think of all of the above history as relating to one football team on one large University campus – schools like the University of Oklahoma and the University of Nebraska were clearly the darlings of their fan base, and a tradition developed of tuning into the Sooners, the Cornhuskers or other big name programs either on radio or television every fall Saturday afternoon (Watterson, 2000). But there are hundreds of other colleges that also played football and were competing for "column inches" in newspapers while negotiating with low wattage radio stations to broaden their fan bases. Small colleges like Mt. Union in Ohio and Amherst College in Massachusetts were known to have strong football programs in their local communities, but not much further.

Until the launch of the internet, small colleges and less well-known universities, struggled to gain the media exposure that seemed to follow the big time programs easily. Although they hired media relations specialists in their athletics departments who churned out the necessary press releases and updated their statistics, it was a challenge to compete against the big time teams both in revenue and in resources. Those teams that were located in a region of the country which offered a professional football team really struggled with getting any coverage, again limiting the amount of exposure a college could receive through traditional media outlets.

The lack of coverage trickled down to affect recruiting and fundraising too, leading schools to hire professionals in those roles to get the message out about their teams. Specialists were hired to design more glamorous brochures, build mailing lists, and host events to entertain potential donors and recruits. Schools adopted the old adage "you have to spend money to make money," some finding they were more successful at this than others. Alumni offices used sporting events to entertain wealthier graduates in the hopes that they would donate to the institution. Relationships with high school coaches were nurtured, as college coaches hoped to develop feeder systems from locally and regionally successful high school programs into their own programs.

LEVELING THE PLAYING FIELD

Spencer (2002) wrote of the potential for nonprofits (the "third" sector) to capitalize on their websites. She writes:

> Non-profits are typically a step behind for-profit and government organizations in capitalizing on new technology. The reasons are fundamental to their operation, lack of funding and technical expertise and a failure to see the importance of the Internet in fulfilling organizational objectives.

Campus athletics departments had developed a finely tuned relationship with the external constituencies in the late 1990s, using the latest email technology and beginning to think about the audio webcasting of their events through various online services. The driving vision was still around bringing people *to* something – a home event, a website, an in person event on campus. It was there campuses could engage their stakeholders. But as broadband technology (as opposed to dial up technology which used traditional telephone lines) expanded and was quickly adopted by thousands of sports fans that wanted the content delivered to them in real time, this began to impact on college athletics departments. Almost overnight, those who were able to upload video clips, provide live streaming of events, press conferences and real time updates of scores were acquiring more and more viewers to their website. Companies provided online counting of site visitors, which allowed for college fundraisers to start thinking of their website as potential revenue space, not just as a space for sports scores. Now, there was potential to make money or "monetize" the campus athletic website.

Except for the big time athletics programs, almost no small college athletics programs saw the opportunity in the early- to mid-2000s to build their websites as anything other than an information resource for teams, individuals, and fans. Some media relations professionals admitted anecdotally that they lacked the funding, the campus-wide integration and even the workload prioritization to effectively manage their websites with engaging new content. One told me "There were simply not enough hours in the day to prepare media guides, rosters, press releases, and maintain websites for every one of our teams." There was little thought given to anything other than providing information at a URL chosen with a snappy name. But the revolution was coming.

With the gradual adoption of spaces on the web like MySpace and Facebook for teenagers and college students, the mainstream media began to tout as a "cultural revolution." Tyler (2002) in his article "Is the Internet Changing Social Life?" differed with that view stating,

> The research reviewed in this issue makes it clear that the nature of people's relationship with others may have changed less because of the Internet than is often suggested. On the contrary, there are suggestions that the Internet may be a new way for people to do old things ... the Internet seems more like a new way to manage long-standing social needs than transformative technology that fundamentally changed patterns of either interpersonal or group processes. (pp. 195–196)

But perception is often reality, and shortly after Facebook, MySpace, and other social networking sites lifted their user restrictions, the floodgates opened. Soon, people of all ages joined to share the daily ups and downs of their lives. College groups were formed, invitations were sent out and advocacy groups were born as the common wisdom became "you have to connect with them where they are," meaning you could no longer expect teenagers and young adults to find your website (other than through Google) – you have to meet them where they are online – social networking sites. Tyler summarizes it when he states that the "Internet provides people with a technology that allows them to engage in activities" with greater efficiencies and a more "tailored" approach to their needs (p. 202).

TOOLS IN THE TOOLBOX

Athletics directors, coaches, alumni relations, and media professionals all need to consider the social media aspect of any outreach effort. Officials on smaller campuses would be well served to integrate athletics into the wider discussion of campus life and recruitment, as both sides need each other more today than ever. There is certainly a fair amount of talk on campuses of integrating all stakeholders – alumni, students, parents, fans, and the campus community; the opportunities to use social media to create efficiencies in this area are substantial.

Knowing that the average person uses the Internet to engage in activities that they like to do more efficiently, what kinds of things do college athletics programs need to be doing both today and in the future? Simply, they need to add some new tools to their toolbox.

Jamie Merisotas, President of the Lumina Foundation, addressed the issue of reinvention when he called upon higher education to utilize technology to create new engagement strategies. He implored leaders to learn from the struggles of the traditional news media, once thought of as the only way to learn the news of the day. Although Internet usage and technology have not made newspapers and magazines irrelevant, they certainly have speeded their decline in influence. Higher education risks that same hard fall if it does not realize that knowledge transference is no longer limited to traditional delivery methods.

> Higher education is, of course, different, but we should not lose sight of the obvious parallels. Economic conditions, changing learning styles, technology...all of these things are transforming the way people acquire and generate knowledge. We would do well to heed the lessons of the news media's experience and get ahead of the curve, making the necessary changes to our business model before circumstances dictate those changes. (Merisotas, 2009)

What tools do you choose? It depends on your target audience, your budget and your desired outcomes. Athletic departments would be wise to consider the following as they seek to collaborate across multiple social media sites, media platforms, and engagement strategies. First, is the activity designed to reduce costs or raise revenue? Although often thought to do both at the same time, the reality is that a strategy is usually one and not the other. Being clear with constituents about what your desired outcome is will help clarify the expected results. If you are fortunate enough to achieve both outcomes, so much the better.

Next, how do you manage multiple and competing interests within your department and your campus? Are there winners and losers in a particular strategy? For example, is your website designed to meet the needs of your internal campus population? External alumni? Fans coming to the game? Potential recruits? Being clear about what the goal is helps a department create a strategy for all stakeholders, not just the ones with the loudest voices. Do you assume that all stakeholders have access to broadband Internet? Should you assume that all stakeholders have access to the Internet at all? Today, there is still a huge cultural and economic divide that exists in the United States that higher education cannot afford to ignore. If your entire strategy is around the Internet, you may be missing a substantial athletic population. How do you reach them?

As you think about your social media strategy, is the goal to drive people to your website or to meet them on their turf? Will you develop a Facebook page, a Twitter feed, or a YouTube channel? How will your stakeholders know you are there – it is a good idea to provide easy links on each page of your site to remind people how to extend their engagement with your teams further through external sites. How will you engage them once they find you? What do you want them to do besides consume information in a different space?

Another good topic to consider at this point is how to address the emerging technology issues like smart phones, applications ("apps") and video broadband. It is important to also think about your brand at this point – does it translate well across multiple platforms? Make sure your website is "smart phone" friendly. When redesigning a website to include social networking, it is important to think about what the technology transfer from print to web to mobile device will do to your content and images.

As technology companies create more "hardware" (i.e. IPods, I Pads, Smart phones, Video on Demand (V.O.D.) portable players), they will seek out "software" to generate content. If you anticipate this development, will you be in position to be an early adopter of this technology and get your athletics program out in front? University of California at Berkeley did just this when they became the first campus to create their own YouTube channel, allowing their message to be broadcast on someone else's platform – for free.

Finally, and probably most importantly, what policies and procedures will you have in place to manage the institution's mission, brand, and philosophy? Do you take into consideration all possible applications for a technology purchase? For example, the Lower Merion School District (PA) decided to purchase webcam technology that could activate a laptop's webcam at any moment. It was bought with the idea that the software would be turned on only if the computer was reported stolen; the reality was that over 56,000 images were taken and recorded of high school students at home, most of whom did not report their laptops as missing. There were no written policies in place to regulate the cameras (Martin, 2010).

ATHLETICS AS THE ULTIMATE REALITY SHOW

Once you have decided the methods of delivery, what should your content look like? Emily Green, president and CEO of the Yankee Group, an independent research and technology consulting firm, speaks to the acronym F.I.R.E. – you should create Frequent, Interesting, Relevant, and Engaging content. There is not a much more engaging topic than sports in this country, and college sports have developed quite a following, too. Since all teams compete in multiple events throughout the season, frequency is an easy match. It seems logical that, when it comes to being a sports fan, you are already interested and engaged. Relevant? Sports are filled with winners and losers – it does not get much more relevant than that! Social Media and all forms of "new" media provide a host of opportunities for you to create fresh, engaging content.

Take a look around and consider the possibilities – as a college campus, there is a host of fresh content created daily. Social media can pitch the human-interest stories, telling your stakeholders why your star athlete chose your institution to continue her career; or why a particular group of athletes participates in a community outreach event. Even finding 2 or 3 of these over the course of a season brings the team into focus in a different way than wins and losses.

Speaking of wins and losses, social media is great for instantly updating folks on game results, but do this carefully. Many of your followers on Twitter may choose to "unfollow" you if they think you are giving them an unwanted play-by-play of a game they do not care about. Also, tweeting inside jokes or minutiae about a sport most are not familiar with will also disconnect you from your audience. Social media is a great vehicle for controlling your message, as long as you are clear in your own mind first what that message is.

Some teams choose to use social media as a way of providing historical context. For example, creating a daily "On this date, John Jones hit his first of what would be 100 career home runs" puts an athlete's accomplishments into context for your followers – it is relevant and interesting information for the average fan. Many coaches, including Duke University's Mike Krzyzewski, speak of each season as its own lifetime – it has a beginning, a middle, and an end, and you start all over again next year. Telling stories using social media allows your fans and friends to follow the season, one interesting tale at a time.

Other anecdotes of ways to engage and use social media come from my colleagues around the country. I utilized several groups on LinkedIn to ask the following question: How have you used social media as a professional tool? I received a number of interesting responses. Here are some:

> (I'm) using Facebook heavily in both Alumni Affairs and Athletics to assist with a data discovery project. That's a nice way of saying our central alumni data base is not as robust as we'd like, and we're using Facebook as a search engine of sorts to capture email addresses and constituent data.
> – VP for Institutional Advancement

> We have created our own athlete social network called _____4life.com. It operates just like Facebook but it is only available to former student athletes. The site allows former athletes to share what they are doing now and provides a portal to post reunion photos and news. We have links to our main website which keeps alumni informed on current athletics news and team schedules. This was just implemented early last year but early returns show more athletes reconnecting in this way. This obviously provides a link to future development and philanthropy.
> – Senior Associate Athletics Director

> In my travels I see quite a few ways of doing things. While it is not social media via a public or community domain; healthcare has certainly engaged this concept with Electronic Medical Records. This will be a major area of future development as Congress mandates EMR concepts, and require all medical providers to engage the concepts, or be penalized. Patients have the ability to access protected medical information and input data, to be seen by approved providers while they can likewise access their medical information from the providers. This will be a major development moving forward-and I see Sports Medicine making significant improvements to facilitate this process for students.
> – Consultant in Sports Medicine

It was important for two reasons:

(1) The "off the resume" references and for other references that the candidate might not even give me so that I can get a more honest assessment.
(2) To learn other history and info – literally where they worked and went to school (location); we recruited on a national level so let's say I want to recruit for a position for the Atlanta Falcons or Tampa Bay Rays, I would investigate if they went to college or ever worked in the Southeast part of the country; this would make my efforts more efficient because I would think twice about contacting someone with no ties or connection to a certain part of the country. – Headhunter

Alumni interaction, philanthropy, medical records, headhunting; all using technology to interface with people in new ways. It seems as if just merely reporting the score and standings has become the old standard; the new standard is building communities of people with common interests online.

SOCIAL MARKETING ACROSS MULTIPLE STAKEHOLDERS

What does a social media platform, a corporate partner, a high profile college athletic event, and a charity have in common? How does 450,000 online viewers sound? The headline said it all: *Coke Zero concert goes live on Facebook*. And it happened *outside of* the mega event known as the National Collegiate Athletic Association (NCAA) March Madness, the men's Division I basketball tournament. How did they pull this off?

Taking a page from the National Football League's Super Bowl playbook, the NCAA in the early 1990s began to add ancillary events to the three games held at the site of the Final Four. What started as a series of athletic challenges for fans morphed into entertainment options that promoted the NCAA's corporate partners. Coca Cola, long time partners of the NCAA, asked themselves "We refresh billions of people – globally – How can we take this event to people globally?" (Smith, 2010, p. 6).

By reaching out in extremely creative ways, they were able to bring a live concert to nearly half a million people worldwide. How did they do it? The complexity of negotiating the rights to broadcast the concert talent in conjunction with corporate partners who had no previous relationship to the talent was a challenge. Requiring unprecedented "rights" clearances from multiple parties proved to be the biggest obstacle, not the actually streaming of the event online.

In a word – social marketing. Each of the partners heavily promoted the event on their Facebook pages in the weeks leading up to the event. Coke, Papa John's Pizza, NCAA, CBS Sports Television, and the artists themselves each encouraged their fans on Facebook to log on and watch the free concert. The most unique idea of all came from the National Association of Basketball Coaches, the umbrella organization of collegiate men's basketball coaches. The group asked every one of their head coaches with a Twitter account to "tweet" to their followers the day before and the morning of the concert. The head coaches had over 30 million followers between them. The morning of the concert, the NABC urged the coaches to tell their followers "to order a Papa John's pizza on Facebook, and take part in the promotion that asks fans to insert the name of their favorite coach in the promo code when they order. Every time a coach's name is entered, $1 is donated" to cancer research (*ibid.*).

In all, media experts measured 70 million impressions were made through the event – all parties benefited from the cross-promotion. As a bonus, participants were permitted to use the video footage from the event on their own sites and platforms as "unique content." Is this the start of many other cross-promotional events using social media? Without a doubt.

PERSONAL BRAND PROMOTION TO BUILD YOUR NETWORK

Much of this chapter so far has focused on what institutions have done and can do to utilize the opportunities in social media. There is much storytelling to be done in intercollegiate athletics about our teams, our players, and our coaches. But athletic professionals are beginning to ask themselves how they can best utilize these new technologies to "brand" themselves in a very competitive job marketplace. How can they tell their own story? By using social media to build and enhance your own personal brand and strengthen your professional network, athletics professionals can help potential employers see the value they bring to a workplace.

How can social media help me build my professional network in athletics? Start with the assumption that athletics is a very small world. It lives by the old adage "it's not what you know, it's who you know." If a resume is about aggregating your work experience to a prospective employer, then social networking sites like LinkedIn present you as a real, multidimensional human being. LinkedIn, sometimes called the "professional" version of Facebook, provides several levels of engagement and access. The most basic level is free, and allows you to build your profile and connect with others who find you online. The next levels enter the paid content/access arenas, giving you greater understanding to the types of people you might be looking for as future employees or even future employers.

One of the biggest advantages to social networking online is the ability to see how your "connections" lead you to other people's connections. It literally is the old adage "six degrees of separation" – you are connected to everyone else in the world through six or less people. Building on the

Table 1. LinkedStrategies, an Online Site Dedicated to Leveraging LinkedIn, Surveyed Those Who Joined the Site and Found the Following Data.

Average Age: 41
Household Income: $109,703
Male: 64%
Household Income $100k+ 53.5%
Own Smartphone/PDA: 34%
College Graduate/Post Graduate: 80.1%
Business Decision Maker: 49%
Executive Vice President/Senior Vice President/Vice President: 6.5%
24% Have a Portfolio Value of $250k+
Job Titles:
   Chief-Level Executives 7.8% (Chief Operating Officer, Chief Information Officer)
   Executive Vice President/Senior Vice President 6.5%
   Senior Management 16%
   Middle Management 18%
50% Are Business Decision Makers in Their Companies (Kievman, 2010)

premise that you find your next opportunity (or your next one finds you) through connections, it is the virtual networking event, happening 24/7/365.

Professionals in collegiate athletics use the network in a number of ways. Once you have built your profile, and start to connect with colleagues (either through self-initiation or as suggested by LinkedIn), you will start to notice that there is a world of affinity groups created within the LinkedIn community. For example, in the world of collegiate athletics administration, the following groups exist:

- Sports Management Institute Alumni
- NACDA (National Association of Collegiate Directors of Athletics)
- Big Ten Athletics Staff
- Intercollegiate Athletics Administrators
- Drexel University Sport Management

There are thousands of groups you can join, all who have message boards, job boards, and discussion pages. Unfortunately, some people choose to use the space for promoting multilevel marketing ideas, etc. but occasionally I have found a good idea or created a new connection because of joint membership in a particular group (Table 1).

For intercollegiate athletics, this kind of market research is invaluable, as this demographic matches closely with the typical college sports fan. Recent data suggests that LinkedIn is adding one million new profiles per month (Hird, 2010).

TWITTER

Another way to engage fans, colleagues, and others is through using Twitter. Twitter provides an excellent opportunity to share small, significant bits of information with folks who have already demonstrated a level of interest in your teams, players, or coaches. It is also a great way to tell an alternative story about you. For example, by day, you might be a mild mannered marketing assistant, but after hours, you are a fantastic source of knowledge about baseball trivia. Believe it or not, there are folks who want to learn what you know. Twitter becomes a quick way to find a recruit like minds. Twitter is the "micro-blogging" avenue for engagement and discussion. Sure, there have been many jokes written about Twitter (why would I want to know what someone had for lunch?), but to a core group of 15 million active users out of the close to 75 million people who have accounts, Twitter has become another way to develop your "personal brand" (Hird, 2010).

Twitter is enough of a phenomenon that the Library of Congress recently announced it would begin to archive every "tweet" published since 2006 (Lohr, 2010). In fact, the Library of Congress has its own Twitter feed (http://www.twitter.com/libraryofcongress). "This is an entirely new addition to the historical record, the second-by-second history of ordinary people," said Fred R. Shapiro, associate librarian and lecturer at the Yale Law School (*ibid.*).

For these reasons, athletics departments have begun using Twitter. Penn State Abington created one in 2008 (http://www.twitter.com/abingtonsports) that publishes scores, great performances, and award winners to a small but loyal group of followers. Larger campuses have individual coaches tweeting to their fans, and sports information directors promote the national rankings of teams on their feeds. But how can you use Twitter to create your own personal brand, and even better, become a "thought leader?"

Those who have mastered this technology say it is changing the way we consume news. Paul Saffo (2008), the futurist academic currently at Stanford University, describes it this way:

> This time the Tweeters are kilometers ahead of the reporters, and Tweets are just the tip of a citizen journalism tsunami. Flickr is filling up with photos posted moments after being taken, and there is already an authoritative Wikipedia page up and running – and being updated in near real-time. I am certain that we will see multiple layers posted in Google Earth at any moment.

For sure, people who use Twitter are setting up their feeds in ways that allow them to customize the way they consume news and whom they choose to consume it from. Since the launch of Twitter in 2005, there have been many seminal moments in how people learned of these events: the crash of the USAir plane on the Hudson River, Michael Jackson's death, and the attempted government takeover in Iran in the summer of 2009. All events involved people on the scene chronicling their personal observations in real time. Saffo calls it a "citizen journalism tsunami," and he is right. Now, traditional news outlets struggle with breaking news stories at the same pace as the citizen journalist. Is Twitter the new CNN? Is the information for either source accurate? Can it be trusted? Who is held accountable if it is not? It becomes extremely important that athletics directors and their staff discuss what is and is not appropriate information to be shared on public sites. Just because you can post it quickly does not mean you should.

Early adopters of this medium began to write about creating your mission and your vision as to how to use the technology. Barack Obama's campaign was the first for a national candidate to embrace the medium as another tool to convey the message, and the campaign's ability to attract followers was key in his successful grassroots presidential campaign. The feed was another way to create a "call to action" – a means for engaging people to do something almost instantaneously. This call to action, or ability to engage, is critical in helping followers understand the value you bring to their lives.

As an example, in my role as a collegiate athletics administrator for over 15 years, I have a unique perspective inside the industry that very few people have. I know the shiny, bright spots of the industry, and I know the naked underbelly that exists, too. I am savvy in the language and the culture of the industry. My particular interest is in the business of college sports, and how it affects the future of the academy. Since I launched my Twitter feed in 2008, journalists around the country who are interested in having an insider's point of view for background information, or to quote for an upcoming story have picked up my Twitter feed.

Besides journalists, I have noticed my tweets attract an interesting mix of people outside of the athletics world. Academics interested in studying intercollegiate athletics have added me to their "must follow" lists so they can stay on top of the latest sports business news. Casual fans that like to follow the revenue and expense side of the house like to read along too. But the most surprising group? Gamblers. Maybe it is because of my account name (@collegeathlete), but I think they believe they are going to get some inside information that will give them a slight edge when they place their bets. Not from me, fellas. Move along, now!

FUTURE SHOCK

When this appears in print, the landscape will have already shifted – that's the challenge in trying to write about an industry that says something is "old" if it was created six months ago. However, since I maintain no personal gain for any of these ideas other than they make sense to me, let me offer some trends to keep an eye on in the next few years. First, integration will evolve and emerge as technologies evolve and emerge. Colleges will continue to feel, like most of the world, that technology is a "black hole" for spending – as soon as you invest in today's latest gizmo, here comes tomorrow's with even more bells and whistles. There will be a constant stream of products (hardware) that will try to merge the best content (software) and get you to pay for it. Chumby, the latest personal internet/information video device that promises to deliver information tailored to your interests in a small desktop/nightstand unit promises to customize the information you want when and where you want it (for only $14.95 per month!). It remains to be seen if people will adopt this, and other new forms of technology, and (more importantly) drop their old habits at the same time.

There is a move afoot to merge social media content with video technology. This is already happening as traditional cable companies like Verizon FIOS put Facebook and Twitter on their screens so people can multitask on their service. Many people who use laptops today will tell you they are "dual-screeners" – they watch television while surfing the Internet. Content providers are already doing this through text message engagement. Relief agencies such as the American Red Cross have discovered a compelling call to action through asking citizens to text their donations to relief efforts to a specific number, allowing them to capitalize on the emotion of the moment. Look for even more organizations to embrace this in the very near future.

As more colleges look for alternative revenue streams to offset sagging state and Federal support, technology would appear to provide opportunities to create paid content. On demand or pay per view video content, live game feeds and other similar productions have allowed college athletics departments to add new dollars to their budgets. Fans from across the country and around the world can log on to view a game for $4.95–9.95 per event, creating an instant new source of income. Obviously, there are production requirements that mandate an upfront infrastructure investment, but it is fairly simple arithmetic to determine where one's break-even point might be. The harder part might be determining what people are willing to pay for versus what they expect to get for free.

Technology leaders are constantly looking for the next great trend to emerge. Green, from Yankee Group, believes that the video game revolution that produced systems like the Xbox, PlayStation and Wii, have captivated and engaged people in their leisure time; she wondered, is there a way to use these existing platforms to merge technologies? An intriguing thought revolves around the merging of these ideas – can colleges create and then compete in these virtual worlds that are born in video game? This may be something to consider when developing an integrated marketing plan. Collegiate teams are already used in video games (like the NCAA Football video games). Consider tying in the sponsors and signage and add another layer of new revenues if you decide to explore virtual games.

Speed always matters and it appears that the new 4G networks will allow for even more wireless capabilities. It remains to be seen if it will finally replace the traditional coaxial cable that has appeared in nearly every home and workplace for the last 30 years. This has profound implications for those programs that choose to partner with a cable distributor like Comcast, Time Warner, or Cox Cable. How should colleges position themselves to be ready for the next wireless revolution?

Apps, apps and more apps – it seems as if the world cannot get enough of specific applications for mobile devices. News outlets have put the number "at well over 100,000" for now – and with open. The strategy comes when determining how to rise above the cacophony. With all of this change going on, how do colleges continue to differentiate themselves from their competitors, reach their prospective students, and speak to their alumni and friends in this new medium? Can they effectively engage and aggregate their stakeholders?

Technology has leveled the playing field for large and small colleges and universities. One thing is certain – doing nothing is not an option. Collegiate athletics departments are compelled to be in certain spaces and places or they risk being irrelevant. In today's marketplace, differentiating oneself is the key to surviving. Not always known for being nimble, the academe and intercollegiate athletics stands at the edge of a revolution – who will be the new King?

REFERENCES

Hird, J. (2010). *20+ mind-blowing social media statistics revisited.* E-Consultancy. Available at http://econsultancy.com/blog/5324-20+-mind-blowing-social-media-statistics-revisited. Retrieved on May 8, 2010.

Kievman, N. (2010). *Why you must master Linked In Strategies*. LinkedStrategies. Available at http://www.linkedstrategies.com/blog/linkedin-stats-why-you-must-master-linkedin.htm. Retrieved on May 8, 2010.
Lohr, S. (2010). Library of congress will save tweets. *New York Times*, April 14, 2010. Available at http://www.nytimes.com/2010/04/15/technology/15twitter.html. Retrieved on May 8.
Martin, J. (2010). *Lower Merion report: Web cams snapped 56,000 images*. Philadelphia Inquirer. Available at http://www.philly.com/philly/news/breaking/20100419_Lower_Merion_details_Web_cam_scope.html. Retrieved on May 8, 2010.
Merisotas, J. (2009). Engaging multiple stakeholders to ensure college access and success for all. Speech given to Governor's Conference on Higher Education, State College, PA March 17. Available at http://www.luminafoundation.org/about_us/president/speeches/2009-03-17.html. Retrieved on May 11, 2010.
Saffo, P. (2008). News no longer breaks – it Tweets. Available at http://www.saffo.com/journal/entry.php?id=964&pg. Retrieved on May 8, 2010
Smith, R. A. (2010). Coke zero concert goes live on facebook. *Sports Business Journal*, *13*(1), 6–7.
Smith, R. A. (2001). *Play-by-play: Radio, television, and big time college sport*. Baltimore: Johns Hopkins University Press.
Spencer, T. (2002). The potential of the internet for non-profit organizations. *First Monday*, *7*(8). Available at http://firstmonday.org/issues/issue7_8/spencer/index.html
Tyler, T. (2002). Is the internet changing social life? It seems the more things change, the more they stay the same. *Journal of Social Issues*, *58*(1), 195–202.
University of Notre Dame Football Archives. Available at http://www.und.com/sports/m-footbl/archive/allambios/nd-m-footbl-gipp.html. Retrieved on May 8, 2010.
Watterson, J. S. (2000). *College football: History, spectacle, controversy*. Baltimore, MD: Johns Hopkins University Press.

ATHLETICS AND SOCIAL MEDIA BLOGS

The Sports Networker. Available at http://www.sportsnetworker.com/
Women Talk Sports. Available at http://www.womentalksports.com/items/read/4/151587
Sports, Media and Society. Available at http://sportsmediasociety.blogspot.com/
The Ocean Agency Blog. Available at http://www.theoceanagency.com/blog/20090720/sports-and-social-media-building-a-community/
College Sports Business. Available at http://Collegeathlete.blogspot.com

PART IV
SOCIAL MEDIA AND ALUMNI RELATIONS

ENGAGING ALUMNI AND PROSPECTIVE STUDENTS THROUGH SOCIAL MEDIA

Eric Kowalik

ABSTRACT

Social media provides institutions an opportunity for a new level of engagement with prospective students, alumni, donors and community members. This chapter begins with an overview of social media in higher education, who is using it and for what, then provides a few talking points to consider with others before beginning a push into social media. The remainder of the chapter includes a few examples of ways in which social media are used to engage alumni and prospective students, including utilizing Twitter as a free SMS service to provide updates to prospective students during their recruitment, creating an iPhone application for alumni weekend as both an information and engagement tool, and using live tweets from alumni during homecoming to provide an authentic look at the day's events.

The Web is changing the focus of modern advertising, which for many years was focused on drawing associations from the physical qualities of products to the unfulfilled yearnings of potential customers.

Erich Fromm (1969) compared modern advertising methods of influence to hypnosis:

> All these methods are essentially irrational; they have nothing to do with the qualities of the merchandise, and they smother and kill the critical capacities of the customer like an opiate or outright hypnosis. (p. 128)

The value of emotion in web copy cannot be overemphasized, as Veloso (2009) states, "People buy on emotion and justify with logic. Emotion is such a powerful element of the online sales process; the most important objective of a salesperson, marketer, or copywriter is to deliver an emotional experience during the sales presentation" (p. 161).

Despite the focus on traditional psychology in the advertising process, the web has created a new type of customer who is becoming immune to the hard sell of traditional marketing. If you need to sell it, it may not be worth buying. You do not need to sell the iPad. It sells itself, you just need to demo it to the customer. What the Web, blogs, and social media reflect is a customer revolt. The Web is a more rational space. The Web thrives in open, questioning cultures. The Web is not about technology, but psychology.

According to McGovern (2010a), a new type of customer is emerging. This customer is less emotional and more rational. This customer does not believe in blind faith. They are on the Web to research, compare, to find out for themselves. They wish to search out the views of others like them who have also bought the product rather than obediently accepting the organization's message.

If you want to be successful in engaging with this sort of customer then you need to think of them as an inquisitive stranger. Relentlessly focus on helping customers understand your product, service, and/or experience – not its advertisements. Marketing your institution should focus on engaging with the customer and showing them the desirable products, services, and/or experiences.

Sure, you can sell a brick. But when the good vibes are gone (and so are you) the buyer is left with ... a brick. That is not a sustainable long-term strategy. Social media provides you the opportunity to humanize stories of students and alumni of your institution, which can create loyalty and earn future business (students), and ultimately their respect (Solis, 2008).

The Conversation Prism graphic (Fig. 1), created by Brian Solis, provides a living, breathing representation of Social Media meant to evolve as services and conversation channels emerge, fuse, and dissipate.

Engaging Alumni and Prospective Students through Social Media

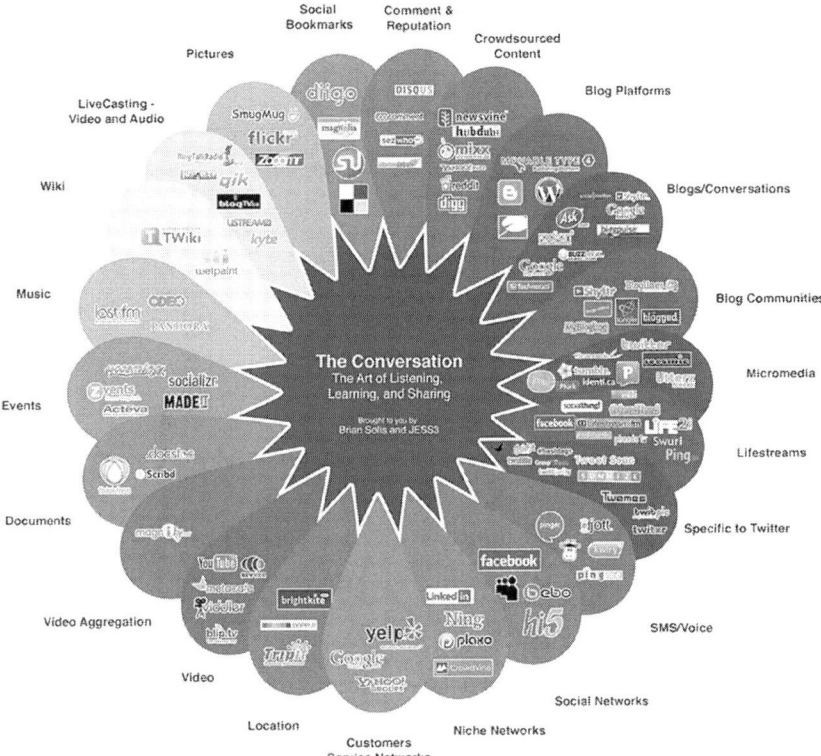

Fig. 1. Citation: "Conversation Prism." Infographic. Brian Solis. Briansolis.com. July 6, 2010. <http://www.briansolis.com>

Your organization is in the center of the prism and whether you are observing, listening, or participating, a conversation about your organizations and its products are always happening and these conversations can impact and influence your business and brand. As conversations are increasingly distributed, everything begins with listening and observing. Doing so, will help you identify exactly where relevant discussions are taking place, as well as their scale and frequency. This dialog can be charted into a targeted social map that is unique to your brand (Solis, 2008).

This chapter begins with an overview of social media in higher education, who is using it and for what, then provides a few talking points to consider with others before beginning a push into social media. The remainder of the chapter includes a few examples of ways in which social media was used to engage alumni and prospective students, including a couple of projects the author worked on directly.

WHERE ARE WE?

Before beginning a discussion on any subject it is important to provide a broader context before delving into the details. Below is a look at the higher education social media environment. In July 2008 higher education Web, marketing, and communication professionals subscribed to the uweb, HighEdWeb, and SUNY CUADnet listservs were asked to complete a survey about their university's use of social media (Reuben, 2008).

The 148 unique responses from 4 different countries: the United States, Australia, Canada, and New Zealand, shed some light on the social media landscape in higher education.

- Over half (53.79%) of the institutions reported having an official Facebook page for their campus, and 20 of them have developed a custom application for Facebook.
- Only 21.9% report having an official presence on MySpace, with only one responder indicating they created a custom application for MySpace.
- Nearly 67% did not have an official Twitter account for their campus, and about 64% did not have an official Flickr account.
- Just over half had an official presence on YouTube and nearly 60% had some form of blogs on their site.
- Only 17% reported using delicious, a community bookmarking website in which users can save Web pages they find and share them with other users.

The survey also asked for input on staff time for managing these social media endeavors and what the intended purposes of these activities were. Respondents reported the overwhelming majority of these tools were maintained by one or more individuals in either their marketing, communications, or public relations office.

Communication with current students and alumni was the most widely reported use and most organizations spent 1–4 h a week updating their Facebook. Those respondents that reported having an official Flickr account, nearly 43% said their marketing, communications, or public relations office maintained their presence and use was split pretty evenly between sharing photos with current students, faculty, staff, and alumni. The majority of respondents reported spending 1–4 h a week adding photos to Flickr. YouTube appeared to be used primarily for recruitment purposes (29.50%), with some using it to share videos with current students and alumni. Most reported spending 1–4 h a week adding videos to their channel.

Despite the survey results showing an active push in higher education to utilize social media for marketing and engagement, some may still be skeptical or skittish of investing time and resources into social media.

Surveys show, however, that more and more prospective students and younger alumni are joining social networks. More than half of America's teens and young adults use social networking sites, and more than one-third of all Internet users engage in social networking (Jones & Fox, 2009).

Although the predominant users of social networking are young adults; three-quarters of adult Internet users under age 25 have a profile on a social networking site (Lenhart, 2009); the popularity of these sites is attracting more and more adult users. In 2005, only 8% of adult Internet users had an online profile; today, that number has more than quadrupled to 35% (Lenhart, 2009).

Social networking site users are also regular visitors, with more than one-third checking their profile page daily and almost another 25% visit every few days. Among teens, these numbers are higher – almost half said they logged into their profile at least once a day and about one-third visit weekly. In one study of college students, males and females were equally likely to have profiles on social networking sites and were found to spend about 3 h each day on the sites (Raacke & Bonds-Raacke, 2008), while two studies reported that the students limited themselves to an average of 10–30 min each day (Ellison, Steinfield, & Lampe, 2007; Valenzuela, Park, & Kee, 2009).

But according to the E-Expectations Class of 2007 Report, 80% of the high school students surveyed said they had not looked for a school they were considering attending on MySpace or Facebook. Only 27% reported having read a blog written by a current student and 21% by a faculty member at a college they were considering (Noel-Levitz, 2007).

Recent research is also showing that "older" users are the fastest growing group in the social media demographic. More than 50% of Facebook's members in the United States are 35 or older, and only 26.8% are 24 or under, according to an analysis of December 2009 visitors by comScore Media Metrix (Stross, 2010). Twitter is also growing rapidly among "older" users according to Nielsen, with 35–49-year-olds making up almost 42% of the traffic to Twitter.com.

So why consider investing in social media? The social media environment contains both your prospective students and alumni, making it a great place to interface with them about your institution and programs. People are also using traditional communication sites and services (think webmail, IM, and discussion groups) less and less and choosing to use Facebook and other social networks instead. Nielsen Online, an analytics firm that tracks time spent online at various websites, issued a report in March 2009 finding that throughout 2008 social networking sites and blogs saw more time spent by users than personal email.

Even if this data still leaves you unconvinced to make a foray into social media, then consider it the 10% of the 70:20:10 resource allocation rule suggested by Dick Damrow: 70% of marketing dollars should go to the programs and media that you know work; another 20% should go to new ideas to be tested; and the final 10% should be allocated to new emerging media (Sevier, 2007).

Do not underfund what already works at your institution to substantially invest in what may not, but at the same time, at least some 10% strategies will be in the 70% area in future years.

Noel-Levitz (2007) suggests that social networking can be a great resource for recruitment efforts, and could be very beneficial to your program. However, they still believe the majority of your focus should be strengthening the experience perspective students have on your official website.

Brad J. Ward (2009), who ran Butler University's admissions office social media efforts, suggests that without a solid website, you are like the homeowner who is building on sand. As a homeowner, you want to make sure your house has a solid foundation. If you build on a bad one, you might be all right in the short run but you are as good as done over time. No one wants to build on a bad foundation, and your social media efforts should be no different.

Social media provides new avenues to reach out to people, connect with them, engage in a conversation and foster a relationship. But currently a prospective student cannot apply to your school through Facebook and a donor cannot give a gift via Twitter.

The end goal is to funnel the individual to your website where they can take action, i.e. apply to your school, get more information, give a donation. Your institution can do the most creative things on Facebook, Twitter, or YouTube, but if the student gets to your site and cannot figure out the call to action, the action that is requested by a marketer's content (either from an advertising banner or website copy) such as how to apply or find information about a degree, you have failed. Do not let the goodwill you have built through social media be destroyed by a poorly functioning website. Before you establish why you are using social networks, examine your foundation, i.e. your institution's website.

TO TWEET OR NOT TO TWEET?

Just because you can do something does not mean you should. Although there are plenty of reasons to have a presence on Facebook, Twitter, or other social media outlets, before jumping in with both feet, take a step back, and evaluate the realm of social media at your institution and ensure you have the necessary support, both politically and staff wise to do it right.

1. *Do you have the resources?* Is there someone at your institution who is a social media practitioner? The kind of person who understands the world of social media networks and how to move among them like a native.
2. *Do you have the experience?* Although the gap is closing, there is still a big difference between surfing the web and marketing an institution. Your social media practitioner needs to not only have a working knowledge of social media outlets, but also know how to interact professionally and sell effectively. Remember, your institution's reputation is always on the line. Davenport University in Grand Rapids, Michigan recruited someone to do just this. The position is Social Media Manager, with responsibilities that include implementing, advancing, and measuring Internet communications and social media for the University.
3. *Do you have the money?* To do social media right, you need to invest time into developing a strategy and design, as well as ongoing updates. Time equals money, and unless you can hire your own social media practitioner like Davenport University, your staffer probably will have other responsibilities. Can you schedule them for the hours required to really manage your social media platforms? Expect to spend anywhere from 1 to 10 h a week when using social media as part of the marketing mix, depending on how many tools you use, how actively they are used by your audiences, and how extensive your presence is in each.
4. *What is your central marketing team doing?* This advice is for departments or schools inside a university. Check with your central marketing team to ensure that your efforts are brand-compliant and not duplicative. Your central communications office may already have a wealth of social media experience you can draw on. Even if they are not doing anything it never hurts to build cross-departmental relationships.
5. *What are the compelling stories?* Find the stories that humanize your institution and its constituents, i.e. students, staff, faculty, donors, etc. If possible create the story in multiple forms, written, video vignettes, and audio stories to provide different ways for visitors to access and distribute your stories.

Consider your answers to these questions before embarking on a social media campaign. There are plenty of ways to engage prospective students and alumni, in the social media realm, and the next two sections provide real world examples of ways social media were utilized to engage alumni, prospective students or both.

ALUMNI

It is important to reiterate that all fundraising, social media driven or not, is about building relationships and communities; stewarding your supporters and asking appropriately (both in terms of amount given and frequency of asks). This is not unique to social media or anything else.

Involved alumni are alumni who will give, and then ask how they can do more. If a college knows how to cultivate and engage its alumni, it is well on the way to financial health and growth. Although the benefits of utilizing social media are plentiful, alumni offices, with limited human and financial resources, can now reach a growing number of graduates. It still requires work, creating a Facebook page and Twitter account is just the beginning.

Unlike a traditional fundraising job, where there is an existing community of alumni donors and friends that have a relationship with the organization, the first day you begin a social media offering, you are not part of a community nor do you have any initial followership. This is why it is important when creating your institutions' social media community to build credibility with in it and cultivate your position.

Technology, while an important component of an effective process, is not as important as the people behind it. Do not hand the task to an intern or entry-level staffer and expect it to succeed. The worst thing an institution can do is put something out there for a few months and then abandon it. You have got to make sure you have the organizational stamina to commit to doing something like this by assigning a senior-level owner to the community.

Information overload is another pitfall. Adding information to a social network is an inexpensive way to alert thousands of people about alumni events or graduates' achievements. But the messages, if they arrive too frequently, can be perceived as spam, poisoning the relationship between the college, and the graduate. Social media is particularly effective in engaging younger alumni who are not responding to traditional marketing campaigns.

Madell and Muncer (2007) while researching people aged 18–20 on why they chose to use certain communication media, especially the Internet and mobile phones for social purposes discovered participants indicated that different communication media afforded them differing levels of control over their social interactions. Research by Shao (2009) into the popularity of user-generated media (UGM) sites such as YouTube, MySpace, and Wikipedia showed that one of the reasons behind the popularity was the sense of control users have over the creation and sharing of content. Traditional marketing campaigns targeted at younger alumni may not be successful because these individuals like control over their social interactions and want the ability to engage in conversation and content creation, something the social media environment can offer.

According to Tolliver Nigro's (2010) interview with Kate Dunn, president of a strategic marketing firm, institutions need to go where their young alumni are and that means incorporating social media into a cross-channel marketing strategy that incorporates social media, not as an afterthought, but as part of a cohesive, integrated approach. Dunn talked of working with clients that were sending the same piece to a 22 year old as they did to a 50 year old. Of course younger alumni were not going to respond to that. For the institutions the question became how to find these young alumni and how to engage them. In most cases they are on Facebook, so once an institution has found them, how do you go about engaging them so that they shall respond to fund-raising efforts in the future? The goal is simply to get alumni talking. It's the difference between a campaign and a conversation.

Once they are talking to you, they are more likely to give when your institution asks. Solicitations are not going to be directly through Facebook, although there will be status updates and reminders on the wall. Facebook's value is getting younger alumni re-engaged with their institution's community. Once they are re-engaged, they are more likely to give. It also makes them more aware of direct mail coming from the institution. Do not start the conversation with a tin cup out saying, "Give me money," that can cause an irreparable break in the relationship. It has to be part of an overall strategy.

In 2006 during my time as Assistant Director of Communication at University of California Irvine's Donald Bren School of Information and Computer Sciences our school wanted a way to create a more dynamic alumni chapter, one that would provide a way to connect the current students with the alumni. The current alumni chapter website was difficult to update and only a few members had access. The Associate Director of Development in conjunction with the Director of Communications suggested creating a blog, which would allow all members of the alumni chapter to create posts.

The goal for the blog was to create an open forum where students and alumni could come for a variety of reasons, i.e. students could seek advice from alumni, alumni could be profiled showing current students what career paths were available for them, and for alumni to reflect and discuss graduate student experiences. During initial meetings with the leadership of the alumni chapter usage policies were established both on how often posts needed to be made and how user comments and interactions would be handled.

When making an entrance into the world of social media, ensure your institution first creates a written and thought out usage policy. You cannot plan for every contingency but it is better to have a sound framework to consult when an issue arises than attempting to make it up on the fly. With ground rules in place and strong support from the school's leadership, the blog was launched. Despite some slow initial growth in the amount of posts, the blog has since grown into a thriving community which has included posts on various topics such as an alumnus documenting his experience attempting to get into business school, insight into careers in consulting, and an alumnus hosting a Thanksgiving get together for fellow alumni.

Including the blog in alumni advertising and the school's other social media endeavors such as their Facebook and YouTube presence have helped sustain and grow the community.

Success with the blog inspired our school to attempt another foray into social media engagement during UC Irvine's 2009 Homecoming in which our school utilized Twitter to allow alumni in attendance to tweet their experiences so those who were not at the event could still get a sense of the experience.

Homecoming is an annual event hosted by the UC Irvine Alumni Association during a Saturday in which there is an evening men's basketball game. During the afternoon there is a street festival with games and activities and each school has a table set up where they can distribute information and as a general meeting point for alumni to reconnect with the school or meet up with fellow alumni.

Live tweeting was advertised to Bren School alumni via the alumni blog and email announcements regarding homecoming. Alums were told that if they were attending the event they could provide a first hand account of their Homecoming experience by sending updates to their Twitter account with hashtag #brenics. Utilizing a free script called TwitterZoid, a page was created on the Bren School website that displayed all mentions of tweets with the hashtag #brenics. The day of Homecoming a large graphic was placed on the Bren School homepage, that when clicked, would take visitors to a page listing all the tweets with the hashtag #brenics.

Only a handful of alumni tweeted their experience but they did a good job capturing the events of the day and the emotion of the basketball game that ended up going down to the last basket.

Unlike an after the fact article in an alumni magazine or newsletter, the raw commentary of real alumni provided a unique personal record of Homecoming in real time for those who could not attend.

Princeton provides another example of utilizing social media to engage alumni by enhancing their experience during the annual alumni reunion. Andrew Gossen, Senior Associate Director at the Alumni Association of Princeton University, shared the experience on the Alumni Futures blog with Shaindlin (2009).

Looking for a way to reduce costs, nearly $10,000 to print 9,500 brochures listing reunion events and activities as well as enhance the reunion experience, Princeton created a mobile friendly site called Reunions Mobile (http://m.princeton.edu/reunions/).

Attendees would be able to optimize their participation, increase their ability to connect with friends and classmates on campus, and keep track of the what, where, and when of events to get the most out of their reunion experience. The site was heavily advertised through traditional marketing methods in order to reach as many alumni as possible. PAW, Princeton's alumni magazine, did a story on Reunions Mobile on their blog, the class reunion chairs were also asked to include it in their final messaging to their classmates, and put it up on their class websites.

During the Reunion event the URL was on posters at reunion headquarters, in heavy-traffic areas around campus and the link was included on the inside cover of the print brochure.

The reunion was held from May 28 through May 31 and according to Gossen between May 22 and May 31 there were:

- 4,170 visits to the mobile site
- 1,590 unique visitors
- 15,368 page views

For context, about 9,000 Princeton alumni (and about 20,000 total visitors) are on campus at the peak of the Reunions weekend. As for the mobile web site: 53% of visitors used the Safari browser on an iPhone, and 65% of users were on some kind of Apple handheld device. From this data Gossen drew these conclusions:

- Reunions Mobile worked well enough to serve as a primary source of information about Reunions for users of iPhones and other higher-end mobile devices.

- The team received positive feedback and constructive suggestions for future versions. Graduating seniors used the site, as did alumni at least back to the classes of the early 1970s.

Princeton spent about $7,000 to build, test, and roll out the site and for Gossen it was well worth the time and effort. For alumni interested in this type of technology, the added value went beyond the utility of being able to access the info on their smartphones. Alumni were also really happy to see that Reunions is evolving in response to changes in the broader social and technological environment.

As smartphones garner a larger share of the market, sites like Reunions Mobile will become an increasingly realistic alternative to, or replacement for, printed brochures and schedules while allowing users to connect with other alumni and the institution. There are already free open source applications such as the Massachusetts Institute of Technology Mobile Web app which allow schools to easily create a version of their website offering up-to-date information, optimized for different types of mobile devices. Viewers can use this mobile friendly version to find people, places, events, course news, shuttle schedules, and more. All you need is a mobile device with a web browser and either WiFi or a data plan.

PROSPECTIVE STUDENTS

The Web reflects a shift to service and, more particularly, a shift to self-service. To succeed in self-service you need a genuine understanding of, and relationship with, your customer. And you must also strive to give them a fast, simple experience.

This is just as true in the real world. According to McGovern (2010b), Starbucks is investing millions in replacing their espresso machines. These machines are in perfect working order, so why are they replacing them? They want machines that are not as high, so that the server and the customer can more easily see and interact with each other. Understanding, relating to and developing empathy for your customer (prospective student) is one of the greatest drivers of clarity in communication and social media is a way to get to truly know your customers.

A look at for-profit colleges shows the benefits of engaging and striving to know about your students. Enrollment in the country's nearly 3,000 career colleges has grown far faster than in the rest of higher education – by an average of 9% per year over the past 30 years, compared with only 1.5% per year for all institutions, according to an industry analyst (Zernike, 2009). For-profit universities now educate about 7% of the nation's roughly 19 million students who enroll at degree-granting institutions each fall. And the proportion rises to 10%, or 2.6 million, if you count students who enroll year round (Zernike, 2009). Just this academic year, the University of Phoenix eclipsed California State University as the second largest higher-education system in the country, with 455,600 students (Zernike, 2009). Harris N. Miller, president of the Career College Association, says if the growth curve for proprietary schools continues, they could be educating more students than any other sector of higher education worldwide by 2020.

For-profit universities spend a lot of money to get students in the door. For the 3-month period ending November 30, 2009, the Apollo Group spent $275-million on "selling and promotional" expenses, or about 20% of its total net (Zernike, 2009).

Although nonprofit educational institutions often do not have similar advertising budgets to get students in the door, the world of social media provides a cost effective way to engage with prospective students and build a meaningful relationship that can increase the odds of a student matriculating to the institution. The initial discussion will hover around whether to build your own social network or become part of a popular existing one such as Facebook.

Steven Infanti, director of communications and marketing at Harrisburg University of Science and Technology (Pa.), is an advocate of colleges creating their own sites. Harrisburg University's single sign-on web portal, Jenzabar Internet Campus Solution (JICS), was implemented in fall 2006. Infanti says the "portal better allows new students to situate themselves as part of the Harrisburg University community" (Sevier, 2007). Admitted students can access a portal just for them, and those who then choose Harrisburg University get access to an enrolled students' portal. Besides institutional information, notes Infanti, the portals offer community checklists for important dates and future plans, chat tools, and other ways to meet people. The portals take the best of social networking and limit it to the Harrisburg University community.

"We want students to connect with each other, our professors, and our administrators. This is the medium to do so. In the future, we will look at giving parents of admitted students their own portal," he said (Sevier, 2007).

However it's very difficult to gauge the effectiveness of social networks beyond running simple traffic reports. There is also the argument that since the majority of prospective students are already on Facebook and Twitter why not engage them where they are instead of trying to lure them to an institutions homegrown social network.

At the Bren School we looked at utilizing Twitter to engage prospective students even if they did not have an account on Twitter or knew what it was. I originally heard of using Twitter as a free SMS service from Brad J. Ward, who utilized it for the same purpose when he was working in the Butler University admissions office.

First, we established a Twitter account, @brenadmissions, which is where we would push updates to students. When creating a Twitter account be specific with the name and do not view it strictly as an admissions tool. An account could also be used as a way to announce athletic content scores without having to sign up with an SMS vendor.

After you get your account, you just need to tell people how to follow and then set up your page. At the Bren School we placed a call to action on our Bren:10 prospective student website and also on the web form prospective students would fill out to request additional information via mail.

Before publicizing this be sure to test it on a cell phone and walk through the process on your own.

1. Student sends a text to 40404 that says follow brenadmisions
2. If student is not on Twitter, then it will ask them to confirm their name
3. Student responds with name
4. Twitter then sets up an account for the student and gives them general Twitter advice
5. Student is notified how to opt out
6. You send your updated news from the Twitter account and it pushes straight to their cell phone.

Students do not even have to know about Twitter. To streamline the process, an institution can utilize Really Simple Syndication (RSS), a web publishing technology that allows end users to automatically receive new digital content from your institution, which can then be added to a site such as Twitterfeed.com to push updates without the need to login to Twitter and make manual updates.

From a marketing perspective this is the best option to get your content in front of a prospective student. When their phone vibrates or rings the student will instinctively look at the message and be reminded of your school. There is no filter, no direct mail piece getting lost in the shuffle on the kitchen table, no phone call that is sent straight to voice mail or email lost in a sea of other messages. This method is a great way to remind students of upcoming admission deadlines, your school's appearance at local college fairs or announcements of interesting speakers or sporting events. You could even hold contests offering free tickets to an athletic event or a bookstore gift certificate if the first correct email response to a trivia question is received.

Remember to be up front about your privacy policy in regards to how you will handle the users data and be sure to explicitly tell users after they have signed up, how to opt out of receiving further messages if they so choose. The Mobile Marketing Association recommends it is fundamental to the concept of control that a subscriber maintains the ability to stop participating and receiving messages when desired (Mobile Marketing Association, 2010).

Flickr, the online photo sharing website, is another tool that can be used to effectively engage prospective students and sell them on the experience of attending your institution. Prospective students are looking for the truth about college life at your institution online and they are definitely bound to look for real photos taken by their peers already enrolled at your university.

Paul Stamatiou, a student at Georgia Tech as well as a popular blogger, explained in February 2005 in an exchange with one of his readers, Michael, that he did use Flickr to get a feel about the institutions he was considering:

> When I was accepted into Georgia Tech, I wasn't able to visit until the summer. I had gotten into a blind agreement, but then I just hit up Flickr and was thoroughly impressed with the photos I found so I wasn't shocked or anything when I finally got a chance to visit. I also did the same thing with the other 9 or 10 colleges (yeah, I applied to a lot of schools) I was accepted into. (Joly, 2006)

Michael, apparently a student from American University, then added:

> Another thing about college + flickr is that University Students are more likely to post and tag photos on flickr than say ... older folks. Using flickr like this is cool because you see the college campus without bias and really get a sense for what the campus is like. Plus, it's a great way to find out about the people who attend the college, which I find important. (Joly, 2006)

One way to showcase your "real" institution is to create a Flickr group and allow users to post photos to it. Amherst College, Simmons College and California State University, Chico are good examples of this concept. Amherst has a webpage in their alumni website devoted to informing visitors of the Flickr group and encouraging them to share their photos and videos with others who have an interest in the college. Each week Amherst selects a photo from the Amherst College Flickr Group to feature on the alumni homepage. The ability to comment on photos posted in the group provides an opportunity to engage prospective students with stories about the events of the photo, whether it is an athletic event or a unique campus experience.

CONCLUSION: IT IS ALL ABOUT TRUST

The Internet originally drew people because of the anonymity it offered (McKenna & Bargh, 2000). Today with the maturation of social networking sites people are shedding that anonymity and are utilizing the Internet to socialize with others (Jones & Fox, 2009).

In the social media realm where individuals have a belief that they do not want to be marketed to, how do you engage them in conversation with the intent of promoting a product or service? Successfully engaging with individuals in social networks requires building trust and relationships, providing value and becoming the go-to resource when that audience is ready to buy what you sell. However the trust you build needs to be largely dependent upon your ability to convince your audience your intent is pure.

Acknowledge that your messages exist within a larger ecosystem that is beyond your control and engage consumers with this in mind. Become an active member of the community, network or environment and participate with the audience to create a genuine trust. Social media is growing in influence, but if you are willing to join the conversation don't view it as a panacea, instead, first establish why you are there and adhere to that purpose.

REFERENCES

Ellison, N. B., Steinfield, C., & Lampe, C. (2007). The benefits of Facebook "friends:" Social capital and college students' use of online social network sites. *Journal of Computer-Mediated Communication, 12*(4), 1143–1168.

Fromm, E. (1969). *Escape from freedom.* New York: Avon Books.

Joly, K. (2006). Flickr, a giant real-time viewbook of college life? Available at http://collegewebeditor.com/blog/index.php/archives/2006/09/08/flickra-giant-real-time-viewbook-of-college-life/. Retrieved on April 6, 2010.

Jones, S., & Fox, S. (2009). Generations online in 2009. Pew Internet and American Life Project. Available at http://www.pewinternet.org/Reports/2009/GenerationsOnline-in-2009.aspx. Retrieved on April 6, 2010.

Lenhart, A. (2009). Adults and social network Web sites. Pew Internet and American Life Project. Available at http://www.pewinternet.org/Reports/2009/Adults-and-SocialNetwork-Websites.aspx. Retrieved on April 6, 2010.

Madell, D., & Muncer, S. (2007). Control over social interactions: An important reason for young people's use of the internet and mobile phones for communication? *Cyberpsychology & Behavior, 10*(1), 137–140.

McGovern, G. (2010a). Customers: irrational sheep or intelligent strangers? Available at http://giraffeforum.com/wordpress/2010/04/04/customers-irrationalsheep-or-intelligent-strangers/. Retrieved on April 30, 2010.

McGovern, G. (2010b). Web design: clarity is more important than persuasion. Available at http://giraffeforum.com/wordpress/2010/03/28/web-design-clarity-ismore-important-than-persuasion/. Retrieved on April 30, 2010.

McKenna, K. Y. A., & Bargh, J. A. (2000). Plan 9 from cyberspace: The implications of the Internet for personality and social psychology. *Personality & Social Psychology Review*, 4(1), 57–75.

Mobile Marketing Association. (2010). *U.S. consumer best practices guidelines for cross-carrier mobile content programs*. New York: Mobile Marketing Association.

Noel-Levitz. (2007). Building an E-Recruitment network: Connecting with college bound seniors in the era of MySpace. Available at https://www.noellevitz.com/NR/rdonlyres/5549FBAC-A1CE-4F27-966C2CE16C6CFB14/0/EExpectationsClassof2007SeniorEditionpdf.pdf. Retrieved on August 1, 2010.

Raacke, J., & Bonds-Raacke, J. (2008). MySpace and Facebook: Applying the uses and gratifications theory to exploring friend-networking sites. *Cyberpsychology & Behavior*, 11(2), 169–174.

Reuben, R. (2008). Survey about the use of social media in higher education. Available at http://doteduguru.com/id423social-media-uses-higher-education-marketing-communication.html. Retrieved on April 6, 2010.

Sevier, R. (2007). Using Social Networking to Its Fullest Potential. *University Business*, 10(5), 25–26.

Shaindlin, A. (2009). Princeton puts reunions on your iPhone. Available at http://www.alumnifutures.com/2009/06/princeton-reunion-iphone.html. Retrieved on April 6, 2010.

Shao, G. (2009). Understanding the appeal of user-generated media: A uses and gratification perspective. *Internet Research*, 19(1), 7–19.

Solis, B. (2008). Introducing the conversation prism. Available at http://www.briansolis.com/2008/08/introducing-conversationprism.html. Retrieved on April 6, 2010.

Stross, R. (2010). Getting older without getting old. *New York Times*, March 7, p. 4.

Tolliver Nigro, H. (2010). Keys to success in social media marketing. *Printing News*, February 1, p. 11.

Valenzuela, S., Park, N., & Kee, K. F. (2009). Is there social capital in a social network site? Facebook use, and college students' life satisfaction, trust, and participation. *Journal of Computer-Mediated Communication*, 14(4), 875–901.

Veloso, M. (2009). *Web copy that sells*. New York: American Management Association.

Ward, B. (2009). Have you checked your foundation lately? Available at http://squaredpeg.com/index.php/2009/03/09/checked/foundation/. Retrieved on July 14, 2010.

Zernike, K. (2009). In shifting era of admissions, colleges sweat. *New York Times*, March 8, p. A1.

AM I INVITED? SOCIAL MEDIA AND ALUMNI RELATIONS

Heather M. Makrez

ABSTRACT

The alumni event everyone needs to be at. "Am I Invited?" will focus on the initial implementation of social media as it pertains to alumni relations, along with the relevance it plays within the advancement world. Social media strategies are a creative and powerful way to connect, educate, and energize those interested in the university. This technology and change in interpersonal behavior allows us the capabilities to create a complex, tightly woven, and diverse university community – a hotbed for innovative ideas, energetic conversation and practical networking.

As the world connects in new ways, so does our student body, so do our graduates and therefore, so do our alumni. We must be able to be part of the conversations because they are happening whether we know about them or not. We need to want to be where our constituencies are getting their information if we want to be productive when trying to reach out to them. The internet has taken over newspapers as a source for world news, especially with the younger generations, and it is quickly approaching the impact of the television. "Nearly six-in-ten Americans younger than 30 (59%) say they get most of their national and international news online; an identical percentage cites television" states the Pew Research Center. The study was done with 1,489 adults over the age of 18 in December 2008.

Why a university engages with SNS is an important question. The justification of investment must be met, and a comprehensive plan for implementation of social media initiatives must be created. Delving deeper into the societal norms and beliefs that need to be institutionalized before one can be truly successful in implementing a strategic investment of time, money, and brainpower. Then looking at key examples on how others were able to be successful at using SNS for alumni relations will prove to be helpful in weaving a practical web of social media initiatives that are effective at creating a virtual community ready to share thoughts, questions and resources. The impact of the experimental uses of SNS within the context of a diverse alumni community – which connects seamlessly to emerging campus-wide initiatives, is a complex and exciting realm to participate in. Challenging one to think out-of-the-box when it comes to finding an answer that suits their specific institutional goals will hopefully inspire a creative, fun, innovative, and interactive flow of ideas, along with the courage to try new things. Be bold. Be brave. Be here. Yes, you are definitely invited!

WHY ENGAGE IN SNS

Technology is not only affecting the way in which illnesses are treated, cars are driven or cities are developed. It is dramatically affecting the way in which people communicate with one other. There is an array of opportunities for institutions to partake in when it comes to sending out their marketing messages to their desired constituency. Conventional marketing mediums such as television, newspapers, magazines, traditional mailings, and the like are all still relevant and effective, however, there is a new "influencer" that should be considered when analyzing an institutions outreach strategy.

The Society for New Communications Research, in 2007, conducted a study of almost 300 communications professionals from all different fields and industries to realize the way in which people were using new technologies to reach a broader audience and how they analyze the impact and measures of success of each initiative. The results were published in their "New Media, New Influencers and Implications for Public Relations" report (Society for New Communications Research, 2008). In this they stated that "social media is rapidly becoming a core channel for disseminating information." Broken down to a more specific number, they state that "fifty-seven percent of this group of early social media adopters reported that social media tools are becoming more valuable to their activities, while twenty-seven percent reported that social media is a core element of their communications strategy."

Institutions such as higher education providers are a part of that population, and are an increasing percentage of the users. In order to create an impactful marketing compliment within the Social Networking Sites (hereinafter referred to as SNS) one may want to evaluate the networks available for usage, determine the resources available to allocate to the cause, the objectives that hoped to be accomplished with the implementation of a SNS strategy, examine some best practices and then try to implement the ones most relevant to the demographic and constituency they are trying to influence. All of these will allow an institution to create a brand community or at least expand an existing one.

This brand community allows one to connect with a desired population regardless of geographic location and based on a shared affinity and propensity for particular behavior, such as event attendance, university philanthropy, and general academic interest in a specific institution. With regard to alumni relations, helping to develop this brand community can be very useful for the entire university. Albert Muniz and Thomas C. O'Guinn (2001) describe brand community as "shared consciousness, rituals, traditions, and a sense of moral responsibility." This is directly applicable to alumni relations and the use of SNS as it helps to create an active community regardless of geographic, financial, or societal boundaries all united for one cause and that is the progression of affordable, high quality, accessible education for future generations.

Although venturing into the brand community realm there are a few basic parameters that will have to be determined. The office will need to decide who will manage the SNS. It is then very important to decide who your audience is, what demographics to they cover. For alumni, an institution will want to know if they are local, what age range they are, and come to discover the types of information they are looking to receive via these mediums. This will impact the way they move forward in creating an impactful social media strategy. Alumni relations, as a function and department, are a direct path to donor relations and therefore, university advancement. Some of the key priorities are donor contact and philanthropy promotion; however, it is important to balance this with alumni benefits and university achievements, and involvement opportunities in order to not alienate those who are not financially able to contribute or who are looking for the access to raw information and insider content.

Key objectives for developing a social media policy within alumni relations may range from fundraising to alumni research to information sharing to alumni activity involvement. Something that is important to remember while trying to achieve all of those objectives is that here is a definite expectation on the SNS for informal yet professional communication. This is a balancing act; therefore it is imperative to start with what the office is comfortable doing in order to keep a focused organizational voice while attempting to juggle new mediums of conversation. SNS take a lot of upkeep and maintenance and some require prompt responses so it is important not to take on more than an office can handle. Even though many SNS are free platforms, there are some costs associated with the implementation of them into a communication strategy: upgrades available – an investment of time, money and staff. Either way it seems to be an important conversation to be in.

Benefits of Social Networking Sites

- *It is where they are.* Alumni are using these SNS whether the university they attended is or not, and they are connecting with other alumni from this same community. It could be compared to there being a party, and even though one may feel left out, it is unwarranted, because there is room for everyone, everyone is invited. The only reason one should be left out is if a conscious decision was made not to engage in this behavior. In these forums, people are discussing news, events, other people, policies, political votes and much more – including you, your institution, your business, and your reputation. If an institution is not engaged they may be missing some of the important things being discussed within their potential or existing brand community. A study conducted by Rapleaf in 2008 with a query of social network usage across the 175 million people that was collected from publicly available social media data. Of the 49.3 million people in the study, ninety percent are within the United States. The study conducted in California found the following statistics on SNS:
    - 120 million social network profiles (total) were found, with each person averaging 2–3 social networks.
    - Women and the 14–24 year old demographic are more likely to use Myspace and Facebook than other demographics (the 14–24 year old demographic represents sixty-five percent and sixty-six percent of total users, respectively).

- Men and the 25–34 year old demographic are more likely to use LinkedIn and Flickr than other demographics (the 25–34 year old demographic represents fifty-one percent and thirty-eight percent of total users, respectively).
  - Despite increased presence of older demographics on social networks, the study reveals that younger people still continue to dominate social media space (Rapleaf, 2008).
- *Cost-Effectiveness*. Though the SNS are usually free to use, they do require resources such as employee time for site management and costs associated with some account upgrades that may be available. There can also be costs associated with creating logos and content for the SNS. However, compared to buying air time, doing large mailings, and paying to have someone else promote your brand, SNS can provide very valuable options and a cost-effective way to reach a larger audience, some of whom an alumni office may not even have a way of communicating with otherwise, due to lack of updated database information.
- *Alumni Empowerment*. Engagement opportunities and event promotion are some of the idea products of this brand marketing initiative. The most successful communities are those with two-way constituency interaction. Allowing those alumni to become invested in the university can take place through SNS. In addition to emailing, which is also not a comprehensive solution, social media channels give another interactive way to promote events, solicit feedback and share news. At the end of the day, active alumni are contributing alumni. Alumni offices are continually searching for new ways to keep alumni engaged. Even if they are not physically attending events on campus, engaging them in this brand community allows the university to develop a broader base of those who have a vested interest in the success of the enterprise.
- *Alumni Research*. SNS provide an additional resource to conduct alumni research. They serve as a tool to assist in updating alumni databases with new contact information. Through social media one is able to reach out, gather email addresses, new contact information, and create more dynamic class note sections of publications because there is constant contact with new ventures and developments in the lives of alumni, just like they are with new developments of the institution – it is a mutually beneficial relationship that can reap a number of benefits of handled the correct way.
- *Alumni Benefits*. SNS provide a sort of convenient mechanism for interactions among diverse groups, across various locations. On a more specific level, social media outlets can also be used to help alumni find

jobs, network with other alumni, spread the importance of staying in touch, and give alumni a voice in the current situation and direction of the university. Social media also provides new ways for a university to be able to interact with their alumni. Some specific examples include: hosting contests, asking opinions, sharing photos/videos, and soliciting feedback from alumni through these networks. This can help improve the services that offered to alumni because you will be able to adjust to what the people want. A university is able to actively engage in a dialogue and make an educated decision in finding out what type of outreach their alumni body is looking to receive, what type of information they want to have access, and what sort of affinity they possess towards the institution – all of which can translate into increased alumni philanthropy.

Using SNS is a way to reach thousands of people all over the world, there is no suitcase, plane ticket or hotel required. The impact of social media on different industries can vary, however, in the Society for New Communication Research's own study they only confirmed the impact SNS could have on the educational community. Of the 19 industries including media, nonprofits, entertainment, health services, retail, computer software and education, education came in sixth with regard to the opportunity to be influenced by SNS (2008). Engaging an institution in SNS is a new way to connect alumni and friends who may not have otherwise had a connection to each other with the ultimate goal of creating a mutually beneficial relationship for all of those linked to one another in these virtual communities.

DRESS CODE: HOW TO BE SUCCESSFUL WITH SNS

The thing to remember is there really is not a dress code, or specific must way to act. The user just needs to be comfortable in their abilities and have clear objectives. When beginning on this journey with SNS it is important to remember that things are always changing, and what works for one group might not work for another. In August 2009, the University of Massachusetts Lowell's Advancement Office began its social media outreach within the division of Alumni Relations. There was no real presence to speak of besides some groups that had been formed at one time by an alumna/us, and the degree of their activity varied depending on the alumni administrator's passion and time commitment. Instead of trying to compete with each of these groups the department decided to work collaboratively with them in hopes of providing assistance with the maintenance and upkeep of an active SNS.

As one navigates through these SNS opportunities, it is very important to survey all opportunities available and see which ones suit your organization the most. Decide which mediums are the most important and beneficial ones to use based on the target audience and resources of the office. Experimenting and discovering which ones will yield the best results is important and will vary slightly among different institutions. Colleague buy-in is imperative to the success of the SNS efforts because it a team effort relying on word of mouth and activity. Colleagues can be a great source of activity generating. Social media activity needs to be dynamic. There is no way one person can know everything that is going on, know everything that will be interesting to everyone, but that can not be a reason to slow the adoption of these new influencing technologies because building that university brand community is imperative to the success and progression of higher education.

It is important to remember that none of these outlets are comprehensive answers to marketing initiatives, but can help enhance the brand community and with regard to alumni relations, help to increase the potential philanthropy opportunities. The same is true with the composition of a successful social media strategy. Social media's effectiveness is multi-dimensional. Just like email has not been able to completely take the place of paper mailings, social media will not be able to take the place of email. A report done by *eMarketer* found that "social media is not a threat to email" and that with their question to respondents "If you had one way to communicate with friends and relatives what would it be?" Seventy-one percent answered email and twenty-nine percent answered social media (2010). However, email did not fair as well when it was up against text messaging – fifty-two percent for email, forty-eight percent for texting (2010).

Once an institution decides on how to move forward in this social media revolution, a number of specifics will need to be developed. There are basic functionalities that need to be set-up especially with regards to creating the alumni Facebook fan page, LinkedIn group, Twitter account, and/or YouTube channel. Although doing this the more office buy-in from the beginning, the more successful the initiative will be. One person or group will have to set-up initial content with the commitment to keep it fresh, relevant and interactive. Then the office will need to enlist the help of other alumni in growing the membership, a few key field organizers and perhaps the university's communication office.

The marketing of these groups is important, some of it may be automatic, and others will be the result of strategic marketing efforts. There may be people out there who want to join the group but have not found it yet. Some specific examples used to make it as easy as possible for them to find the new SNS are through email and hyperlinks on more popular websites, having alumni sponsors – asking them to join and then ask them to suggest it to their friends – organize a few "friendzies." This would be where one creates an event over a determined amount of time and ask people in the network to suggest the page to friends in their network and have those connections do the same. Once they start growing the impact can be exponential just due to the complex way in which the degrees of separation become smaller, the more connections one is able to make. Then this brings one back to the importance of buy-in from all parties involved. The more people committed to promote these SNS the more dynamic and profound the impact will be in enhancing the brand community.

ANALYZING IMPACT

Using SNS is an investment of time and resources and in order to create a comprehensive, sustainable plan, there must also be some analysis of the benefit and impact of these activities by an institution. The New Influence study stated that the top criteria for evaluating a person's influence in online communities and social networks are participation level, frequency of activity and prominence in the market or community (2008). As part of the matrix for measurements of success, one must also look at how much SNS drives people to the university website, does it increase attendance at specific events, does it increase donor support through online donations, and does it cause people to sign up for other online communities and what are the interaction activity levels on each site. With web analytic tools, some built into the SNS themselves, and others based off of the office's in-depth interaction with the university's web team, one may be able to come up with answers to some of these questions. The University of Massachusetts Lowell was able to release the statistics below displaying how people discover http://www.uml.edu. Two months after implementation, Facebook and LinkedIn were driving people to the website just like Google, Bing and other search engine sites (Table 1).

The comparison table above shows the increase in homepage hits over the course of nine months. The more usage of Facebook and LinkedIn there is, the more they are able to drive users (alumni) back to the university's

Table 1. Referring Sites to http://www.uml.edu April 2010 v. October 2009.

Visits Pages/Visit	August–October 2009	January–April 2010
Source	Visits Pages/Visit	Visits Pages/Visit
uml.edu	1,246	3,635
massachusetts.edu	50	31
umasslowell.com	N/A	26
linkedin.com	13	20
facebook.com	10	15
admin.alumniconnections.com	19	11

website and alumni homepage, on which there are news articles, press releases, event information and giving opportunities. The table shows that viewers are spending more time on the university's main website looking around, and attracting prospects that might not have been found otherwise. This is good for not only fundraising, but event promotion and university news and marketing. Since word of mouth is one of the most positive influences in a student's choice of higher education institution, the more one can spread the word about the great things a university is doing, the better it will be for continued growth.

Speaking of university growth, there seems to be a significant link between alumni relations and admissions. This relationship has allowed the two offices to find compatible and beneficial ways to interact with one another through SNS. Alumni are constantly looking for new ways to be engaged with the university and admissions always needs new ways to recruit new students, therefore, the two departments are able to join forces to recruit alumni admissions volunteers via social media and have made a LinkedIn group aimed at that audience. For example, the University of Massachusetts Lowell has had alumni attend college fairs and call accepted students to encourage admission and answer any questions the prospective student may have. Social media is allowing them the easy access to alumni all over the country and the world to help increase their campus diversity based on the outreach alumni can have on potential students from all over the world.

As a university moves forward in engaging with SNS it is valuable to use a multifaceted mechanism to add a dynamic element to the creating of these virtual communities. Using Facebook to link to a YouTube channel to showcase a new alumni business, or student accomplishment is a great way to increase viewer activity and hopefully evoke some emotion or response.

Advertising events on these SNS through event pages or RSS feed technologies is an effective, quick, low-cost marketing mechanism to reach a broad audience of alumni, whether it is a guest speaker, a commencement reception or a sporting event. SNS allow the alumni office a hands-on tool to inform their alumni community. They also create avenues of immediate contact that an alumni office can have control over without waiting for a print/mail house or graphic designer. The university is able to disseminate relevant information in a simple way and perhaps draw attention to future advertisements increasing participation, and hopefully growing that virtual community and enhancing the brand identity of the institution at the same time.

EXAMPLES OF SUCCESS

If you do not go up and introduce yourself to the host, they may not know you were even there. With this new medium, the ways are still being paved. Sometimes you have to take a risk in order to get noticed in the crowd of people. Find the way to make that impression when walking in the door. Examples to highlight like the admission one above are easy to find. Universities are constantly trying to find new ways to use social media to make an impact. There was also the India event example in the LinkedIn section. The way to rise to the top is to find your own efficient way. The path less traveled can sometimes work in your favor. The *Social Media Examiner* is quoted as stating that after reviewing a report compiled by social media professionals entitled "The State of Social Media Marketing," the most important thing to come away from this report with is that the "least-tried tactics often seem to work the best" (Porterfield, 2009).

This supports the success behind this new campaign the University of Massachusetts Lowell tried in order to increase our fan/viewer/supporter base. They decided to put a daily goal on their fan page – 1,000 fans by a specified time. It was a risk because they were posting for the world to see that we would make this goal. One wants to make that goal. What happened? People rallied. Energy built and they passed their goal! A strategy was developed. This is why it is important to take risks and experiment with social media. There are some techniques to help along the way, such as event promotion, question asking, and picture posting that can illicit feedback and interaction, but there is much room for development of new techniques as the technology and ability levels move forward.

There will be many skeptics in the beginning, and using them as a catapult for success can be one of the biggest promoters. At UMass Lowell there was a definite reluctance for the investment in social media as an administrator's responsibility, but after much hard work, there was a shift in this perception. The reasoning for this shift in confidence was partly from a very tangible case study. The university, like many others, was making a strong shift to promote international education. Included in this were initiatives such as study abroad programs, finding and accepting more international students, and international partnerships, along with increasing our international alumni network. In April 2010, they had their Chancellor, engineering professors and deans attend an event in Mumbai, India. As one might have guessed, they wanted to make sure there was a good turnout. The alumni database, in its present state, did not have comprehensive data, never mind correct mailing addresses for invitations to this event overseas. Aside from what it would cost to mail to India, they would not even know where to send them.

Therefore, a few months ahead of time, they started using social media to research their alumni. They focused on using LinkedIn Alumni groups to solicit email addresses and contacts of alumni interested in staying in touch with the university. They used what is called "In Mail" to reach those they found through searches who were not in the LinkedIn alumni group. It was an added cost for the upgraded capability to send those special messages, but proved to be worth the investment. (With LinkedIn, if you want to send messages to people that you may not be connected to, you can send an "in mail", but in order to do this you must upgrade your LinkedIn personal account from a free one to a subscriber's monthly fee at either the business or premium level.

The results of this SNS effort yielded a large alumni event in India and future ones are being planned. This caused the administration to see a tangible result of social media outreach efforts and buy-in from the top was achieved. If SNS can help provide a university with valuable information, they can also help a university provide information to people who are looking for access to real, immediate, and raw information, than it can help create a valuable influencer. If alumni or friends wanted polished articles with multiple sources or strategically marketed sales adds they would read the newspaper. If they want polished speeches and press releases they would turn to the television or world news/media websites. SNS gives institutions and industry leaders the opportunity to provide that middle ground – a unified organizational voice unaccompanied by some lightly censored material. It serves as a way to grab their attention while feeding them valuable, important information while allowing them the courtesy of a response.

The balance that must be achieved is between the instinctual desire of a company or institution to push data or objective marketing materials. If one does that they are "missing out on the opportunity to establish meaningful relationships" with their investors and is a "sure-fire way to lose followers quickly" (Porterfield, 2010). Social media is a relationship. The most successful relationships are those with open lines of communication. There is no doubt the uncensored side comes with some obstacles, but they must be examined and solutions can be found.

SNS EXAMPLES: FACEBOOK, LINKEDIN, TWITTER, AND YOUTUBE

With regard to SNS like Facebook where users have profiles that generate the ability to connect with other people, places, and organizations, it is important to become aware of the opportunities that already exist on these sites. The university would want to survey the fan pages and groups that already exist that pertain to the organization or institution. It will be a great research tool allowing an institution to become acquainted with what is going on out there on the SNS. After some initial research is done, an educated decision on how to proceed can be made. Look at the membership and then decide if there is one worth cultivating or if the university should branch out and start their "official" alumni fan page. If it is worth cultivating an existing group or page – ask if there are any helpful ways that the university can be involved without having to start a new virtual community.

If this does not work, it is still possible to start funneling support toward a new fan page or group should the office decide to create it. Once established, the alumni fan page will need to grow-Fan pages have been found to reap larger benefits because of the functionality of data analysis tools and advertising capabilities. Fan pages are usually better for long-term relationships with your fans, customers, and readers (Cohn, 2009). Groups are also directly connected to the administrator of that particular group, fan pages are more discrete – which means that whatever goes on in the group could potentially reflect on that profile (Cohn, 2009). Fan Pages are indexed by search engines like Google (Oltersdorf, 2010). Fan pages are more open and accessible, and therefore, more beneficial for a university alumni relations office to solicit feedback, have user interaction and tract effectiveness and outreach ability.

With regard to LinkedIn there are many benefits for using this forum. It tends to be a great compliment to SNS that are heavily friend-based platforms and in-house alumni/client databases and networks. LinkedIn groups allow you the capability of directing information to targeted groups of people. The use of subgroups has become very popular as well. A university is able to grow their alumni SNS group, whilst also giving people the opportunity to connect with one another based on their affinities. For example, the UMass Lowell Alumni group has subgroups for residence life alumni, engineering alumni, student activity alumni, and other departments. Universities such as Penn State and University of Michigan have been able to grow their networks to over 20,000 alumni members.

Reasons for getting involved as an alumni office with these alumni networks are multidimensional in the areas that they can reap benefits to the university, but there are also exponential benefits to not only being involved in the discussion, but in being an administrator or manager of the community. One of the easiest to highlight is the ability to capture updated alumni contact information that is knowingly being shared with the manager by those requesting to join the group. There may be alumni who have not had the time, need, or desire to update a school about their change in contact information, but through the management of these groups, and outreach by alumni to be in contact with their alma mater, there is now the capability to update alumni records while engaging in SNS activity. For example, when one requests to join a LinkedIn group there is a disclaimer that the SNS has on the sign-in page that explains that by registering to be an SNS group member you agree to have your name and email address accessible to the official representatives of the group and to be listed as a group member in your LinkedIn profile and search results.

Another benefit of being a group administrator on LinkedIn is the ability to post news articles and discussions, and make them "featured." This means they will appear at the top of the list. The great advantage to LinkedIn is that no matter how large your web department or marketing department is the manager of these groups has the presence in each member's inbox that is exponentially greater than it could be otherwise. There is no waiting for production meetings or publication requests to process. It is immediate and time-effective. To illustrate this, when people join a LinkedIn group they are able to pick how often they want to get updated from the group – daily or weekly – this means that each time LinkedIn sends them an update, they see your name and the articles, discussions or events that one might post to their email inboxes. There have been numerous times where I have met alumni at events, and they already feel like they know me. The posts made by the administrator reach thousands of people – depending on how large their group is – at least weekly.

The University of Massachusetts Lowell experienced developing co-ownership of a SNS group which turned into a very successful partnership. There was already a Plastics Engineering Alumni group in existence with a great base, and they were able to join as co-administrators. Once co-ownership was established the university was able to use some of its resources to help increase the promotion of the group, and it grew exponentially. Anthony Gasbarro is a plastics engineering alumnus from the University of Massachusetts Lowell. He started a Plastics Engineering Alumni LinkedIn group and this is what he had to say about it:

> A few years back I was introduced to a website called LinkedIn by a friend of mine. I was intrigued by the concept – it was described to me as a "Facebook for grownups" and I found it to be just that. It was a way for me to keep in touch with people that I communicated with professionally. Being in a technical sales role, it was important for me to connect with my customers and to create relationships with them – I found this to be a wonderful tool to do just that. I had a desire to be in touch with my University – the University of Massachusetts Lowell and more importantly with the Plastics Engineering Department that I graduated from. The department head uses the group as a place to keep people informed to what's going on at the school, and the alumni use it as a means to communicate with one another. There are several things that have come up as side-benefits to creating the group and being involved in the group. The first benefit is that I personally get to see a list of every person that joins the group. The second is that I have found that people I do business with on a daily basis are fellow alumnus of the Plastics Engineering Department and this has help build our relationships. (A. Gasbarro, personal communication, April 15, 2010)

As one transfers over to discuss another type of SNS that relies heavily on RSS feed technology, one should note that Twitter may work better for one university over another, or one department in an institution better than another, depending on the university's constituency, geographic location (if the university is in a major city this may be very beneficial) and the university's other office initiatives. In *The Social Media Examiner*, they reported on a new study by *eMarketer* that surprised them with regard to Twitter usage predictions. The study found that "In 2009, there were 18 million U.S. adults who accessed Twitter on any platform at least monthly. That represents a two hundred percent increase over 2008 levels. And the article went on to suggest that usage will reach 26 million U.S. adults in 2010, a further forty-four percent climb" (Porterfield, 2009).

In respect to partaking in all of the social media outlets and combining this with efficiency, a balancing act must be put into place. Sharing only some of the relevant pieces of news or events, may prove to be more beneficial than linking everything from all of your SNS. Each venue offers users a different functionality. Some allow you to resend what someone has shared, others allow the user to RSVP to events, and still more help engage in sharing video or picture information. With regard to the RSS feed technologies, and Twitter specifically, in order to get the most out of Twitter one may want to be able to tag (#-hash tag) certain words so that they are picked up in RSS feeds. For Facebook and LinkedIn this is not necessary. If all of the accounts are linked to show the same status updates, the hash tags can become a cumbersome for those not on Twitter. Owing to the different nature of each social media outlet and the targeted desired outcome and expectations of the constituencies present in each venue. When issuing status updates and information sharing it might be helpful to keep each venue's assets in mind. Twitter has a strategic, concise, press focus. LinkedIn has a professional development, networking focus, and Facebook has a more laid back, informal, dynamic focus.

Finally, the discussion of video SNS sites is important because these allow the user a whole new resource which customers/alumni/viewers find very enchanting. YouTube, for example, can be a very dynamic instrument. It can compliment all of the above mediums with visual effects. As an alumni office, one could host video contests, share student documentaries, post commencement or other event footage. You can share live-streaming of events that alumni from other parts of the world may not be able to attend, and one can use YouTube to help illustrate the need for alumni participation with new community building/branding efforts. YouTube can be linked to each of the previously mentioned sites to enhance news posts, entice people to attend an annual event, or even solicit alumni for an annual gift in a new way. At a university, using YouTube allows offices to share resources and footage/video on different SNS which in turn helps unify that organizational voice among departments while engaging in a rich tool of visual engagement.

As a university tries to figure out the best way to implement a SNS strategy using various SNS it is important to look to other institutions for examples of success with this relatively new technology. The University of Massachusetts Lowell between 2009 and 2010 has tried many different techniques, some more successful than others. Below is a list of examples:

- Holiday Song Contest 2009 – as the LinkedIn group was gaining steam we decided to try something different. Remember: No risk. No reward.

So we posted the lyrics of "Let is snow" hoping that we could have a little contest and people would chime in to complete the song. Alumni did. They even started making up their own verses about the University of Massachusetts Lowell. There were nine comments from alumni on the song contest. For example, "Cumnock stairs are icy, Sig O's eggnog is spicy, Snowball fight in the quad-OH! Let it snow, Let it snow, Let it snow!" (LinkedIn, UMass Lowell Alumni Group, 2009).

- On SNS they promoted their first residence life alumni reunion that became so popular we had to make it its own fan page. Comments from alumni were gathered, volunteers to help recruit former residence life staff were discovered, and alumni were tagged and codes attributed to them in their alumni database. The office was able to pull an extensive invitation list because of that, and as a result, had a great event with feedback from the alumni that they wanted to have another one that was even larger. There were over a hundred alumni attend the first annual reunion and are all looking forward to the next one when more people plan to attend.
- Posted alumni e-newsletters for the campus and individual departments, as well as their published alumni magazine on these websites. It provided easy access to university communications.
- They worked to create and post electronic surveys to capture data and opinions from alumni who might not have otherwise received these opportunities.
- Event attendance at annual events increased with the promotion through social media. They receive numerous comments from alumni who were happy to learn of all of these events that other departments were starting to advertise through the alumni office. The alumni office got numerous requests from deans who understood the importance and relevance of SNS and wanted to use them to help promote their own departmental functions and initiatives.
- Alumni who have been hard to reach in the past, have been reaching out for various reasons through social media and as an alumni relations professional, the administrator of the sites is able to facilitate contact between major gift officers and prospects on many different occasions, providing a great medium for connection and relationship growth.
- On April 28, 2010, the alumni office posted a paragraph and article link about the student solar decathlon team that was chosen to be part of the 20 university-led teams that design, build, and operate the competition's solar-powered houses are the heart of the U.S. Department of Energy Solar Decathlon. Two days later they received a response from an alumnus, grateful for the education he had received here and willing to help out in any way.

To compliment this list of successful examples from UMass Lowell with some other research take a look at a study done on the reasons why people engage with SNS. The study was done by the market research firm Chadwick Martin Bailey and iModerate Research Technologies with over 1504 consumers over the age of 18 and spread out throughout the United States. The study was then quoted again in the *eMarketer* report we spoke of earlier demonstrating what motivates the institution's constituencies to "like" the office's fan page on Facebook.

They found that 25% wanted to receive discounts or promotions. Twenty-one percent of them were customers of the company. Then 18% had a friend who liked or supported the brand, and 10% interacted via SNS because they found it to be fun and entertaining. All of the others joined for reasons like gaining exclusive access to content, because it was recommended, to join in with others like them, and about 1% answered because they either worked at the company or owned stock in it (eMarketer, 2010). All of these can be directly applied in alumni relations terms. People join in the virtual communities because they are alumni of the university, because a friend recommended them to it, because they may find alumni exclusive deals or breaking news before anyone else through the SNS membership.

It is important to remember that these posts and interactions are successful for two reasons. The attitude going in is representative of the expectations of the constituents in that they are people looking for raw, exciting, uncensored (to a point) information that they can not get in the newspaper. And, secondly, that the information we are posting is relevant, insightful and begs for their feedback and participation.

Since there has not been much discussion around the crossroads of SNS, now might be the time to briefly state that even though people may fear bad comments or opening their institution up for criticism, know that it is happening whether someone from the university's administration is in the theoretical SNS room or not. It is better to know the bad things people think about the current situation, than to believe that there is no need for change or to learn about the need when it is too late. It is also important to note, that if a controversial comment is posted on one of the SNS, the best way to proceed to in a thoughtfully crafted response to the poster, not an immediate deletion. That does not make the problem go away. In 2009, there was a case referenced in *Alumni Futures*, an online site and consulting resource aimed at helping higher education institutions invest in and deploy social technologies, from Ohio State University where they did just that and deleted the comment and then were advised by their legal department that they should reinstate the comment. It is important to note that "free speech" is important in online forums (Shaindlin, 2009).

Some more of the realities of implementing informal behavior whilst keeping control and consistency of an organizational voice can cause many to withdraw from SNS. There will always be those comments that one might want to immediately pull down. However, careful consideration must be taken and a critical thinking solution achieved because it may turn out that addressing the comment head-on helps alleviate future problems from boiling up. For example, at the University of Massachusetts Lowell if messages are received where alumni are inquiring about how one might address something they consider to be a problem, some may say not to answer, but what they have found is that by answering some of the not-so-positive questions they help turn a potential negative situation into a positive one because the university is now in control of the issue. Whether it is alumni, friends, customers or even family, people look to SNS for this interaction – these relationship building – opportunities. The content included on the sites must entice the readers to come back for more (Simone, 2010). Giving your constituency reasons to come back and setting the bar high on these expectations makes your SNS's that much more valuable. It is like giving a dog a treat while training them to sit or stay. Good content will help create a pattern of behavior (Simone, 2010). It is important to remember no matter how extensive the social media policy is that is aimed at developing a brand community; there are expectations out there that need to be met in order to be successful.

- Be spontaneous
- Be creative – do not be scared. Be brave.
- Be honest. Be bold.
- Reach out – select a social network and grow the base quickly.
- Find comfort in not having control – you have to realize that you do not have control over opinions expressed via social media in order to embrace the beauty of it.
- Make a good first impression with lots of versatility.
- In order to do that, one must know the audience, who is looking, why are they looking and identify who should be there that is not.
- Time equals success. Static pages are not popular pages, just like boring parties do not last all night.
- Invest in the future – the relationships that the university is able to build now through social media efforts, may in turn end up being some of the biggest returns on investment the university could make. They may turn out to be future donors or may encourage other future donors based on the amount of contact touches the institution was able to make with the help of SNS, especially with those that they may not have had otherwise.

- Learn from others and adapt as one moves through stages of SNS implementation.
- Have fun!

SNS PLANNNG 101- TOOLS

Some Quick Things to Keep in Mind

Things to Keep in Mind
We must maintain the spirit of the sites – The success is based not on the free financial aspect of the advertising, but on the "free nature" of the media.

- Raw
- Quick
- Interactive Information

Official Logo or appropriate photo
Video Policies
Videos should not contain content that:

- is unlawful, harmful, threatening, abusive, harassing, torturous, defamatory, vulgar, obscene, libelous, invasive of another's privacy, hateful, or racially, ethnically, or otherwise objectionable;
- shows nudity, partial nudity, or adult content;
- shows illegal acts;
- harm minors in any way;
- endorses a vendor or a product;
- References alcohol or drugs, shows participants drinking or under the influence of alcohol or illegal substances.

Social Networking Interaction Policies

- Comments are welcome on University of Massachusetts Lowell social networks. Although the way in which comments are handled is up individual site owners there are some guidelines to which all commenters should adhere.
- Comments should not include swearing or profanity.
- Personal attacks against others will not be tolerated.
- Comments should not be defamatory or libelous.
- Site owners reserve the right to edit or delete comments that do not adhere to the guidelines above.

- Some site owners may choose to moderate all comments before they appear.
- No sending of spam.

DISCLAIMER

"The views and opinions expressed in this page are strictly those of the page author(s). The contents of this page have not been reviewed or approved by University of Massachusetts Lowell."

REFERENCES

Cohn, M. (2009). Facebook Fan Page v. Groups. Available at http://compukol.com/blogs/compukol/facebook-fan-page-vs-group/

eMarketer.com. (2010). Social not a threat to E-Mail. Available at http://www.emarketer.com/Article.aspx?R = 1007626&Ntt = social + media + report&No = 8&xsrc = article_head_sitesearchx&N = 0&Ntk = basic

LinkedIn. (2009). UMass Lowell Alumni Group, December.

Muniz, A. M., Jr., & O'Guinn, T. C. (2001). Brand community. *Journal of Consumer Research*, *27*(4), 412–432.

Oltersdorf, J. G. (2010). Facebook Fan Pages v. Group Pages. Available at http://www.snackbox.us/blog/2010/1/18/facebook-fan-pages-vs-group-pages.html

Porterfield, A. (2009). Social media examiner. 5 Must-read social media marketing studies. Available at http://www.socialmediaexaminer.com/5-must-read-social-media-marketing-studies/

Porterfield, A. (2010). Social media examiner. *New Study Reveals* (January). Available at http://www.socialmediaexaminer.com/new-study-reveals-facebook-better-than-twitter-for-marketers/

Rapleaf. (2008). Study reveals gender and age data of social network users. Available at http://www.rapleaf.com/business/press_release/age

Shaindlin, A. (2009). http://www.alumnifutures.com/

Simone, S. (2010). The three essentials of breakthrough content marketing. Available at http://www.copyblogger.com/content-marketing-essentials/

Society for New Communications Research. (2008). New Media, New Influencers and Implications for Public Relations. Available at http://sncr.org/wp-content/uploads/2008/08/new-influencers-study.pdf

TWITTER IN HIGHER EDUCATION: FROM APPLICATION TO ALUMNI RELATIONS

Jon Hussey

ABSTRACT

In four years, Twitter has grown from a fledgling text message-based start-up company to a powerful communication tool embraced by companies worldwide as a mandatory marketing tool. This chapter outlines the growth of the service, how it has changed communication, and the basic knowledge needed to use the service. The chapter expands on that basic knowledge to demonstrate how the service can be used in a higher education setting. Based on the overarching principle that all social media should involve two-way communication, this chapter provides a basic strategy for departments in all colleges and universities – admissions, media relations, career center, alumni, and more – to Act *and* Interact *on social media to boost school pride, develop relationships, and build brand equity. Finally, because social media is an ever-evolving medium, this chapter outlines some of the cutting edge uses of Twitter that are likely to develop over the next five years.*

What are you doing? That was the simple question Twitter asked and thousands of prospective students, current students, and alumni are answering the question daily. From the moment a prospective student tweets, "I'm going to apply to ... ," a digital relationship can be developed that will connect them to your college or university throughout their life. Many higher education professionals have recognized the opportunities Twitter affords them and, as of June 2009, are using Twitter at a far higher rate than the average Internet user – 30.7% versus 10.7%. (Magna, 2009) Whatever their reason for signing up – to network or share ideas with other higher education professionals, as a marketing tool, or to communicate directly with students and alumni – this group is ahead of the curve in recognizing the advantages to Twitter in the higher education community. Their participation continues to deepen as 71.8% of faculty says they are likely to increase their use of Twitter in the next year (Magna, 2009). Despite that growth, the 56.4% of higher education professionals who are not on Twitter have little to no knowledge of the service. Whether you are a university marketer using Twitter for specific campaigns, a college web professional sharing ideas and inspiration with colleagues across the country, or an alumni leader who thinks only celebrities use Twitter, this chapter will provide a broad outline on what Twitter is, how it can be used in higher education, and how some of your colleagues may already be using it. I will walk you through the unique opportunities for engagement that Twitter offers and how to build a university-wide Twitter strategy to successfully develop relationships in all aspects of university life.

WHAT IS TWITTER?

In September 2009, amidst debate in Washington, D.C. over health care and the economy, *Newsweek* writer Aku Ammah-Tagoe (2009) wrote about a new power player in the debate. "Suddenly, all of Washington is atwitter," he proclaimed. The chapter outlined how Senators and Representatives are using the social network, Twitter, to connect with their constituents in a way never before seen. In truth, the phenomenon goes well beyond Washington. In 2010, 60% of registered Twitter users come from outside the United States and countries like India (nearly 100% increase since the beginning of 2010) and Columbia ("300% after politicians like Piedad Cordoba Ruiz began using Twitter as a platform to speak to constituents") are demonstrating rapid growth (Sanford, 2010).

The microblogging site – which allows users to post 140-character updates – has grown to 106 million users in April 2010 (Waters, 2010) since its inception in 2006. What started with a simple question has grown to create a lasting impact on world events. In the spring of 2009, Iran's Mahmoud Ahmadinejad won a disputed presidential election and citizens took to the streets to protest what they believed was a corrupt election process. With the government allegedly restricting the use of blogs, websites, and text messaging, the Iranian public turned to Twitter. Millions of people around the world received live updates of the protests and the alleged police and government abuse (Berman, 2009).

That international event demonstrated the power of Twitter to a public still unfamiliar with the service, though many prominent news stories – local, national, and international – before and since have been broken on the social network. When the US Airways Flight 1549 crash-landed in the Hudson River, it was a Twitter user on a ferry who provided the first image of the downed plane and its passengers (Cellan-Jones, 2009). In 2008, when terrorists attacked in Mumbai, Twitter provided a real-time account of the horrors with an estimated 80 tweets every 5 s detailing the dead and injured as well as information on how to donate blood for the wounded (Busari, 2008). That role in some of the world's most memorable events in recent years has acted as a catalyst to help Twitter reach a growth of 300,000 new users every day (Waters, 2010). Nearly 60% of journalists use Twitter to research stories (Cision, 2009), 65% of *Fortune* Global 100 companies have Twitter accounts (Burson-Marsteller, 2010), and 94% of marketers with social media experience are using Twitter (Stelzner, 2009).

Professionals are not the only ones using Twitter. According to the Pew Internet & American Life Project (Fox, Zickuhr, & Smith, 2009), 1 in 5 Internet users are now on Twitter and 55% of 18- to 49-year-olds are using the service. Middle and high school, college, and graduate school-aged users (13- to 34-year-olds) make up 59% of Twitter's 106 million users (Quantcast, 2010). So it should come as no surprise that the world of higher education has turned to Twitter to attract undergraduate and graduate students, connect with alumni, and improve the experience of current students.

TWITTER BASICS

Unfortunately, Twitter does not come with an instruction manual. That could be why, according to a NielsonWire (Martin, 2009) story, 60% of the

U.S. Twitter users leave the service after 1 month. So before diving into the world of Twitter, it's important to have a basic understanding of the service. Known as a microblogging social network, Twitter allows you to share information with your friends or followers 140-characters at a time. However, the service has a language of its own that is important to learn in order to get the most out of your experience. For example, there is a "tweet," "re-tweet," "at-reply," "direct message," "hashtag," and more.

Below is a basic explanation of the key elements of Twitter usage:

- *Tweet* – a 140-character (or less) status update on Twitter.
- *At-Reply* – A conversation with a follower, which is done by preceding your message with @USERNAME (e.g. @AmericanU).
- *Re-Tweet* (RT) – Used to re-share a status update by someone you are following. If @auwebmanager (that's me) posted something you find interesting, you can post that from your own profile by typing, "RT @auwebmanager" and the message you want to re-share.
- *Direct Message* – A private message between yourself and one of your followers. This can only be done if you are following someone on Twitter and they are following you back. Unlike regular Twitter updates, which can be seen by anyone, direct messages are private and can only been seen by the two parties involved.
- *Hashtag* – A hashtag is a word or abbreviation added to a Twitter update based on the subject being discussed in the update. The word is preceded by #. For example, in discussing Twitter in higher education, a status update might appear like this, "I am learning about #Twitter in #highered." This tagging allows other Twitter users to follow all mentions of specific topics of interest. Anyone can create a hashtag simply by using # before a word or abbreviated phrase. Be sure to make it unique to your school or subject so it is not confused with another subject.

Armed with the basic language of Twitter, the easiest way to build your knowledge and prepare to develop a Twitter strategy for your university is to jump right in and create a personal Twitter account. Keep in mind, in today's infinitely connected, always-on society, your personal account will double as your professional account. Behave on Twitter as you would in any professional setting.

Many higher education professionals are already on Twitter, using it to share ideas and develop relationships with others in their field. They have found a balance between sharing professional advice and ideas and sharing information about their life and who they are. To the uninitiated, Twitter is nothing more than a place to talk about what you ate for lunch. It is so much more. However, even the most seasoned user of Twitter – one using it to its fullest potential – sometimes shares these little details of life. Sharing your hobbies, passions, and moments of your daily life will humanize you and help you to develop relationships on Twitter. Create your account, start following other higher education professionals (you can find lists of them on websites like http://listorious.com), and find your own balance between personal and professional. Once you are comfortable, it's time to start thinking about resources, execution, and strategy.

PLANNING AND TECHNOLOGY

Althoguh social media is known for its casual nature, any higher education professional interested in using Twitter for their university should approach it with the same level of organization and analysis that they would for any other university-wide project. The first step is to identify the reason for starting a university account and your goals and then begin to develop the infrastructure to meet those goals.

Forget all of the hype you may have heard about social media being the perfect marketing tool. Twitter – and social media in general – is not a panacea. However, coupled with high quality traditional marketing or student/alumni relations, it can help to build relationships with your audience, break down barriers between administration and students or alumni, and develop trust.

Before you can get into the day-to-day management of your Twitter accounts, it's important to recognize the basic decisions to be made and tools needed to be successful in the endeavor. The first, seemingly mundane, decisions to consider when developing a Twitter strategy can be some of the most important: a memorable name for your account(s), a logo design consistent with the university brand, and short, catchy hashtags for your audience to use when tweeting about your university. Social media should be easy for your audience or they will not embrace your efforts. If your account name is too lengthy (i.e., your full university name), many Twitter users will be less inclined to type it out. This is not because students are lazy. The millennial generation grew up with the Internet, instant messaging, text messaging, and now smart phones. Their language in these media is casual and brief.

Some examples of university twitter names include: @GWTweets (George Washington University), @AmericanU (American University), @BU_Tweets (Boston University), @Fordhamnotes (Fordham University), and

@IUBloomington (Indiana University Bloomington). These abbreviated names can also be used as hashtags for your users. To let your audience know what hashtag to use when referring to the university, simply start using it in your tweets. They will pick it up and begin using it themselves.

Perhaps the most important decision is your logo or account profile picture. We all know what the Nike swoosh looks like and identify it immediately with Nike. You are not Nike. But that does not mean you cannot create a strong image or logo that will not be confused with anyone else. On Twitter, many users identify other users by their image, not their name. As they watch a never-ending stream of information from the people they follow, the image could be the only identifying mark they look at. Make it distinct. As universities expand their Twitter presence, some will have more than 50 schools or offices using the service. If you are not organized, multiple accounts could be using the same university logo, making it very hard for your audience to differentiate in a quick glance.

With accounts registered and logos developed, the final step in understanding the tools of your success is the technology. Twitter is a website, much like Facebook, where you log in to your account, interact, and follow the stream of updates from those you follow. However, Twitter uses an open Application Programming Interface (API), which means other software developers can create applications that integrate Twitter. These applications are being developed at a rapid rate and many of them offer features and usability that far exceeds Twitter.com. Below are the two most popular Twitter applications and some of their features:

- *TweetDeck* – Allows users to manage multiple Twitter accounts within a desktop application instead of the Twitter.com website. TweetDeck can be broken into multiple column views, including lists, at-replies (referred to as mentions on TweetDeck) of your account name, Twitter searches ("Your University"), direct messages, new followers, and more.
- *Hoot Suite* – An online application like Twitter, Hoot Suite can only be run in your web browser. It offers many of the same features as Tweet Deck, including multiple accounts, simultaneous tweets from multiple accounts and one-click at-reply, re-tweet, and direct messaging. One feature unique to Hoot Suite has made it popular with businesses and higher education professionals – scheduled tweets. This allows users to plan tweets days or weeks ahead of time and schedule the tweet to go out automatically at a specific date and time.

Both applications have their advantages and disadvantages, so which one you choose to use is a matter of specific needs and personal tastes.

At many universities or higher education offices, a single person is in charge of multiple Twitter accounts. Because Tweet Deck is a desktop application offering multicolumn and account view, a single user can keep it open at all times during the work day and read, tweet, and interact in between other daily tasks. Other users prefer to plan individual tweets ahead of time and schedule them through Hoot Suite.

There is a wealth of other Twitter tips, tricks, and applications to help you understand and manage Twitter, but do not get too bogged down in the technical elements of Twitter and its applications. Instead, build a stronger understanding of the content your individual audiences want.

CONTENT STRATEGY

Twitter, and social media as a whole, has grown into a phenomenon in the past decade because it connects people in real time in ways that email and other media cannot. Every university has an abundance of information to convey to prospective students, current students, faculty, staff, alumni, and the surrounding community. A university's news can include research, faculty and student accomplishments, new programs, new faculty, events, campus updates, student internship opportunities, alumni updates, and academic profile information.

The traditional method of getting this information to your audience has been brochures for prospective students, emails to current students on campus life and other information, a university newspaper, an alumni magazine, and the university website. Most of these vehicles for university information will not disappear, but they have had to evolve to adjust to the growing importance of web and social media marketing in higher education. That evolution has been fueled by prospective students, 84% of whom say they depend most heavily on university websites in their research (Ashburn, 2007).

A decade ago, the university website was a place where prospective students could find general information about the school, its campus, and the academic programs it offered. There was a news section – often consisting of press releases – housed under media relations or university communications. The website was updated infrequently, with only a handful of pages updated more than a few times a month. Today, universities are creating dynamic websites that include more storytelling, videos, live updating events calendars, RSS feeds users can subscribe to, and interactive virtual tours of the campus. More than ever, prospective students and alumni expect to be able to interact with a university and its content.

That's where Twitter comes into the picture. With Twitter, your audience can interact in real time with information coming from the university. And the university can interact with information coming from its prospective students, current students, alumni, faculty, and staff.

With university Twitter accounts, there are two equally important elements to a content strategy: you must *ACT* and *INTERACT*.

ACT by providing your followers with the content they want. Tweet at least once or twice a day with news of interest, events, rallying points about the university, photos, interesting stats (student–teacher ratio), and anything else your audience might like. Not sure what they like? Social media is casual. Just ask your audience what it likes.

INTERACT by watching what your audience is saying, re-tweeting their updates, or simply congratulating them on their accomplishments. A little interaction between a university account and any member of your university community can go a long way toward strengthening pride and loyalty to your institution.

Convinced yet that Twitter can help your university? Here's how this simple strategy of *ACT* and *INTERACT* can play out across many offices and units across campus.

UNIVERSITY COMMUNICATIONS

Much of higher education is moving to a decentralized publishing and communications model. Schools, colleges, and departments within a university have their own marketers, writers, and events coordinators. That's good news for the university communications department that was previously charged with identifying all of the news and events campus-wide, writing about it, and distributing it to the appropriate audiences. The role of a central university communications office has changed, but the workload has not. Instead of distributing all of the news and information, the central communications office is managing it – assuring that it is consistent in tone, voice, quality, style, and brand identity. The communications office has to manage Twitter content in the same way. The best way to manage the university's overall Twitter presence is to set a good example with the overall university Twitter account.

The university's main Twitter account will likely have the most followers, and therefore, it will need the most content and will receive the most scrutiny. Twitter is a casual place, but when your audience feels you are not providing valuable content, it can be harsh and dismissive. So the first thing to do is to identify the staff members available to update the account regularly and find a source for consistent content.

Act

Students today are busy and are always mobile. They have a full courseload, work internships, and are involved with myriad student groups and extracurricular activities. Twitter allows you to bring the university news and events to them where they are, rather than depending on them visiting your website. For external audiences, particularly alumni and the surrounding community, many of the events and activities at the university go unnoticed. With a university Twitter account, these audiences can stay up-to-date on the latest happenings with mobile applications on their iPhone or Blackberry.

Capturing all of the news and events at the university will be easier for some universities than others. Today, many colleges and universities have websites with a Content Management System (CMS) that includes news and events aggregators. This means that while 10–20 schools and departments across the university are publishing news and scheduling events, they can all be found in one central location thanks to taxonomy built into the site. Most of these news and events aggregators will include an RSS feed, which – with the help of an RSS reader like Google Reader or Bloglines – will allow you to follow all news and events published university-wide in real time. As news and events come through your feed, send them out through Twitter. Not only will your audience stay informed about everything that is happening at your university, if you include links, you are driving more people to your website.

If your university website is not set up with a news and events aggregator, you will have to do it the old fashioned way – talking regularly with marketers and events organizers.

Interact

Some university Twitter accounts provide news and events – nothing more – and are highly successful. Others choose to expand their content, have some fun, and interact. The university's main Twitter account will not be as conversational as other offices and departments, but that should not prevent the manager from posting photos (even from a camera phone) of the campus or events. Experiment with different kinds of posts – interesting statistics, university history, class information not found elsewhere. Shake up the content a little and then watch how people respond to the different types of updates. You can adjust based on reaction.

And if you are bold enough, interact. When people ask questions – and they will – answer them. If a student, faculty or alumnus posts their own accomplishment, re-tweet it. That member of the university may have 50 followers on Twitter, while the university account will likely have 1,000–10,000. Re-tweeting their accomplishment will share it with the entire university community and create a sense of pride for everyone.

Monitoring Your Brand

One of the most important reasons for using a Twitter application, rather than Twitter.com, is the ability to display several columns of content at one time. This feature will allow you to keep two or three columns open with Twitter searches for your brand. These searches, which work like real time Google Alerts, will display any mention of your search terms by a Twitter user. Choose search terms that are frequently used by your community, including your full university name, an abbreviation of your university commonly used, the university president's name, and any other important term you would like to follow. Keep an eye on these mentions and you will have a sense, day-to-day, of the current sentiment toward your university. Brand monitoring on Twitter has become a job of its own in many businesses. Banks, airlines, chain restaurants, and corporations have all hired social media managers whose job it is to follow these brand mentions on Twitter and Facebook and interact. Have a bad meal at a restaurant? Mention it on Twitter and within a day you are likely to get a message from a company representative.

Higher education should be no different. This is the day and age we live in. And the Twitter audience – particularly the younger demographic – expect a timely response to their question or complaint. Not every rant on Twitter deserves a response, but when there is a helpful solution or a person's bad experience can be turned around with a simple response or apology, be there to offer it.

Twitter searches also can be particularly effective for emergency communications. If there is an incident at your university or an event that has potential to become troublesome, create a new search for relevant keywords and watch the stream carefully. Journalists are finding that news is broken regularly by people on scene who post to Twitter (as evidenced by the news stories mentioned earlier). If you are following a happening through the right search terms, you could be the first to find out and will be in a position to enact the appropriate emergency response.

Building Lists
Think of Twitter as a community – because that is the most accurate description of how the service functions. Rarely in the past was there one place where prospective students, current students, staff, faculty, and alumni all gathered. Sure, more of them gather on Facebook, but Facebook does not function in the same way. Fans on Facebook cannot be grouped into different categories in a fan page. With Twitter lists, followers of the university account can be grouped into convenient lists such as: students, faculty, staff, alumni, schools and colleges, offices, and student groups. Lists can take some work to compile. One of the easiest ways of differentiating between followers is to simply send a tweet, "at-reply with your status as student or alumni, we are creating lists." This approach creates more interaction between the university and its audience as each person who at-replies will be sharing their university affiliation with all of their followers as well.

If you begin creating lists and leave them as public, rather than private, all of your followers will be able to see your lists and follow them themselves. Twitter's current search function for finding friends and associates delivers mediocre results, so the university's Twitter lists could be the best place for your university community to find each other on Twitter.

Return on Investment (ROI)
There is a lot to absorb when tackling a Twitter strategy for an entire university. There is a new language to learn, staff to train, and technology to master. So it's only natural to ask, "Is it all worth it?" For many who work in social media, the return on investment is visible every time someone says thank you for an answer to a question they posed or when a student or alumnus proclaims their love for your university on Twitter (it happens all the time). But that might not go so far in a board meeting.

Luckily, many Twitter applications have ROI tools built in. Tweet Deck and Hoot Suite automatically connect to link shortening tools like http://bit.ly or http://ow.ly. Create an account at these sites and link that account to your Tweet Deck or Hoot Suite account, and you will be able to track every click-through from Twitter to your website or wherever you may link. Both bit.ly and ow.ly also offer geographic, browser, and other data that can help you hone your Twitter content. They will also keep track of all conversation on Twitter related to each individual link.

If that is not enough ROI data to present, dig into your website data through Google Analytics or whatever analytics software you may be using. Check the number of page-views a story or site has received and look at the referring site. With many pages, stories, or announcements, there will be a considerable jump in traffic due to social media, Twitter included.

All of this data can help to show a user almost instantly what is effective use of time on social media and what is falling flat with your Twitter audience. Once the content has been crafted based on early ROI data, goals and objectives can be developed to determine if the time spent on Twitter and the subsequent results (web hits, positive audience interaction, or consumer relations) are meeting the overall objectives of the university. These can best be tracked through performance indicators outlined in research by Owyang and Lovett (2010) who track consumer advocacy, satisfaction with consumer relations, and collaboration with customers.

MEDIA RELATIONS

Public and media relations are evolving with technology. The entire industry is reexamining its primary vehicle – the press release. Sure, PR professionals still have lunch with journalists to develop relationships, they still send press releases (maybe not by fax anymore), and they still call journalists to pitch stories. But technology and social media have changed the game. Now public relations professionals talk about the "social media release" and PR 2.0. They are using the technology and the openness of social networks to provide journalists with more engaging and better content. A press release today will include video, links to more relevant information, photography, and will often be search engine optimized to gain the most possible exposure online.

It's a new era of public relations, but at its core it is still about building relationships with journalists. And no service is more tapped into journalists than Twitter. Whether it was fueled by the epiphany that was the Iran election, or another news event on Twitter, journalists are on the bandwagon. Large percentages of reporters in every medium – newspapers (49%), magazines (61%) and Web (73%), are using the service regularly (Cision, 2009). University media relations offices can use Twitter to follow journalists, develop relationships, and provide useful content in a timely manner.

The easiest way to find journalists online is through a specific publication's website, or Twitter directories like http://listorious.com, http://www.wefollow.com, or http://mashable.com/twitterlists.

A media relations strategy on Twitter should be more interact than act. The primary goal will be to develop online relationships with targeted reporters and use those relationships to provide assistance with faculty experts, campus stories, or pitches. But strictly relationship-building will not result in a Twitter stream that anyone wants to follow and read.

Act

Your audience should be reporters, so act by providing regular tweets that are of interest to reporters. If a faculty expert is in the news, tweet about it and provide a link to the chapter. If a journalist sees that another journalist used your faculty expert, it will reinforce that faculty member's expert status. Most media relations departments track media mentions daily and send reports to each school or department with a list of their mentions. The work is already being done. Simply take the extra step to send each article, video, or radio clip out on Twitter. The media account will also borrow content heavily from the overall university account. News and events on campus that are relevant to current events may pique the interest of a reporter. The media relations office will, of course, link to press releases in tweets, but often a well-written story taken from the university account can be more compelling.

Interact

Media relations professionals have for years depended on services like BurellesLuce, Vocus, or Cision to provide media contact lists and basic information (beat, interests, and background) on journalists. Again, social media will not replace these services. It can, however, do a better job than these services at giving a glimpse into the interests of individual reporters. No matter how much research the people at a media monitoring company do, their information can become outdated quickly. Following a journalist on Twitter allows media relations professionals to see, day-to-day, where a reporter's interests lie.

Follow a single reporter for a week on Twitter and you will know what stories he is pursuing, trends he is watching, and maybe a new hobby he has taken up. That is a lot of very powerful information as you try to pitch, share stories, or develop a relationship. Maybe the political reporter you have been trying to pitch for months shares your love for organic food. That information would not be available in a media monitoring service, but it might come up frequently on Twitter. Social media is successful because it allows people with common interests and passions to connect. Even if it's a business relationship, these common interests can go a long way to successful relationship building and pitching.

Develop reporter lists of your own and follow them with individual columns in your Twitter application. An overall reporters' list will be a helpful catch-all that could expose larger trends in the media, but it is equally important to develop strong lists in categories important to your institution. It depends on the office's goals, but helpful lists could include: by publication type (newspaper, magazine, radio, television, and academic journal); or by topic (politics, science, arts, and environment). If the media relations Twitter manager is great at multitasking, include all of those categories. Just be ready to follow 15–25 columns of Twitter content.

ADMISSIONS

"Just toured [your university]. Amazing. I can't wait to go." "I can't decide between [your university] and [your rival university], what should I do?" These tweets, and others like them, are commonplace on Twitter. Ever wonder what prospective students are thinking while taking an admissions tour? Now that they all have smart phones, many are telling you what they are thinking while they are still on the tour – you just have to be listening. Prospective students today begin touring schools already pre-loaded with a wealth of information. By junior year in high school, they are receiving materials from colleges and universities, they have studied dozens of websites, and have talked with their friends and family members. With all of that information to absorb – much of it very similar – it's tough for one university to stand out.

Traditionally, colleges and universities stand out based on their brand identity, marketing materials, athletics programs, or even a mascot. But the millennial generation is cynical about marketing. They do not trust it. What they want is a sense of belonging at your school and they have to feel that they came upon that feeling organically. Sounds like a tall order, does not it? But it can be as simple as being in the same sandbox with them.

Act

Flip through the brochure, viewbook, or marketing materials your university admissions office sends to prospective students. It's full of scenic campus images, student testimonials, information about academic programs and majors, numbers and statistics, and anything else that sets your school apart. It's attractive, the language is well crafted, and it probably took a long time to put together. But every other school is doing it and prospective students likely have a stack of 10–12 of them. Deconstruct that information and feed it out on Twitter in approachable, natural language through several admission Twitter accounts. Create an overall admissions Twitter account and encourage each of your admissions representatives to create their own accounts. Now you have separated yourself from the bunch – at least until every admissions office has jumped on Twitter.

Millennials are attached to their smart phones. They are accessing information at all times during the day from any location. Although the shiny viewbook is collecting dust on their desk at home, your admissions office, or an individual admissions staff member, can feed prospective students bits of information to entice them to come to your school. A photo of campus filled with students, a quote from a student who found their calling, a success story about a freshman doing great things at the university – each is a great way to get a prospective student interested in your school. In a brochure, those stories are stagnant. Words sit on a page. On Twitter, the entire university community, and any member of the Twitter public following your admissions account can read it. If you send out a student testimonial and that student re-tweets it, and his or her friends re-tweet it, there is a clear sense of community being demonstrated. And prospective students see that. A simple 140-character piece of content from your brochure has now been reinforced by people they trust – students – and in turn, they will begin to trust you.

Interact

Trust is also built through interaction. Remember, millennials expect, almost demand, interaction. Like the university communications office, admissions should be following a Twitter search for any mention of the university. If you are following these mentions, and you see tweets about your school by prospective students, follow them. If they just applied, say thanks and offer to answer any questions they may have. If they just got accepted, congratulate them and offer to answer any questions they may have. That brief interaction will have an impact. Twitter is about conversation. When a prospective student sees that the university they just applied to taking a one-on-one interest in them, it will set your school apart.

Watch what prospective students are tweeting about, their interests, their passions, and begin to cater your content based on their interests. That does not mean you have to hold separate conversations with hundreds of prospective students. Instead, if you spot several students tweeting about the environment, it may be time to send out a tweet about the university's green initiatives or science programs. If several students ask a similar question, send out that information with a link to your website.

Many admissions offices have student ambassadors who run tours of the campus and are available to prospective students as a resource. Encourage your student ambassadors to get on Twitter or identify those who are there already. If they are willing to become ambassadors on Twitter as well, create a student list under the admissions account. Refer prospective students to the admissions student list on a regular basis.

Once a prospective student sees that your school is speaking its language, using the same technology, and not afraid to allow them to talk directly to other students in the same age group, their trust will be solidified. They may even go home and open up that shiny brochure again.

CAREER SERVICES

Higher education is about the pursuit of knowledge and becoming a well-informed and well-rounded citizen. At least that's the answer many professors and higher education professionals would give. Ask a prospective or current college student and it's more likely they will say, "I need a college degree to get a decent job." A university career services office or career center aids students in that pursuit. If a student seeks help, the career center will provide them with advice on resume writing, interviewing, and networking. If they want an internship during their time at the university, the career center will provide them with internship listings, helpful resources, or contacts. Students develop a bond with the career center staff that pushed them along the path to a successful career. There's one hitch, students have to walk in the door and ask for help to receive any of these services.

Some forward-thinking career center offices are using blogs. They are blogging about the current job market, internships available in the community, resume writing, networking, all of the advice they would provide a student who walked through the door. Others host student blogs, where current students share their internship experiences or advice about job searches and interviewing. It's all useful information that builds trust and reaches students (who are interested) without them physically visiting the office. They can visit the website or follow the RSS feed. Why not put that information in one more place where students hang out.

Act

Identify all of the resources your career services office provides and think of how to disseminate it clearly through Twitter. Listen to the feedback of the students who come into the office for advice. What did they find particularly helpful? What sites are they looking at when they are searching for internships? Take the most successful advice and tips you are already providing and provide it in 140 characters with links back to your website.

Working on Twitter is nothing new. Many higher education professionals worry that it will be a drain on time and resources. But if your office is functioning well, and knows its strengths, Twitter is as simple as boiling all of those tips and resources down into one important, impactful – and casual – sentence. A successful Twitter account could potentially be run by a single person in less than an hour a day, but in many cases it will take more time and more staff. A significant 64% of marketers use social media for 5 h or more each week and 39% for 10 or more hours weekly (Stelzner, 2009). Fortune 100 companies have an average of 4.2 Twitter accounts per company and send out an average of 27 tweets each week (Burson-Marsteller, 2010). These stats would suggest that, depending on the size of your university, it would not take more than two or three staff members in a Career Services office – or any university office – to maintain a similar output.

For a career services office, take all of that great information you provide, take off the administrator hat, and send tweets as if you were talking one-on-one with a 19-year-old. Tell them, "a cool new internship opened up at Discovery," and provide a link. If you are blogging, announce that your latest blog post is up and ask them to comment. Finally, look for local businesses on Twitter. Begin following them. They will be a key to how a career services office can interact with students in a way that is unparalleled in any other medium.

Interact

More than most offices at a university, career services has a personal relationship with students. The staff is involved in a very important part of a student's life. If you can help them land that great internship that leads to their dream job, they will remember you, and the institution, for the rest of their lives. Twitter provides an opportunity to build on those relationships. Your tweets will be full of helpful information, advice, and resources, but students will have questions. Be sure to have a well-informed staff member available on Twitter to answer these questions in a timely manner. Like the admissions office, it's helpful to identify former or current students who have found internships or jobs through the career center and create a list of them on Twitter. Refer students to the list so they can talk to peers about their job hunt. Most importantly, develop relationships with local businesses on Twitter and begin introducing your students to them. Twitter can be a virtual networking event and your office should be the one with connections, introducing the young, shy future intern to the company representatives.

According to *Socialnomics – Social Media Blog* by Erik Qualman (2009), 300,000 businesses now have a presence on Twitter. That number continues to grow as smaller businesses see companies like Comcast, Dell, Jet Blue, and Whole Foods that have had both financial and customer relations success through Twitter (Swartz, 2009). Most of those accounts are run by one or two people who also understand that Twitter is about building relationships and many of them are looking for interns.

If you have a student who is interested in marketing jobs, send them a tweet with the Twitter names of a few marketing firms that are looking for interns. If you do not have the time to match individual students to individual businesses on Twitter there are other methods. On Twitter, there is a hashtag #FollowFriday or #FF for short. Every Friday, people on Twitter recommend other useful Twitter accounts to follow. A career services office can use Follow Friday to suggest any number of businesses to students. If you have developed a lot of relationships with local businesses, each tweet can be split up in categories (e.g., #FF media edition, #FF financial edition, and #FF arts edition).

A simple introduction on Twitter can mean a future career for a student.

ALUMNI RELATIONS

If your university Twitter presence has been consistent, by the time a student graduates, he or she will have had a rich relationship with multiple university Twitter accounts for four years. Recent research shows that 92.2% of students highly engaged in social media (more than an hour a day) and 73.4% of students who use social media less than an hour a day rate their connection to their friends at their university as high or very high (Junco, 2009). Those numbers have a greater implication for alumni relations when taken in the context of previous research on social integration and institutional support, which found, "the greater the level of social integration, the greater the level of subsequent commitment to the institution" (Braxton, Sullivan, & Johnson, 1997). When they walk across the stage at commencement and head out into the real world, the engagement should continue.

An alumni relations and development office has the unenviable job of fostering loyalty to the school while also soliciting donations. Young alumni, who are still paying off student loans, can become annoyed by calls for donations. That's due in large part to the fact that the call for money may be the only contact they have from their university after they graduate. However, if an alumni relations Twitter account continues to provide news, events, and networking opportunities to graduates, the strong relationship will continue throughout their lives and the call for a donation would not seem so out of place.

Act

Alumni tweets should be about providing information that will reinforce pride in the institution and be of value to your audience. Tweet news stories from the alumni magazine and link to articles in the news that feature alumni. Give them content that will show what their former classmates are doing today and they will feel every bit as much a part of the community as they did when they were in school. Support that feeling by sending out the occasional campus photo. When spring hits, tweet a photo of students spread across the quad so alumni can reminisce about their time there. At big events, send out tweets and photos so alumni can feel like they are still on campus. We are all a little sentimental and nostalgia is powerful.

Build lists of alumni from each state, region, or country. Provide them with a network of other alumni they can communicate with any time on Twitter and alert alumni about upcoming events being held in their area.

Interact

Show alumni that you still care. Re-tweet. It's that easy.

Once you have identified your alumni on Twitter and you have lists built, follow all of them. Keep track of what they are doing. When they get a new job, they'll probably tweet about it. Congratulate them and re-tweet it so that your university community on Twitter knows of their accomplishments. Use "Follow Friday" to highlight alumni to the rest of the community.

It makes a huge difference when an alumnus knows their school is watching their progress in life.

THE FUTURE

Administration

Some higher education leaders, including presidents, deans, and provosts, are on Twitter. But a search for higher education administrators on Twitter reveals that even the largest Twitter lists of presidents, deans, and provosts consist of 49 (Stroble, 2010), 44 (Rudolph, 2010), and 38 (American Council on Education, 2010). That is hardly a large percentage considering there are more than 4,000 universities and colleges in the United States alone. However, with the growth of social media and the expectation of interaction, higher education leaders are missing valuable opportunities if they are not using social media.

With higher education administration, transparency can go a long way to building support. If the university president is on Twitter, answering the occasional question, distributing campus news, and updating the campus on the state of the university, faculty, students, and staff will recognize and applaud that openness. A Twitter account for the provost, president, marketing leaders and others, can also help to portray your institution as a leader in the field. A major driver in rankings and evaluation of institutions of higher education is review from peers. If your administration is on Twitter, providing insight, answering questions of higher education journalists and bloggers, or talking with peers in other institutions, it will build awareness.

Unlike most other accounts, where there is an expectation of at least one tweet a day, a higher education leader will not have to dedicate as much time. There is an expectation of interaction, but the community knows you are busy. Even a tweet a week will do.

In the Classroom

Blame it on the University of Phoenix, the popularity of the podcast, or the evolution of high-quality, reasonably priced video and audio technology – the classroom lecture has gone viral. It's an uncomfortable subject for some faculty who see lectures as intellectual property. However, the faculty that have embraced an open courseware model are fueling a movement that is unlikely to die.

Sites like iTunesU (http://www.apple.com/education/itunes-u/), the Open Courseware Consortium (http://www.ocwconsortium.org/), and http://academicearth.org give anyone with an Internet connection access to video lectures, class notes, assignments, and syllabi from some of the top colleges and universities in the country on just about any subject.

A handful of open and innovative teachers have recognized this trend and seen a role for Twitter in the open courseware environment. Dr. Monica Rankin, a professor of History at the University of Texas at Dallas has been fielding interest from educators across the country since a video was posted on YouTube about her use of Twitter in a U.S. History class in the spring 2009 semester (http://www.youtube.com/watch?v=6WPVWDkF7U8).

Rankin created a hashtag for the class, displayed the Twitter stream of notes and comments of students during every lecture, and used her graduate assistants to monitor the conversation and feed her relevant comments, questions, and discussion. According to Rankin (2009), "the twitter experiment was successful primarily because it encouraged students to engage who otherwise would not."

That alone is reason enough to start using Twitter in the classroom. But it can become so much bigger. If this treatment of Twitter in the classroom becomes the norm, there will be hundreds of thousands of hashtags – open to the public – with notes from every class member on the material they are studying in class. With the aforementioned opencourseware sites, staff members have to organize the videotaping of lectures, get syllabi and assignments from professors, and compile notes on each class. To bring all of those notes to the entire world through Twitter, all it would take is to identify class hashtags and create a website that served as an aggregator of all class associated hash tags.

Going to class through Twitter may be years away – and it may never happen – but it is already a brave new world in higher education. And Twitter is fueling this new world in every aspect of university life.

CONCLUSION

Twitter use in higher education is not going away and the 30.7% of higher education professionals using Twitter (Magna, 2009) are the trendsetters leading a new era of real-time, interactive communication. They may have started a university Twitter account a couple of years ago to test the waters and explore its uses. When they started, Twitter – or social media in general – was probably not part of their job description. Today, universities are following the success of businesses like Comcast – which has 10 employees dedicated to social media (Swartz, 2009) – by adding social media skills to job requirements and recreating websites to include social media plugins and Twitter landing pages. Higher education Twitter lists appear among the most popular lists on Listorious (Listorious, 2010). Hash tags like #highered, #edtech, and the *Washington Post*'s #wpcollege are used daily by higher education professionals to share experiences, inspiration, and ideas for previously unexplored uses of Twitter. Many of the same people are doing more than meeting virtually, they are attending conferences like EduWeb and HighEdWeb and joining groups like Social Media Club EDU to bring together hundreds of higher education professionals and students to share best practices and teach the uninitiated.

Although more higher education professionals begin to see the value of Twitter, so do the 300,000 people joining the service daily. As Twitter grows, it continues to evolve to meet the demand and needs of new users with expanded features and better usability. Developers continue to create applications that make Twitter easier to use, easier to understand, and more effective as a business and communications tool. By the time this chapter is published, there could be features of Twitter aforementioned that have completely changed. However, the key to Twitter's success – the reason so many higher education professionals and their audiences have adopted it – will never change. Twitter allows everyone in a higher education community – students, faculty, alumni, and staff from every office across campus – to *act, interact,* and develop a community.

REFERENCES

American Council on Education. (2010). Presidents & chancellors: College & university presidents & chancellors. Twitter. Available at http://twitter.com/ACEducation/presidents-chancellors

Ammah-Tagoe, A. (2009). Who's winning the Twitter wars? *Newsweek*. Available at http://www.newsweek.com/id/214982/page/1
Ashburn, E. (2007). Prospective students rely on campus visits and web sites to learn about colleges, Report Says. *The Chronicle of Higher Education*. Available at http://chronicle.com/article/Prospective-Students-Rely-o/13774/#
Berman, A. (2009). Iran's Twitter revolution. *The Nation*. Available at http://www.thenation.com/blogs/notion/443634
Braxton, J. M., Sullivan, A. V. S., & Johnson, R. M., Jr. (1997). Appraising Tinto's theory of college student departure. In: J. C. Smart (Ed.), *Higher education: Handbook of theory and research* (pp. 106–164). New York: Agathon Press.
Burson-Marsteller. (2010). The global social media CHECK-up 2010. Burson-Marsteller. Available at http://www.burson-marsteller.com/Innovation_and_insights/blogs_and_podcasts/BM_Blog/Lists/Posts/Post.aspx?ID=160
Busari, S. (2008). Tweeting the terror: How social media reacted to Mumbai. CNN. Available at http://edition.cnn.com/2008/WORLD/asiapcf/11/27/mumbai.twitter/index.html
Cellan-Jones, R. (2009). Twitter and a classic picture. BBC. Available at http://www.bbc.co.uk/blogs/technology/2009/01/twitter_and_a_classic_picture.html
Cision (2009). 2009 Social media & online usage study. George Washington University and Cision. Available at http://us.cision.com/news_room/press_releases/2010/2010-1-20_gwu_survey.asp
Fox, S., Zickuhr, K., & Smith, A. (2009). Twitter and status updating, fall 2009. *Pew Internet & American Life Project*. Available at http://www.pewinternet.org/Experts/~/link.aspx?_id=6C747837133C4A54A4D0351E2683478B&_z=z
Junco, R. (2009). *Teaching teens to Twitter: Supporting engagement in the college classroom*. Presentation at the Harvard Berkman Center for Internet & Society Luncheon Series. Cambridge, MA.
Listorious (2010). Listorious: Higher education. *Listorious.com*. Available at http://www.listorious.com/tags/highereducation
Magna (2009). Twitter in higher education: Usage habits and trends of today's college faculty. *Faculty Focus*. Available at http://www.facultyfocus.com/wp-content/uploads/images/twittersurvey_facultyfocus.pdf
Martin, D. (2009). Twitter quitters post roadblock to long-term growth. *Nielson Wire*. Available at http://blog.nielsen.com/nielsenwire/online_mobile/twitter-quitters-post-roadblock-to-long-term-growth/
Owyang, J., & Lovett, J. (2010). *Social marketing analytics: A new framework for measuring results in social media*. San Mateo, CA: Altimeter Group.
Qualman, E. (2009). Social media ROI: Socialnomics. *Socialnomics – Social Media Blog*. Available at http://socialnomics.net/video/
Quantcast (2010). Twitter.com – quantcast audience profile. Quantcast.com. Available at http://www.quantcast.com/twitter.com
Rankin, M. (2009). Some general comments on the "Twitter Experiment." *University of Texas at Dallas*. Available at http://www.utdallas.edu/~mrankin/usweb/twitterconclusions.htm
Rudolph, N. (2010). UPresidents. Twitter. Available at http://twitter.com/NikiRudolph/upresidents
Sanford, M. (2010). Growing around the world. *Twitter Blog*. Available at http://blog.twitter.com/2010/04/growing-around-world.html

Stelzner, M. (2009). Marketing industry report: How marketers are using social media to grow their businesses. *White Paper Source*. Available at http://www.whitepapersource.com/socialmediamarketing/report/

Stroble, B. (2010). Higher ed leaders: Presidents, chancellors, deans. Twitter. Available at http://twitter.com/websterpres/higher-ed-leaders

Swartz, J. (2009). Businesses use Twitter to communicate with customers. *USA Today*. Available at http://www.usatoday.com/tech/news/2009-06-25-twitter-businesses-consumers_N.htm

Waters, A. (2010). Just the facts: Statistics from Twitter chirp. *Read Write Web*. Available at http://www.readwriteweb.com/archives/just_the_facts_statistics_from_twitter_chirp.php

ABOUT THE AUTHORS

Jill Beard is a Library and Learning Support Manager at Bournemouth University, a service which includes libraries, learning technology, and academic skills development. She has written extensively over many years on a wide range of subjects and is currently co-editing a book on Digital Library Environments in Higher Education (Ashgate, 2010).

Melanie Booth is the Dean for Learning & Program Assessment and the Director of the Center for Experiential Learning & Assessment at Marylhurst University. She specializes in teaching, learning, and assessment in higher education; adult learning and development; service-learning and social action; Prior Learning Assessment; and the educational use of social media in higher educational settings. Melanie utilizes various social media tools to mentor and advise her students as well as to facilitate workshops and courses for various departments on and off campus. She is on the Board of the Adult Higher Education Alliance and has consulted at several institutions regarding teaching, learning, and assessment of adult learners in higher education. She and Art Esposito co-taught Introduction to Social Media Communications: Facebook, YouTube, Twitter, & More (http://marylhurst20.wordpress.com/).

Melissa Bowden is a subject support librarian for Law at Bournemouth University. Melissa received a masters degree in Information Management from the University of North London. Her information experience is in education, having worked in both FE and HE libraries. Melissa is especially interested in social media and legal information provision.

Arthur Esposito is a director of Discovery (Undeclared) Advising at Virginia Commonwealth University (VCU) and has been advising first-year and undeclared students at VCU since the summer of 2004. He specializes in encouraging student engagement and the promotion of his advisees becoming active participants in their own collegiate opportunities, educational planning and career goal-setting. Art has also dedicated much of his research to identifying effective ways of engaging students in web-based environments – meeting them "on their own turf" – and attempting to "socialize" them into viewing their educational career as the same sort of interesting and compelling experience as is their online world of social networks and Web 2.0 platforms. He is the creator and proponent of an advising approached referred to as Supplemental Virtual Advising and brings five years of successful implementation to bear on the presentations and workshops he delivers. Art is an active member of the National Academic Advising Association (NACADA), regularly presenting at Regional and National conferences, as part of NACADA Webinars and as a member of the NACADA Consultant and Speaker Service. He has also spent the past two years on the steering committee for both Undeclared and Exploratory and Technology in Advising Commissions. He and Melanie Booth co-taught Introduction to Social Media Communications: Facebook, YouTube, Twitter, & More (http://marylhurst20.wordpress.com/).

Neil Ford is a subject librarian for Health and Social Care at Bournemouth University. Neil received a masters degree in Information and Library Studies from University of Wales, Aberystwyth, after research into staff attitudes toward technology uptake in the UK public libraries. Neil's library and information experience includes health, public, and commercial libraries. In his current role Neil is especially interested in the use of Social Media in delivering Information Literacy materials.

Philip Griffiths is a reader of Energy Storage Integration in the School of the Built Environment, University of Ulster. His research work includes developing energy storage systems for buildings, advanced glazing materials, and pedagogic research into e-learning and the use of social networking.

Leslie Hitch is a Senior Faculty Fellow at Northeastern University College of Professional Studies and Teaching Fellow at Swinburne (Australia). With an MBA and an Ed.D., she specializes in higher education studies. She was Director of Northeastern's Academic Technology Services; Vice President Harcourt, Inc.; Executive Development Director, Babson College; Director Simmons College Communications Management Program; and has managed strategic planning for several colleges.

Jon Hussey is a manager of Web Communications for American University. He is in charge of the home page of the university's recently redesigned, award-winning Web site and the university's social media efforts. The first person to develop an office Twitter account, he successfully built the @aumedia account to develop relationships with students and alumni as well as news media. Since creating that account, he has brought the @AmericanU Twitter account from 21 fans in September 2009, to more than 3,000 fans today. He has worked with the admissions, alumni relations, career center, and human resources offices, as well as all of the schools and colleges to develop unique Twitter accounts and strategies.

Eric Kowalik is a web developer with over 10 years of experience in the field of higher education. For six years he worked as Assistant Director of Communication at the University of California's only school of computer science. There he helped launch and manage the school's social media presence on YouTube, Facebook and Twitter, utilizing these tools to increase engagement with prospective students and alumni. Currently he is an instructional designer at Marquette University, working to incorporate social media to enhance online teaching and learning. He holds a B.A. in Journalism from Marquette University, and a M.S. in Instructional Design and Technology from California State University-Fullerton.

P. Charles Livermore is an eBrarian at St. John's University, New York, received his undergraduate degree from the College of Wooster in Ohio, holds a masters degree in library science from Columbia University and an M.B.A. from Rutgers University. As a part of the Systems and eServices Department, Professor Livermore serves in Reference, instruction, faculty development workshops presentation and web support.

Heather M. Makrez is the associate director of Programs and Alumni Services at the University of Massachusetts Lowell where she also received her bachelors degree in History and masters degree in Regional Economic and Social Development. Her thesis was entitled "The Importance of International Education in Higher Education." She has been a trustee for the University of Massachusetts system, and has worked at both the President's office and Dartmouth campus. In addition to being in Alumni Relations, Heather also consults other university departments on the best practices and new innovative ideas of using social media in the most effect ways. Currently, she is enjoying the fast-paced environment of higher education advancement while living close to Boston, MA.

Bree McEwan earned her PhD from Arizona State University in 2009. She is an assistant professor in the Department of Communication at Western Illinois University. Dr. McEwan's research interests include the formation and maintenance of social networks. Her previous research has focused on the relationship between freshmen social networks and freshmen's persistence at the university.

Nicolle Merrill holds a B.A. in French from the University of Oregon and an M.A. in Culture, Communication, and Globalization from Aalborg

University in Denmark. Her writing interests lie at the cross sections of international education, digital ethnography, and social entrepreneurship. She is the University Relations Manager for GlobalCampus and specializes in Internet recruiting. GlobalCampus is a social enterprise created to make the international market more transparent for students. She was recruited for her current job through Twitter, blogs occasionally on international education topics, and connects to her coworkers abroad on Skype daily.

Nicola Osborne is the Social Media Officer for EDINA, a JISC appointed national data centre based at the University of Edinburgh. Nicola acts as an evangelist for new technologies, advising EDINA projects, and services on current social media tools, practice and opportunities, and contributing to organisational strategy in these areas. She is also currently undertaking the innovative M.Sc. in e-Learning with the University of Edinburgh.

Nancy Richmond currently holds a variety of roles as a career counselor, educator, presenter, and consultant. She has substantial experience in helping students and higher education professionals in using technology during the career development process. Nancy's expertise includes assisting higher educational professionals use social media to solve problems, share information and stay current with new trends in the marketplace. She has been working in higher education for over 10 years at Boston University, Northeastern University, and currently at Massachusetts Institute of Technology. Nancy created the LinkedIn group "Career Counselor Technology Forum" to connect career counselors around the world which now has over 500 members. Several of her recent presentations and webinars have included Using Social Media for your Job Search, The Value of LinkedIn, Using Social Media for Professional Development, and Why Use Twitter. Nancy is enrolled in the Doctor of Education program at Northeastern University and has a Master's of Education in Counseling from Boston University.

Beth Rochefort is an instructional designer and adjunct faculty at Northeastern University. She works with faculty across all disciplines to develop online and hybrid courses for Northeastern University Online. She holds a B.A. in Journalism and Graphic Design from Northeastern University, an M.Ed. in Education from the Harvard Graduate School of Education, and is currently pursuing her Ed.D. at Northeastern University.

Penny Schouten has worked for the past 20 years in study abroad, media, and education. She is a social media specialist as well as a branding and website design strategist. She received her MPS degree in Humanistic/International

Education at SUNY New Paltz and her M.Sc. from the University of Westminster in E-Business. As Marketing Coordinator for Study Abroad at SUNY New Paltz her pioneering use of social media was recognized during the Forum on Education Abroad's Standards of Good Practice review process. She has been interviewed by various media on using social media in international education and co-authored the article "Instant Connections" published in NAFSA's International Educator magazine. Penny is currently a member of the NAFSA Education Abroad Technology Taskforce, Co-Chair of the Technology Special Interest Group and NAFSA Region X Communications Manager.

Anthony Wall joined the University of Ulster as a research assistant in 1999; he was appointed as a lecturer in 2000 and a senior lecturer in 2007. His research areas include the Private Finance Initiative/Public-Private Partnerships, performance management, intellectual capital, students entering higher education, and social networking sites. Anthony has worked for both local and central government and also in the private sector.

Charles Wankel is associate professor of Management at St. John's University, New York. He holds a doctorate from New York University. He serves at Erasmus University, Rotterdam School of Management, on the Dissertation Committee and as Honorary Vice Rector at the Poznań University of Business. He has received numerous awards from the Academy of Management, including the 2010 Service Award of its Organizations and the Natural Environment Division. His recent books include *Teaching Arts and Science with the New Social Media* (March 2011), *Educating Educators with Social Media* (2011), *Cutting-Edge Social Media Approaches to Business Education* (2010), *Being and Becoming a Management Education Scholar* (2010), *Emerging Ethical Issues of Life in Virtual Worlds* (2010), and *Global Sustainability as a Business Imperative* (2010). He is the leading founder and director of scholarly virtual communities for management professors, currently directing eight with thousands of participants in more than 70 nations. Charles has taught in Lithuania at the Kaunas University of Technology (Fulbright Fellowship) and the University of Vilnius (United Nations Development Program and Soros Foundation funding). Invited lectures include Distinguished Speaker at the Education without Border Conference, Abu Dhabi and Keynote speaker at the Nippon Academy of Management Conference. Corporate clients include McDonald's Corporation's Hamburger University and IBM Learning Services. Pro bono consulting assignments include total quality management programs for the Lithuanian National Postal Service.

Laura A. Wankel, Ed.D. Vice President for Student Affairs has been at Seton Hall University since 1995. While at Seton Hall she has also held titles of Vice Chancellor for Student Affairs and Vice President for Student Affairs & Enrollment Services. During her tenure she has been responsible for a variety of services and programs including Undergraduate Admissions, Student Financial Aid, Student Accounts, Registrar, Dean of Students and Community Development, Public Safety and Security, Student Health Services, The Career Center, Disability Support Services, Student Counseling Services, Housing and Residence Life and Athletics & Recreational Programs. Before coming to Seton Hall University, Dr. Wankel served as Assistant Vice President for Student Affairs at SUNY Purchase from 1987 to 1995. From 1983 to 1987, Dr. Wankel was Assistant Dean for Campus and Residence Operations at SUNY Purchase. Before that, she served in student affairs positions at the University of Pittsburgh.

Dr. Wankel has been an active NASPA Student Affairs Administrators in Higher Education member at both the regional and national level. She has served as a program reviewer for several NASPA national conferences, member of the Region II Advisory Board, Pre-Conference Program Coordinator and member of the 1994 national conference committee. She has also been on the editorial board for the NASPA Journal and currently serves on the editorial board for the Journal of Student Affairs Research and Practice. Additionally, she has recently been elected as Regional Vice President for Region II of NASPA and serves on the NASPA Board of Directors.

Dr. Wankel holds a bachelors degree in American History from SUNY Oneonta where she graduated magna cum laude. She holds a M.Ed. from the University of South Carolina and an Ed.D. in student personnel administration from Teacher's College, Columbia University. Dr. Wankel also received a certificate from the Institute for Educational Management (IEM) from the Harvard Institute for Higher Education. Dr. Wankel has served in a consulting capacity to a number of education-related projects, including, Learn and Serve America and the Corporation for National and Community Service (AmeriCorps).

Dr. Wankel has a chapter on crisis management in Understanding Student Affairs in Catholic Colleges and Universities that is based on the tragic residence hall fire at Seton Hall University. She is co-editor of Reading the Signs: Using Case Studies to Discuss Student Life Issues at Catholic Colleges and Universities in the United States. She also serves on the Board of Directors of the Association of Student Affairs at Catholic Colleges and Universities (ASACCU), and has presented on issues in higher education nationally as well as in Lithuania and Japan.

About the Authors

Karen Weaver is the Director of Athletics, Intramurals and Recreation at Pennsylvania State University – The Abington College. She received her doctoral degree in Higher Education Management from the University of Pennsylvania. Her research focus centers on the business of college sports and television, with a particular interest in new media technologies. She has presented her research at symposiums in Paris, France and the United States. She spent 16 years as a collegiate head field hockey coach, with 10 of those years as a coach in NCAA Division I. Her teams made five post season appearances and won an NCAA National Championship while going undefeated, the first team to do so. She served as the broadcast announcer and assistant producer for men's and women's field hockey at the 1996 Centennial Olympic Games in Atlanta, Georgia. She is currently working with the Big Ten Network as a color analyst.

SUBJECT INDEX

Alumni, xvi–xviii, 3, 25, 49, 71, 85, 96, 100–101, 105, 127, 129–132, 134–135, 137, 141, 144, 147, 167, 191, 194–196, 199–200, 202, 206, 211–215, 217–223, 225, 229–247, 249–251, 253, 255–257, 259, 267–268, 270, 274–275
Ambient Intimacy, 89, 100
American College Testing Programs, 5
American Red Cross, 205
American University, 225, 253, 274
Amherst College, 193, 225
Apex Learning, 78

BBC News, 131
Bebo, 56, 58–59, 61–62
Blackboard, 77, 109, 134, 137
Blog, xvi, 31, 33–36, 43–44, 46, 60, 90, 95, 98, 100, 128–129, 133–137, 140, 161, 171–172, 174–178, 180, 183, 215, 219–221, 265–266
BlogTalk Radio, 134
Bournemouth University, xiv, 105, 107, 111–113, 118, 120, 122, 273–274
British and Irish Association of Law Librarians (BIALL), 122
Brizzly, 173
Butler University, 216, 224

California State University, 223, 225, 275
Career Management, xv–xvi, 147–159, 161–163
Career Resilience, 150
CNN, 204

Collaboration, xiv–xv, 89, 105–107, 117–118, 123, 142, 151, 260
College Sports Business, 204
Comcast, xviii, 206, 266, 270
Content Management System (CMS), 54, 63, 257
Continuing professional development (CPD), 107, 122–123
Copyright, 3, 25, 49, 71, 85, 105, 112–113, 127, 147, 167, 191, 211, 229, 249
CoverItLive, xvi, 172–173, 175–176, 181
Creative Commons, 114, 177
Creepy Treehouses, 91, 96

Davenport University, 217
Delicious, 108–109, 114
Digital ethnography, 25, 27–31, 45, 179, 276
DoesFollow, 178
Donald Bren School of Information and Computer Sciences, 219
Duke University, 198

EduWeb, 270
Efficiency, 243
Enrollment management, xiii, 3, 25, 49, 51, 53, 55, 57, 59, 61, 63, 71, 85, 105, 127, 147, 167, 191, 211, 229, 249
Epistemic frames, 80
EventBrite, 170

Facebook, xii, xvi, 3–4, 7–20, 25–28, 31, 37–39, 42, 44–46, 50, 53, 56–58, 62, 64, 88, 90–101, 112, 115–117, 122, 128–130,

132–136, 139–143, 148–153, 157–160, 163, 167, 171, 195, 197, 199–201, 205, 214–220, 223, 232, 235–237, 240, 242–243, 245, 254, 258–259, 273–275
Flickr, xvi, 50, 114, 129, 132, 134, 143, 167–168, 170, 172–173, 175, 177, 203, 214–215, 225, 233
Folksonomy, 109
Fordham University, 253
for-profit colleges, 222

Genome Island, 73
George Washington University, 253
Georgia Tech, 225
GlobalCampus, 27, 32–36, 43, 45–47, 276
Google, xviii, 44, 71, 115, 121, 132–133, 138, 140, 160–161, 176, 187, 195, 203, 236, 240, 257–258, 260
Google Reader, 121, 257
GoogleTalk, 139

Harrisburg University of Science and Technology, 59, 223
Hashtags, xvi, 33, 43, 47, 115, 167, 172–174, 181, 253–254, 269
Health, 113, 120, 130–131, 136, 218, 234, 250, 274, 278
Higher Education Academy, 107
Higher Education Research Institute, 9, 14
HootSuite, 142

Indiana University Bloomington, 254
Interprofessional, 120

JISC Repositories and Preservation Program, 170

Learning Management Systems, 97, 137
Learning technologist, xv, 106–107, 123
Librarian, 71, 80, 82, 113, 120–122, 203, 273–274
Linden Labs, 72

LinkedIn, xii, 33–36, 38–39, 42–44, 88, 91, 94–95, 98, 101, 129, 132, 134–135, 137, 139, 148–153, 157, 159–161, 199, 201–203, 233, 235–244, 276
Listorious, 253, 261, 270
listserv, 12, 36, 43

Mentoring 2.0, xiv, 85, 87–89, 91, 93, 95–97, 99–101
Michigan State University, 9
Microblogging, xiv, 105–107, 114–115, 118–119, 123, 153, 171, 251–252
Microsoft, 78
Mumbai, 239, 251
MySpace, 4, 26, 38–39, 51–52, 140, 195, 214–215, 219, 232

NCAA, 200, 206, 279
Netnography, 29
Netville, 12
Networking, xii–xiii, xv, xvii–xviii, 3–4, 7–11, 13, 16, 19–20, 26, 28, 30, 38–39, 41–42, 44–46, 49–51, 53, 64, 86, 106–107, 113, 115, 127, 130, 133–134, 137, 140–141, 144, 147–162, 168–169, 171, 175, 183–184, 191–192, 195, 197, 201–202, 215–216, 223, 226, 229, 231–232, 243, 247, 264–267, 274, 277
Nike, 254
Ning, 38, 57–58, 88, 129, 173

Open Courseware Consortium, 269
OpenKnowledge Scotland, 176
Orkut, 38–39, 44
Oxford University, 53, 180

Pageflakes, 121
Papa John's Pizza, 200–201
Pew Research Center, 9, 229
PlayStation, 206
Princeton University, 221
Profile Pages, 158

Really Simple Syndication (RSS), 95, 113–114, 121, 172, 187, 224, 238, 242–243, 255, 257, 265
RepositoryFringe, 170, 172
Retweets, 34–36, 43, 45
RSS, 95, 113–114, 121, 172, 187, 224, 238, 242–243, 255, 257, 265

Second Life, xiii, 71–73, 75–79, 81, 129
Simmons College, 225, 274
Sistine Chapel, 73
SL Globe Theater, 73
SMS, 211, 224
Social bookmarking, xiv, 88, 105, 107–114, 123
Social capital, 3, 6, 12–14
Socialnomics—Social Media Blog, 266
Soda.sh, 173
St. John's University, 74–77, 80, 275, 277
Stanford University, 80, 203
Starbucks, 222
State University of New York, 136
SUNY Broome Community College, 137
Surveillance, 13
Surveymonkey, 30, 33

Tag, 33, 38, 108, 110, 112–114, 160, 173, 225, 243
Teaching, xi, 32, 53, 55, 57, 71, 87, 109, 112, 116, 118, 120, 122–123, 273–275, 277
The Ocean Agency Blog, 207
The Sports Networker, 207
Time Warner, 206
Toronto, 12
Transformative Learning, 87
TwapperKeeper, 176, 184
tweet, 116, 120–121, 128, 131, 160, 178, 180–181, 183, 200, 203, 217, 220, 252, 254–256, 258–259, 261, 263–264, 266–268
Tweetdeck, 116, 121, 142, 173, 254
Twitter, xii, xvi–xviii, 4, 25–28, 31, 33–39, 42–47, 91, 107, 109, 114–122, 129–137, 139–142, 148–154, 160–161, 163, 167–168, 172–173, 175–183, 185–187, 197–198, 200, 203–205, 211, 214–218, 220, 223–224, 235, 240, 242–243, 249–270, 273–276

United States Holocaust Museum, 73
United States State Department, 135
University of California, 77, 131, 197, 219, 275
University of California-Berkeley, 131, 197
University of California-Irvine, 219
University of Massachusetts Dartmouth, 26, 32
University of Nebraska, 193
University of Notre Dame, 192
University of Oklahoma, 193
University of Phoenix, 223, 269
URL shortener, 35, 44
US Airways Flight 1549, 131, 251
UStream, 134

Verizon FIOS, 205
Virtual learning environment (VLE), 54, 63, 65, 109, 111, 113, 118
Virtual Networking, 202, 266

Weak Ties Theory, 149
Web 2.0, xiv, xviii, 50, 53, 62, 85–86, 88–89, 99, 110, 112, 119, 141, 274
Wii, 206
Wiki, xvi, 135, 138, 170, 172–173, 176
Women Talk Sports, 207
Wordle, 181–182
WordPress, 273–274
World of Warcraft, 173

Xbox, 206

YouTube, 26–28, 37–38, 44, 50, 56, 60, 88, 95, 112, 116, 129–130, 132, 134, 137, 143, 197, 214–216, 219–220, 235, 237, 240, 243, 269, 273–275

Printed in the USA/Agawam, MA
July 23, 2012